CHINESE DREAMS
Pound, Brecht, *Tel quel*

Chinese Dreams
Pound, Brecht, *Tel quel*

Eric Hayot

THE UNIVERSITY OF MICHIGAN PRESS
Ann Arbor

For my parents

First paperback edition 2012
Copyright © by the University of Michigan 2004, 2012
All rights reserved
Published in the United States of America by
The University of Michigan Press
Manufactured in the United States of America
⊗ Printed on acid-free paper

2015   2014   2013   2012   4   3   2

A CIP catalog record for this book is available from the British Library.

Library of Congress Cataloging-in-Publication Data

Hayot, Eric, 1972-
    Chinese dreams: Pound, Brecht, Tel quel / Eric Hayot.
       p. cm.
    Includes bibliographical references and index.
    ISBN 0-472-11340-2 (alk. paper)
       1. Chinese literature—History and criticism.   2. Pound, Ezra,
    1885-1972.   3. Brecht, Bertolt, 1898-1956.   4. Tel quel.   I. Title.
    PL2262.2 .H39 2004
    895.1'09—dc21   2003012776

ISBN: 978-0-472-03486-4 (pbk. : alk. paper)
ISBN: 978-0-472-02493-3 (e-book)

Preface to the Paperback Edition

The publication of this paperback edition, some years after the initial appearance of *Chinese Dreams,* offers like all retrospectives an occasion for reevaluation and judgment. I had not anticipated—the book does not anticipate—the tremendous changes in the fields into which the book intervened, which now locate the work in a radically different intellectual space than the one to which it was first addressed.

Looking back, it is clear how deeply the book was influenced by the ongoing debates about Said's concept of Orientalism, which had had such an impact on postcolonial scholarship of the 1980s and 1990s. That impact was only belatedly being felt in discussions of East Asia. Now, of course, the debates are over. Their disappearance was occasioned, as such disappearances often are, by a triumph. The end of the debate is a sign of Said's slow drift into normativity—a space in which, becoming unconscious, the critique is no longer recognized as such.

Accordingly, though one of the book's major stated concerns—the question of how to parse relationships between unequals defined manifestly by appreciation and love, rather than by fear and loathing—remains for me at least a matter of ongoing and vital import, the relative weight of the analytic categories to which such an analysis applies has changed. Whereas in 2004 it seemed crucial to at least try to work out the value of Chinese dreaming along a scale that would measure its ethical and political acceptability—a working out prompted not only by Said but by the competing version of positive East Asian Orientalism described by such proto-nationalist critics as Zhaoming Qian—in more recent work (and not just my own) the question of ethics has largely dropped out of the picture. Figuring out who had a correct or good relation to China, and who didn't, no longer feels useful. Since one of the major arguments of the book was that it indeed was not, I experience this change with some satisfaction, though I have no illusions about my own impact on it.

Chinese Dreams appeared, in 2004, in a sort of no-man's-land between a number of different potential academic fields: modernist studies, Chinese studies, and Asian American studies. Each of those fields has since expanded, partly owing to the transnational turn in literary studies, so that the book now lies, in the Venn diagram, in the set composed by the intersection of those three areas, rather than in the open space between them. From this perspective, as in its relation to ethics and Orientalism, *Chinese Dreams* once again seems to have inhabited a threshold region of scholarly change. I claim no special perspective for that inhabitation, but I think it explains why, for me at least, rereading the book as a stranger, some features of the book's concern feel very much "over," while others feel still quite relevant and even new.

The new seems most present in two ideas, both of which emerge in the conclusion. Together they comprise the fundamental justificatory condition for the book. Both appear as a result of the work done in the chapters on Pound, Brecht, and *Tel quel.* The entire labor of those chapters aimed, finally, to earn the right to claim that those two ideas are true.

They are, first, the concept of sinography, and second, the philosophical importance of the *manifest* content of the aesthetic work, particularly when it comes to Europe's relation to China. Sinography, which got a fuller run-out in introduction to the 2008 collection *Sinographies: Writing China,* which I co-edited with Haun Saussy and Steven Yao, involved the simple assertion that the history of China needed to be written with far less effort toward the production of *accuracy*—whether referential or political—and far more toward the description and comprehension of the complex life of national, political, economic, ethnic, and historical ideas. That the history of China is always a history of "China"—even in China—is guaranteed as a premise by the analysis done in *Chinese Dreams.* Scholarship informed by that truth appears both in the edited collection *Sinographies* and in a wide variety of work in contemporary Chinese studies today. At Washington University in Saint Louis in 2008 the distinguished historian William Kirby, who has been the head of the East Asian Languages & Cultures department at Harvard, opened a conference on China by remarking on the number of upcoming talks that had put *China* in quotation marks, and went on to theorize the state of Chinese Studies as a field on the basis of this new willingness to put pressure on the historical and referential stability of its organizing concept. (I know that Kirby had not read *Chinese Dreams*—the anecdote illustrates the general movement of the field—and came, at the time, as a total surprise to me.)

As for the importance of the manifest content (in the Freudian dream interpretation model, the content that one passes through in order to reach the significant, latent content): the most important and historically unusual representational capacities of China in the Western context stem from its ability to function as a particular type of manifest content, allowing China to generate, as I wrote in *The Hypothetical Mandarin,* a particular kind of "example-effect." China's role as a special kind of philosophical and cultural limit, and the impact of that limit on the entire history of Western philosophical and economic modernity, merits the attention of all those who wish to understand the history of China. That the People's Republic's recent, eternally re-announced, "rise" to economic prominence appears to give that project a new impetus is not, as the narcissists and paranoiacs imagine, a justification from the *outside* of the concept of "China," but one firmly ensconced in it.

State College, Pennsylvania / January 2011

Preface

I used to say, to hell with martyrs' palms, all beacons of art, the inventor's pride, the plunderer's frenzy; I expected to return to the Orient and to original, eternal wisdom. But this is evidently a dream of depraved laziness!
                                                            —Arthur Rimbaud

It reflects the force of expectations people have about identity and scholarship that ever since I started thinking and writing about China and the West some eight years ago, I've been asked every once in a while if I'm part Chinese. (I'm not.) My answer usually prompts this follow-up: "Why are you interested in China?"

What that question asks for is a story, a story of how I became interested in a culture that is essentially *not mine*. As a question, it reflects a series of expectations about the things people like to think about, and how they come to like to think about them: people expect other people to study things that come from cultural identities or formations that are essentially *theirs* (nationally, ethnically, sexually, in terms of gender or class formation). When that pattern gets broken, there's some sense that the fascination or interest produced there must have happened in some unique or intriguing way—in a manner that does not simply retell a story everyone already knows. Like Tolstoy's happy families, perhaps, those who study their own cultures have motivations that are all more or less the same. But those who study cultures not their own apparently each come to that study in their own little way.

In 1994 I decided, toward the end of a lengthy intellectual turn towards the cultural ramifications of Western imperialism, that I ought to learn a non-Western language. The best way to afford this was, at the time, to live at home, so I moved back in with my parents and looked up the summer catalogue of courses at Ohio State University. They offered Chinese and Japanese, and I chose the former for reasons that remain unclear to me, though I think they had to do both with an interest in Marxist theory and a sense that China would, in the next decade or so, become an important thing to know about, economically and politically (on that latter score I was more right than I would have imagined). Classes were six hours a day, and I loved them, coming home at night and dreaming in Chinese after only a few weeks. The following summer, I went to Tianjin to study language and the Peking Opera. Two years later, just having started writing a dissertation, I spent a year in Beijing, learning more Chinese, attending classes in comparative literature, and—not atypically for foreigners in China today—appearing several times on television as a singer on variety shows or, once, as a commentator on the U.S. soccer team's chances in the 1998 World Cup. Out of that experience comes, at least partially, this book.

One response to such a story remarks that, despite the perhaps-charming specificity of its details, it remains very much a cliché. The fascinations of China's language, its people, and its geopolitics have long motivated Westerners to visit China, prompting a variety of similarly "unusual" stories about their interactions with Chinese people and Chinese culture. Some of the more prominent historical motivations for such travel have faded: China no longer presents, as it did to Jesuit missionaries in the seventeenth century and Protestant ones in the nineteenth, a vast challenge to biblical history (though it remains an important reservoir of potential converts). But other motivations remain as vibrant in our century as they were hundreds of years ago. Figures as disparate as Leibniz, Ezra Pound, and Jacques Derrida have all, at one point or another, hitched their intellectual wagons to the aesthetic and political intensities of the Chinese language;[1] more prosaically, some become interested in China through Buddhism, Taoism, or even kung-fu (as did my roommate in Beijing in 1997). Behind many of these fascinations flits the specter of the "ancient and wondrous East," source of fairy tales, fantastical travel narratives (the earliest of which was Marco Polo's), delicately sexualized fantasies (Giacomo Puccini's *Turandot*), postmodern iterations of narrativity (Italo Calvino's *Invisible Cities*), and contemporary political or military intrigue (the 1997 Richard Gere spy thriller, *Red Corner*).

Secondary literature on such Western encounters with China has, in the past fifteen years, enjoyed something of a bull market. Colin MacKerras's *Western Images of China* appeared in 1989; J. A. G. Roberts's two volumes, *China through Western Eyes* (nineteenth and twentieth centuries), were published in 1992; Zhaoming Qian's *Orientalism and Modernism* in 1995; Robert Kern's *Orientalism, Modernism, and the American Poem* in 1996. Other contributors to the field include Haun Saussy (*The Problem of a Chinese Aesthetic*, 1993, and *Great Walls of Discourse*, 2002), David Porter (*Ideographia*, 2001), Ming Xie (*Ezra Pound and the Appropriation of Chinese Poetry: Cathay, Translation, and Imagism*, 1998), Steven Yao (*Translation and the Languages of Modernism*, 2002), Yunte Huang (*Transpacific Displacement*, 2002), Zhang Longxi (*The Tao and the Logos*, 1992, and *Mighty Opposites*, 1999), Lisa Lowe (*Critical Terrains*, 1991), and Marie-Paule Ha (*Figuring the East*, 2000). Worthy of separate mention is the immensely important ongoing work of Rey Chow, who in *Woman and Chinese Modernity* (1991), *Writing Diaspora* (1993), *Ethics after Idealism* (1998), and *The Protestant Ethnic and the Spirit of Capitalism* (2002) has relentlessly pursued the most difficult and most compelling questions that come out of the encounter between China and the West.[2]

In 1998, popular historian Jonathan Spence waded into the debate with *The Chan's Great Continent: China in Western Minds*. Seeking at the close of his book to explain the ongoing Western fascination with China, Spence writes: "The curious readiness of Westerners for things Chinese was there from the beginning, and it has remained primed, over the centuries, by an unending stream of offerings. Precisely why this should be so remains, to me, a mystery. But the story we have traced seems to prove that China needs no reason to fasten itself into Western minds" (241). This is very much a non-answer to the question "why China?" Though in the first sentence Spence asserts that the West's interest in China "was there from the beginning," at the end of the second sentence the *reasons* for that fascination are declared a "mystery." By the third sentence he has concluded that China "needs no reason" to fascinate the West. But no matter how unsure they may be about the specific origins of the West's interest in China, these sentences—especially in their attribution of activity and passivity—carry with them a more general theory of both the West and the China that fascinates it. While Spence's West has a certain "readiness . . . from the beginning," it remains primed *by* Chinese offerings; it is China that "needs no reason to fasten itself" into the Western mind. In the passive construction of the first sentence ("primed . . . by") and the self-reflexive infinitive of the second, active one, China is given the grammatical position of the actor ("China needs no reason to fasten itself," yes, but when it does fasten, it fastens *itself*). Whatever the rationale behind the West's readiness—which, "there from the beginning," may have a genetic importance—Spence suggests that China does something to keep such readiness "primed"; in other words, the West, though ready for China, does not necessarily decide its own fascination.

Does such a scenario not confirm China's most tantalizing stereotype? China—mysterious, irrational, evocatively provocative—beguiles. Such a characterization may be the inevitable result of asking "why China?" If China fascinates the West, then the natural reaction is to attribute that fascination to something particular—undefinable, but particular—about China itself, to say, Yes, China fascinates because it is this way, or that way. And looking down the long list of Westerners fascinated by China, the temptation to make that particular fascinating aspect of China the *same one*—to make it some ontological marker of what we believe to be historical Chineseness—is practically irresistible. Many Westerners interested in China, including some of those discussed in this book, have taken this route, pointing to some apparently unchanging, essential aspect of China or its culture (the peasant character of the people, the landscape, the ideology of its writing system, the texts of classical Confucian thought) as the driving force behind their interest.

The trouble with such explanations—indeed of any general answer to the question of "why China?"—lies partly in the annoying lack of similarity among different people's Chinas. The early Qing dynasty China of many Jesuit missionaries bears little resemblance, geopolitically, to the humiliated signatory of various "unequal treaties" in the nineteenth century, which in turn does not look much like the cultural-revolutionary China of the early 1970s. Add to this the changes in the West, throw in a consideration of the cultural or biographical factors in play for individual authors, and it becomes clear that we have many different Chinas, many of them incoherent to other members of their species (if species there be).

While there is a certain appeal to the retreat to specificity and the idea of innumerable Chinas, each one uniquely tied to a particular historical or cultural circumstance, such a retreat simply moves the ontological maker over onto the West. If one no longer acknowledges China's referential stability, it is easy enough to replace that instability with a stereotyped West whose major characteristic is that it invents Chinas, for whatever reason deemed to be one of its essential features: the West fascinates itself with China because of its imperializing drive, its scientific curiosity, its penchant for exploration, its insistent pursuit of otherness—each of these there "from the beginning," much as Spence believes the West's "readiness" to be. The simplest response to such a conception of the West simply explodes the stereotype with specificity. The West is no more the same every time it interacts with China than China is when it interacts with the West.

Why, then, China? The question is probably a bad one, or rather, it is good only inasmuch as it opens up discussion about the relation between geopolitical space—an area on the Pacific side of the Eurasian landmass with a more or less continuous history of being conceived as a political identity—and the realms of thought. As far as *Chinese Dreams* is concerned, the mapping or reading of myths—tracing the specificities of China through their various permutations—is a useful exercise in intellectual history and cross-cultural reading; it has something to teach about the ways the West has thought itself through its articulation of a set of ideas named "China." At one level, to be sure, by finding "Chinese dreams"[3] in the work of Ezra Pound, Bertolt Brecht, and the writers of the Parisian journal *Tel quel,* this book both assumes and assigns similarities among those myths; by putting together the texts it does the book theorizes a more general commonality to the "Chinas" it reads. And yet I have tried not to let that general theory do anything other than occasionally interrupt the more specific stories each text tells, rather than shape the readings from the beginning. Each chapter is staged so that the text has, whenever possible, the last word—if not directly in the reading then at least when it comes to the more general question of "why China?" It's precisely the movement between an understanding of these stories as at least partially generic—as being to some extent alike—and an appreciation of their sometimes exquisite unlikenesses that provides, for me, the clearest understanding of the stakes of reading and making meaning.

Chinese Dreams focuses on three groups of texts, each organized around an author or group of authors. Chapter 1 opens with the strange fact of Ezra Pound's translations of Chinese poetry in *Cathay,* published in 1915. History's judgment that Pound, despite knowing no Chinese, translated the poems better than anyone else ever has, sets the stage for a series of questions about how Westerners come to "know" China, and how much of that knowledge is the ghostly reflection of their own desires. As it approaches Pound's translations, the chapter is especially concerned to discern "Chineseness," to ask what in Pound's modernism may have been literally Chinese, or may have been taken as Chinese. Following up on *Cathay*'s national origins, much of the latter half of the chapter discusses the immense buildup of critical discourse on the question of Pound and China. That discourse, sometimes more clearly than Pound's own work, points to some of the stakes of the "Why China?" question in our time, particularly around the difficulties of the West's orientalism and its critique, inaugurated by Edward Said. Particularly as it focuses on *Cathay*, criticism's attempt to decide the poetry's national origins—English or Chinese?—frames one of the political dimensions of East/West literary criticism. Tracing the way "Pound and China" criticism has struggled to define Pound's interest in China relative to both orientalism and modernism, this opening chapter establishes a staging ground for the next two.

The second chapter centers on the work of the German playwright Bertolt Brecht (though as I eventually remark the idea of "Brecht" as a single author is itself a hotly contested issue). After looking at Brecht's translations of Chinese poetry, I consider the ways in which a certain ideology of Chinese translation, possibly carried over from Pound, shapes the reception of Brecht's "Chinese" poems. Much of the discussion addresses Brecht's "*Verfremdungseffekte in der chinesischen Schauspielkunst*" (1936; translated by John Willett as "Alienation Effects in Chinese Acting"). It argues that one ought to understand Brecht's famous *Verfremdungseffekt* at least partially by looking at its "Chinese" origins, and particularly Brecht's experience of "strangeness" (*Befremdung*) as he watched a performance of Chinese Peking Opera in Moscow in 1935. Unlike Pound, who seemed happiest when truly getting down to the genuine Chineseness of things, Brecht wishes to rid the Chinese alienation-effect of its original Chineseness, and make it fully his own. But can you have "Chinese" acting without China? Or is a measure of its Chinese "strangeness" always left behind in the experience, like a taste in the mouth?

From Brecht I turn to the Parisian avant-garde journal *Tel quel*, which was at the center of a certain radical version of French Maoism in the late

1960s and 1970s, and whose interest in China culminated in a two-week trip there in April and May 1974. For the Telquelians—Julia Kristeva, Philippe Sollers, Marcelin Pleynet, Roland Barthes, and François Wahl—China became the name of both the "revolution in action" and the "revolution in language" that they believed were not only inextricably linked but also on the verge of taking place. As *Tel quel* moved into Maoist politics, those politics were made to stand in for a more general aesthetic theory stemming from the group's literary poststructuralism. But the trip to China in 1974 would, rather than reinforce this political radicalism, disrupt it; the group's reminiscences of that trip in light of a recurrent reference to Brecht and to Chinese theater lead us to ask why it proved to be such a disappointment. Following the return from Beijing, the Telquelians outgrew and eventually repudiated their Chinese interest; their charged writings on China run through a wild, wide gauntlet of emotions, culminating most intoxicatingly in Julia Kristeva's fierce nostalgia for the lost opportunities of *Tel quel*'s revolution.

Though each chapter centers its readings around texts by Pound, Brecht, and the members of *Tel quel,* the chapters are not *about* those authors in a strict sense. In the first chapter, for instance, my subject is not simply the particular manner in which Pound related to China but rather a broader field of discourse called something like "Ezra Pound and China," which includes not only Pound but other English translators, as well as American, English, and Chinese critics working on Pound's relation to China. In short, I am reading a discourse that stretches well past the particular work of the author Ezra Pound to address the more general stakes in the presence of "Chineseness" (genuine or mythical) in Pound's work; I am not giving a definitive statement on whether or not his China was truly Chinese. The same is true for Brecht and *Tel quel;* throughout the book I differentiate as little as possible between "primary" and "secondary" texts (including the text of actual China itself). As for the choice of these three focal points: there could have been others. In the twentieth century, the French writer Victor Segalen is one obvious choice, as is the American Pearl S. Buck. Ultimately, the book begins and ends where it does because the aim was a linguistic and temporal diversity across the twentieth century—and the recognition of "major" authors—that might begin to suggest some of the larger contours and importances of the "China" question.

Throughout *Chinese Dreams,* the idea that the meaning of "China" remains in many instances very particularly *constructed*—and rarely in the same way twice—is observed with as much rigor as possible. But this brings up another problem: in a book on Western understandings of China, attention might be paid not only to the vagaries of "China," but also to variations in "the West"—the object whose interests in things called "Chinese" is the subject of the book. To theorize a "West and China" requires remembering that even as the question of how the West defines China becomes important and interesting, any definition of China by the West depends, intellectually, on an unstated theory of the West. While I have looked quite specifically at how each author presents a China, I use "the West" and "Western" in a relatively unreconstructed manner to refer to Western Europe plus North America. There is thus an imbalance between the text's attention to the various Chinas and Chinesenesses it encounters and its use of "the West" and "Western," two concepts that remain, to some extent, undisturbed. The West's "West" is, in one sense, the name of the book's limits.

This nod, then, to limitation: As Jan Hokenson has remarked, the meaning of the word *West* differs immensely depending on its linguistic and cultural context. For the French, the *tradition occidentale* refers quite precisely to the intellectual and philosophical traditions leading from the ancient Greeks into Europe, and does not include the United States. But *occidental(e)* almost always gets translated as "West" in English, with no mention of the different valences of this word in English and French.[4] In another context, for the Idaho-born Pound, who identified deeply both with his American wildness and the European intellectual traditions, the West might have included both at the same time but not in the sense in which the currently undifferentiated words *the West* have come to refer, at the end of this century, to the combination of capitalist formation and cultural/political preference that now enables one to see the United States and Western Europe as part of the same larger thing. As for Brecht, though he lived in the United States for years during World War II, he concerned himself primarily with Europe (both Western and Eastern) and its traditions.

"Chinese dreams" is thus a topic whose geographic origins can be taken two ways, either via a focus on its dream-space China, or the West, its dreaming subject.[5] But the second word, "dreams," also merits attention. It is given weight and a certain reading by the quotation from Rimbaud that opens this preface: "I expected to return to the Orient and to original, eternal wisdom. But this is evidently a dream of depraved laziness!" Rimbaud's take on the Chinese dream highlights its status as a cliché. "Depraved" translates *grossière*—crass, crude, even ignorant or stupid; the dream is "lazy" because it involves little original thought. The (self-)mockery in Rimbaud's tone jibes well with a certain style of dream-reading, wherein a stance taken up just outside the dreamer's lust-blinded field of vision allows for a rich appreciation of the foolishness of desire.[6]

Given the theoretical sophistication of contemporary literary criticism, such a stance is readily available to those who wish to take it up vis-à-vis those Westerners who dreamed through China. In the decades since the publication of Said's invaluable *Orientalism,* critics have learned to look a certain way at texts that deal with encounters between the West and the rest, and in turn have understood more about how constructions of otherness work, and how the invention of otherness inevitably grounds a sense of self. From that perspective, the orientalism of the authors in this book—their seemingly crass laziness, the manner in which their fantasies about the East shaped and were shaped by their own worldview—is obvious. One could wonder, then, how could these writers have been so . . . *orientalist?* How could Kristeva have imagined that the Chinese people had no unconscious? Did Ezra Pound really repeat that old saw about ancient Chinese wisdom? This obviousness often produces a critique that's basically ironic at the author's expense, one that begins with an "ah-ha," as in "ah-ha, I've caught you being a hypocrite, or a fool, or blind to your own desires." I think at this point such critiques are wearing a little thin. Probably they were, in the parlance of the times, always already worn thin. What such critiques hear is always more than what the text gives, always the text's secret. Instead of figuring out what in the text is new to these texts—what their secrets are—I have tried to hear what is new to me, and therefore to learn something *from* the texts, not just something *about* them. So if the book seems, at times, to be defending the work of those texts it reads, it is partly, I think, because it tries to take dreams and dreaming seriously.

In a discussion of David Henry Hwang's play *M. Butterfly* Rey Chow remarks that while fantasy has been recognized as central to orientalist preoccupations, "the problem of fantasy . . . is usually dismissed moralistically" (*Ethics,* 75). Moralistic critiques of Western fantasies about the East depend on the unstated premise that truthful communication devoid of misperception is possible. What is more interesting, Chow writes, is to understand fantasy (and dreams) as "not simply a matter of distortion or willful exploitation, but rather as an inherent part of our consciousness, our wakeful state of mind" (76). We currently live in a culture—both academic and otherwise—that strikes me as especially inimical to such a consideration of dreams and fantasies. The vast majority of dream discourse involves explaining or revealing the dream's hidden meaning, treating the dream as a cipher to be translated into a language that is, in the light of day, sometimes shameful, sometimes perverse, but especially and inevitably *ordinary*. What such criticism forgets is that everyone dreams, and that one of the conditions of dreaming is precisely that one does not know one is doing it. For the authors in this book, China named in its dream-state a wild, incandescent experience of thought, an experience that allowed them to bend the limits of what they believed it was possible to know. *Chinese Dreams* aims, then, to record not only the causes and effects of that Chinese dream—its practical shapes, its shifting sources of origin—but also to acknowledge the lived experience of its opaque, undomesticating imagination.

My teacher and friend Jane Gallop deserves a good deal of the credit for this book; it was she who suggested, upon my return from Tianjin in 1995, that I write a dissertation having something to do with China, "since you seem to have liked it there so much." I owe her an immense debt of gratitude, both for that idea and her subsequent advice, criticism, and support, which continues to sustain me. I have been lucky to have had many wonderful teachers, including Kevin Michael, Phil Courier, John Glavin, Bruce Smith, Amy Robinson, Henry Schwarz, Gregory Jay, and Herbert Blau, all of whom contributed to my becoming a literary scholar. This book has benefited from their influence as well as from the generous help of Marcus Bullock, Rey Chow, Panivong Norindr, Kathleen Woodward, and Michelle Yeh, who commented on some portion or all of the text.

The most difficult challenge in getting from the dissertation to a book lay in framing the work so that it took part in a larger conversation on

China and the West. Timothy Billings, Christopher Bush, Haun Saussy, and Steven Yao showed me where the best parts of that conversation were. Without the talk we shared—in Palo Alto, Montreal, Columbus, Austin, New Haven, Boulder, San Francisco, Philadelphia, San Juan, San Diego—the book would have been much longer in the writing. Many of these ideas were worked out in conversation with other friends, including Christian Gregory, Astrid Henry, Kelly Klingensmith, Emily Littleton, Tim Lynch, and Jake York. I am grateful to those at the University of Michigan Press, including Ingrid Erickson, Allison Liefer, Marcia LaBrenz, LeAnn Fields, and the Press's anonymous readers, who worked on my behalf to improve the manuscript. Megan Massino made putting together the index easy and fun. I was helped along the way by fellowships from the Graduate School at the University of Wisconsin–Milwaukee, and a year-long Boren Fellowship from the Academy for Education Development, which allowed me to spend 1997–98 in Beijing. *Chinese Dreams* was completed at the University of Arizona, where both my colleagues and students continue to astonish me with their generosity and brilliance; I owe a debt of gratitude to Susan Hardy Aiken, Laura Berry, Charlie Bertsch, Sean Cobb, Bill Epstein, Larry Evers, Amy Kimme Hea, and Greg Jackson for their friendship and support. I reserve a special thanks for the incomparable Xu Bing, whose art speaks precisely to those intersections and encounters that motivate my work, and who so graciously offered to illustrate the book's cover.

Ted Wesp—*mon frère, mon semblable*—has been for eighteen years my closest friend and ideal reader. Di Chunyuan has been everything else. Their trust and friendship are an honor whose dimensions remain, for me, immeasurable.

Part of the first chapter appeared in *Twentieth Century Literature* 45, no. 4 (1999). Its editors have generously given permission to reprint it here.

Contents

Chapter One   POUND

*N*o figure of twentieth-century literature has had a more public relation to China than Ezra Pound. From the early moments of his career in London to his final days in Italy, Pound made China part of his general project to rethink the nature of the West, to discover in poetry the best that humans had ever said or thought, painted or sung, and renew it. In London Pound first translated Chinese poetry into English, and through that poetry developed an aesthetic theory rooted in a broader, mistaken understanding of Chinese writing. Later, Pound intertwined Chinese characters and philosophy with his Cantos, published translations of Confucian texts, and partially explained his interest by insisting that the texts belonged as much to him as to the Chinese. These ideas stayed with him till the end of his life: a BBC film taken of Pound in the 1960s shows him carefully explaining to the camera the pictorial relation between the Chinese characters for "sun" 日, "wood" 木, and "east" 東, an idea that had first surfaced for him in an essay he edited and published in 1918, some forty years earlier *(Ezra Pound).*

The material Pound provides to the scholar of "Western images of China" offers itself up as a complex, variegated tapestry of errors, misperceptions, half-truths seen and unseen, flashes of pure genius, and great poetry. It has been the subject of a vast literary critical discourse. Following Pound's literary canonization in the 1950s, scrupulous attention has been paid to his readings of Chinese history, the sources of his Confucianism, and especially his translations of Chinese poetry. The books and essays thus produced range from meticulously researched discussions of Pound's original source material—John Nolde's *Blossoms of the East,* for instance, compares every single line of Pound's 1940 "Chinese History Cantos" with Joseph-Anne-Marie de Moyriac de Mailla's thirteen-volume *Histoire Générale de la Chine*—to more theoretical work on the role of the East in the construction of Western modernism—of which this book is only one example. Between the practical and the theoretical appear a number of takes on Pound's techniques of translation, ranging from the critical (L. S. Dembo) to the comparatively neutral (Wai-Lim Yip), all struggling to decide how far Pound saw into China, and what, if anything, his vision means for Anglo-American poetry.

How a book takes its place within this network is a delicate subject. Much of the criticism centers on the question of whether Pound got it right or wrong, but I do not decide that question here. Neither am I trying to demonstrate (or refute) the genuineness of China's influence on Western modernism. I will not, along the way, identify and amend ethnocentrisms or errors of translation under the assumption that my own perception is "authentic" (instead "authenticity," and the claims made for and against it, will be one of the subjects of the reading). This is not a reading of Ezra Pound's relationship to China.

It is rather a reading of the still-living subject of "Pound and China," a subject that forms itself not only in the texts of Ezra Pound and his contemporaries, but also under the shadow of the critical discourse that has been built around Pound's *Cathay,* his *Cantos,* his translations of the *Shi jing,* his various remarks on Chinese poetry and Chinese writing. On the subject of the possible values of China (and "China") in the West, critics have as much to say as Pound himself; my reading aspires to understand and sometimes name the historical shifts in the kinds of questions deemed relevant to the subject of Pound and China. In doing so I am tracing a more general critical history of the relationship between "China" and Western thought.

Is there still more to say about Pound and China? The flood of books on the subject shows no sign of abating; the questions and ideas at stake in the original debate apparently remain both relevant and provocative. Haun Saussy writes, "China has always been, is always still, in the process of being invented; but does one invent it in whatever way one pleases? 'China' names a country, of course, but it more accurately names an international culture; and 'culture' is the identity-tag of a question having, these days in North America at least, a moral as well as an epistemological side" (*Problem,* 4). If the question of knowing China (and I take knowing as a kind of inventing) has moral and epistemological dimensions, then its ongoing relevance ought to be clear, and the ensuing conundrum complicated indeed: What if the very process of "knowing" itself were premised on some a priori sense of what it would mean to "know" this country, this international culture, this felt expression of true poesis, this thing called "China"?

With questions like these, it is not surprising that we are still talking about Pound, and that we might try to read the ways his knowing China has been repeated or refused, elaborated or worked through, by critics interested in "cultural" questions. It is possible that the history of Pound's invention of China (a history that includes, I am arguing, its own criticism) might set the stage for a discussion of the nature of inventing—or knowing—itself.

Frame: Orientalism and Modernism

In 1995 Zhaoming Qian published *Orientalism and Modernism: The Legacy of China in Pound and Williams,* a book that lays out Qian's claim that China's substantial influence on both the principles and principals of Anglo-American modernism has been sorely overlooked. A year later, Robert Kern published *Orientalism, Modernism, and the American Poem,* an attempt to discover why China catalyzed the poetic experiments of a series of important American poets—Pound among them.

This coincidence, the "orientalism" and "modernism" repeated, signals the appearance in "Pound and China" of the obligatory and vital gesture toward Edward Said's landmark 1978 book *Orientalism. Orientalism* is a damning critique of the West's literary and political production of the Orient, which the book claims helped justify and extend Europe's colonization of the East. It is also one of the major attacks on Western literature's claim to political autonomy. Said insists that the literary academy's separation of literature from politics has concealed the former's cultural and political contribution to imperialism, and goes on to suggest that the West cannot seriously study its own literature unless it considers that literature's relation to its political and social context.

Both *Orientalism and Modernism* and *Orientalism, Modernism, and the American Poem* invoke in their titles the specter of a certain reading of modernism, a reading that would argue that the modernists' fantastic and ill-informed treatments of China (both books discuss China at length) were intimately related to the West's imperialist designs on that country during the eighteenth and nineteenth centuries. But both books seek to deflect or dismiss such a reading by arguing that the stakes of representation in modernist poetry—and particularly in Pound's representations of China—were more complicated than allowed for by a simple, politicizing understanding.

Standing in for Pound in the argument—this in both books—is his friend T. S. Eliot, whose role as the representative of critical modernism depends largely on one sentence, which appeared in his 1928 introduction to Pound's *Selected Poems:* "Pound is the inventor of Chinese poetry for our time." This entrancing declaration has exerted such an influence on Pound scholarship that it is nearly impossible to find work in the field that does not cite it. And yet, as Kern points out, Eliot's remark, "often quoted as unqualified praise, . . . actually seems intended to indicate the limits of what Pound had accomplished" (3). Eliot had written,

> As for *Cathay,* it must be pointed out that Pound is the inventor of Chinese poetry for our time. I suspect that every age has had, and will have, the same illusion concerning translations, an illusion which is not altogether an illusion either. When a foreign poet is successfully done into the idiom of our own language and our own time, we believe that he has been "translated"; we believe that through this translation we really at last get the original. . . . His [Pound's] translations seem to be—and that is the test of excellence—translucencies: we *think* we are closer to the Chinese than when we read, for instance, Legge. I doubt this: I predict that in three hundred years Pound's *Cathay* will be a "Windsor Translation" as Chapman and North are now "Tudor Translations": it will be called (and justly) a "magnificent specimen of XXth Century poetry" rather than a "translation." Each generation must translate for itself.
>
> This is as much as to say that Chinese poetry, as we know it today, is something invented by Ezra Pound. It is not to say that there is a Chinese poetry-in-itself, waiting for some ideal translator who shall be only translator. (14–15)

If *Cathay* was not, however, a clear window onto the East, its opacity was dazzling enough to make it look like one; Eliot says at both the beginning and end of this quotation that Pound effectively "invented" Chinese poetry for his readers. In calling the poems "translucencies" and *Cathay* a "magnificent specimen of XXth Century poetry," Eliot makes clear the degree to which the sheer force of Pound's language makes its China believable and real. Eliot is thus in the difficult position of making two points at once: first, that *Cathay* is not Chinese poetry, and second, that it is great poetry. The effect of the second of these points is to make the first hard to hear. It is precisely because the poems are so good

4

("magnificent specimens") that they seem so Chinese, and so Eliot must insist again and again that they are not.

In claiming that Pound has invented Chinese poetry, Eliot carefully lays out the difference between what Pound has done and actual Chinese poetry. He emphasizes that Pound's successful representation of China will only last a few hundred years, and insists that "each generation must translate for itself." The illusion of Chinese reality will fade with time. At the same time, Eliot insists that no one will ever perfectly translate Chinese poetry—he does not want the reader to imagine he is criticizing Pound for not achieving perfection where someone else might do so. Accordingly, in the last sentence here he insists that there is not "a Chinese-poetry-in-itself" waiting for a better translator. Perhaps because he is uninterested in China, Eliot never says whether actual Chinese poetry is Chinese-poetry-in-itself, or whether a Westerner might ever read that. He is more concerned with what the West knows, and how it knows it.

Eliot's reaction to *Cathay* finally eludes the knotty problem of actual China with the following: "It is probable that the Chinese, as well as the Provençals and the Italians and the Saxons, influenced Pound . . . on the other hand, it is certain that Pound has influenced the Chinese and the Provençals and the Italians and the Saxons—not the matter *an sich,* which is unknowable, but the matter as we know it" (17). By "matter *an sich,*" Eliot means the actual Chinese or Provençals; he is saying that Pound did not literally influence those people but instead influenced the English idea of who those people are. By differentiating between the matter as such and the known, Eliot can acknowledge both the impossibility of a literary production of "real" China *and* the powerful creative effect of Pound's version of it (emphasized by Eliot's surprising use of "Chinese" and "Provençals"—as though Pound had actually influenced the people rather than the poetry).

In attempting to strip the veil of Chinese authority from Pound's *Cathay,* Eliot was responding to two kinds of reactions to the small book of translations. Positive reaction to *Cathay* was likely, as Eliot suggested, to believe that Pound had really at last gotten the original, that he had perfectly translated the nuances of Chinese culture and poetry into English. Negative reaction to *Cathay,* on the other hand, often insisted on Pound's failure as a translator, blaming him for over-Anglicizing the poetry by intentionally ignoring its literal meaning, or by misunderstanding various words or concepts. Eliot met both of these reactions with a certain skepticism and the same response: Pound's *Cathay* is not Chinese, and shines because it is brilliant, English poetry.

A half-century after Eliot called Pound "the *inventor* of Chinese poetry," Said declared on the first page of *Orientalism,* "The Orient was almost a European *invention*" (emphasis added). Like Eliot, Said was discussing the powerful reality-effect of Western representations of the East. In some way, Said was naming the process Eliot had identified in 1928: the tendency for the West to believe that its literature and art accurately represented the Orient as such. Unlike Eliot, however, Said gives this process a moral and historical twist, declaring that orientalism allowed the West to justify its imperialist exploitation of a good chunk of the world from the Enlightenment through World War II. For Said, orientalism means "the enormously systematic discipline by which European culture was able to manage—and even produce—the Orient politically, sociologically, militarily, ideologically, and imaginatively" (3).

Like Eliot, Said interests himself more in the constructedness of the Western Orient than the Orient-in-itself. He writes that "the phenomenon of Orientalism as I study it here deals principally . . . with the internal consistency of Orientalism and its ideas about the Orient (the East as career) despite or beyond any correspondence, or lack thereof, with a 'real' Orient" (5). In other words, Said's concern is the development and existence of "the Orient" *as the West knows it.* But he also wants to link what the West "knew" about the Orient with what the West did in the Orient, and so he worries about the degree to which the West's Orient seemed real. He writes that the "Orient is an idea that has a history and tradition of thought, imagery, and vocabulary that have given it reality and presence in the West" (5). While the Orient is an "idea," Said also recognizes that it has a "reality" and a "presence" that make it appear to be an accurate reflection of the East as such.

Unlike Eliot, for whom the reality-effect of Pound's translations worked primarily as a thought-problem or an exercise in ontology, Said's concern with the West's Orient ultimately returns to the "real" Orient. The West's Orient develops its "reality and presence" by virtue of the way it affects the minds of Westerners who then behave a certain way in the "real" Orient, producing effects on the people and governments that live there. The myth of orientalism thus returns to its source and becomes real, like some absurd self-fulfilling prophecy. Said's interest and belief in the "real" Orient thus requires him to differentiate between the Western idea of the Orient—which only becomes real when it returns East in the form of Western imperialism—and the actual people and countries in the East, who have a reality whether the West thinks about them or not.

> [I]t would be wrong to conclude that the Orient was *essentially* an idea, or a creation with no corresponding reality. . . . There were—and are—cultures and nations whose location is in the East, and their lives, histories, and customs have a brute reality obviously greater than anything that could be said about them in the West. (5)

In declaring the "brute reality" of Eastern nations and cultures "obviously greater than anything that could be said about them in the West," Said reveals his deeply pessimistic take on the possibility of any fair or reasonable Western representation of the East, which must always come up short of the Orient's "brute reality" (or as Eliot would put it, the Orient *an sich*). Said's subject in *Orientalism* is the persistence of the Western belief that its knowledge of the Orient corresponds perfectly to the Orient's brute reality.

Said's use of *real* and its cognates in these early pages of *Orientalism* indicates the difficulty of differentiating the West's Orient from the Orient *an sich*. Within the space of a page, Said writes that the West's Orient has a "reality and presence in and for the West"; he says that nations in the East have a "brute reality" greater than what the West says about them; finally he declares that orientalism (that is, the West's Orient) exists "beyond any correspondence, or lack thereof, with a 'real' Orient" (5). This last "real," in scare quotes, sums up the ambivalence with which Said deploys the term, both for and against orientalism, emphasizing its power on the one hand (it has a "reality and presence"), its limitations on the other (the "reality and presence" are *in and for the West;* the East has a "brute reality" orientalism cannot touch), and finally, both: whatever reality the Orient has in that final instance, it is not real, but "real"—contingently, not-quite-real; real as we know it.

Since *Orientalism*'s publication in 1978, any number of critics have taken up its challenge. Examining the degree to which the ability to say things about the West depended on an assumed civilizational superiority, these critics show how texts repeat and develop Western fantasies about the East. An Orientalist reading of Pound might try to understand *Cathay*

7

as a document of imperialism, typical in many ways of a Western fantasy of the aestheticized, natural East. Such a reading might interest itself in how *Cathay* participated in a social discourse that legitimized, say, British investment in Chinese railroads, and would begin, perhaps, with a look at the general state of cultural knowledge about China in 1915. Though such a reading could never have occurred to Eliot, it springs from the idea he shares with Said: that the West could invent and shape a believable, real-seeming East.

Making Eliot's declaration on Pound the representative statement of modernism turns the pairing orientalism/modernism into less of a binary and more of a vaguely disturbed equivalence. At the very least, it suggests that the most obvious critical methodology promised by such a pairing— using Said as the key to unlock Pound—cannot proceed in any simple or uncomplicated way. This theoretical assumption is well borne out in the practice of Zhaoming Qian and Robert Kern, each of whom offers a certain resistance to a direct application of orientalism to modernism. It is Kern who most explicitly identifies Said and Eliot together. After remarking that Eliot's phrase "Pound is the inventor of Chinese poetry for our time" tends to be separated from the rest of its paragraph, Kern goes on to show that Eliot's influence on subsequent "Pound and China" criticism might be measured by the degree to which readers have ignored the context of the paragraph for the seductiveness of his declaration. By understanding Eliot's position as similar to Said's rather than opposed to it, Kern is able to incorporate elements of both critiques into his own take on Pound. In *Orientalism, Modernism, and the American Poem*, he writes, "What Pound provides in *Cathay*, as Eliot suggested long before Edward Said formulated his conception of 'Orientalism,' is not Chinese poetry itself but 'the matter as we know it'" (156). Following Eliot, Kern writes that "Pound's *Cathay* is . . . largely an event within Anglo-American literature" (4). Later, in a nod to Said, Kern also acknowledges "Pound's subcareer as an orientalist" (155), and the degree to which he participated in a very traditional Western understanding of the East.

Kern ultimately steps away from both Said and Eliot, adopting a more understated and moderate position on the possibility of Pound's knowledge of China, or at least of the Chinese language. In his introduction, Kern questions the notion that *Cathay* had almost nothing to do with the "real" East:

[W]hat . . . is the bearing of Chinese itself upon the accomplishment of these [Pound's] goals? From the standpoint of Eliot's distinction between "Chinese-poetry-in-itself" and Pound's translations, such a bearing would hardly seem to exist. But it is also clear that Pound got something from Fenollosa—even if it was only a shock of recognition, an awareness that they shared an interest in the same qualities or capacities of language—and that Pound's discovery of Chinese constituted a breakthrough in his own work. (5)

The phrase "Chinese itself," which appears in the first sentence, indicates Kern's belief in the existence of something like "real Chinese," a concept rejected by Eliot and generally uninteresting to Said. But it is perhaps the difference between "*Chinese* itself" and "*China* itself" that allows Kern to posit the influence of a "matter *an sich*" on Pound's *Cathay*. Indeed, the primary focus of his book is to trace the influence of a Western romance with the Chinese *language* rather than the Chinese culture or nation, and to look at the poetic effects of such a romance. Accordingly, he is willing and interested to show that a Western perception of Chinese writing invoked orientalism. But he also wants to posit an actual Chinese influence on English poetry. He writes, for instance, of "the degree to which *Cathay* provided a *genuine* opening to Chinese poetry and culture" (156; emphasis added).

At the same time, Kern is quick to contextualize the West's interest in Chinese as part of the history of its orientalism. *Orientalism, Modernism, and the American Poem* situates *Cathay* in a broader tradition of Western translations of Chinese poetry. And yet it does not go so far as Said might in decrying these Western gestures as inevitably caught up in the justification of imperialism: "We may feel . . . that there are important differences, in terms of sensitivity to Chinese culture, for example, between a poet and translator like Pound and a liberal colonial administrator turned scholar like Giles" (157). Kern's tentativeness here—especially with "We may feel"—indicates the difficulty of holding to such a position. Having held it, he quickly moves on to say that translations of Chinese generally exhibit ethnocentrism, without ever indicating who, Pound or Giles, was more sensitive to Chinese culture. And yet the suggestion that one might differentiate among Western texts about the East, being more critical of some than of others, allows Kern to discuss Pound's Chinese influences in a relatively sanguine manner. While his contextualization of Pound in the history of Western literature and scholarship about China effectively acknowledges and enacts an orientalist criticism, Kern's stronger interest lies in the aesthetic and poetic effects of China on modernist Anglo-American poetry.

Kern's relatively tentative approach to Said—he seems to be sure Said is relevant to Pound and China, but not especially interested in making an astringently orientalist critique—is in fact typical of much work on Pound and China today. Like Kern, Xiaomei Chen takes exception to the pressure of "vulgar" orientalism-critique. The title of her 1994 essay, "Rediscovering Ezra Pound: A Post-postcolonial 'Misreading' of a Western Legacy," indicates her intention to surpass the postcolonial reading (identified in the essay mostly with Said and post-*Orientalism* criticism). Chen opens by suggesting that an essay on Ezra Pound may, in a "postcolonial era," be "politically incorrect" (81), and goes on to note that "'Misunderstanding' of the Other in a historical past—although subject to attack in a later age when a new language of theory needs proof for its own 'political correctness'—may nevertheless be considered as exceedingly fruitful and constructive within its own cultural dynamics" (82). Chen argues that Saidian orientalism fails to take Pound up in his own cultural context, where his various errors of translation or understanding allowed him to produce interesting knowledge. This leads to her larger claim that "misunderstanding" or "misreading" is the natural form of all cross-cultural encounters: "'Misunderstanding' (in quotation marks) means a view of a text or a cultural event by a 'receiver' community which differs in important ways from the view of the same text or event in the community of its 'origin'" (83).

In this, Chen takes up the essential point made by Eliot and Said while refusing the moral judgment usually connected with orientalism. Since "misunderstanding" always occurs across cultural boundaries, she suggests, there is no point in lamenting it; rather we should try and understand how it occurs and what its consequences are. Accordingly, Chen announces that she will perform a willful "misreading" of Pound, in which she insists, contra Pound, that much of what he thinks of as Confucian philosophy in his Cantos is in fact Taoist. Chen concludes her essay by emphasizing again the necessarily hybrid nature of encounters between cultures: "because the desire for the exotic necessarily takes its point of departure from conditions within the 'home' culture, the discovery of the culturally alien is not based on the nature and function of those elements in their own, indigenous environment" (103). Here Chen defuses the orientalism-critique by naturalizing it; it would be foolish, she is saying, to believe that the West might know the East as anything other than an "invention." If "Pound and China" arrived, in the mid-1990s, somewhat late to *Orientalism,* it seems to have done so only to take the time to wonder about the relevance of an orientalist critique.

But Chen's claim that everything is a misunderstanding effaces the relatively subtle distinctions around the word/concept "reality" on which both Said and Eliot depend. For instance, though Eliot seems to create a relatively sharp distinction between matters *an sich* and matters as they are known, he ultimately undercuts that difference when he describes the effect of translations as "an illusion that is not altogether an illusion." Unlike an illusion, and unlike a thing that is not at all an illusion, an "illusion that is not altogether an illusion" lives and breathes somewhere between the matter as we know it and the matter as such. It is real and unreal at the same time, like a dream. The only way Eliot can really describe what happens in *Cathay* is to combine the categories that he uses to differentiate between things: an illusion that is not altogether an illusion. This ontological complication suggests at least one way out of the apparent bind of orientalism, a way to acknowledge that a representation can be a truth and a lie at the same time. If it is hard to hold onto the sharp theoretical distinction between constructed and genuine knowledge, we are obliged to work somewhere between a desire for the "real truth" and a sense of its radical impossibility. This is, in the end, the most difficult thing. When the experience of the real world comes in the form of the illusion-that-is-not-altogether-an-illusion, the hybrid product of what is and what we know, we ask two different questions. First, is it constructed? And second, is it true? Eliot's "illusion that is not altogether an illusion" suggests the difficulty of answering either one of these in the absolute affirmative.

Like Eliot's, Said's sense of the burdens of representation can be made to speak a complexity greater than the one Chen assumes it has. In *Orientalism,* Said never says the West should *stop* representing the East. When he declares the "brute reality [of Eastern nations and cultures] obviously greater than anything that could be said about them in the West," he puts the West in a difficult position, one it cannot escape simply by shedding the burden of representation. Even when the representation is in every way accurate, it still must confront the strictures of orientalism. For instance, if I reproduce (as Pound did) Chinese poetry's tendency to make each line a complete sentence in my English verse, I am taking something from "genuine" Chinese poetry, and yet I am still (if I announce to the world that my methodology is Chinese) participating in a Western invention of China—I am helping the West create a China "as it knows it." While any single Western perception of China may be accurate and true to real China, it is also necessarily inflected to some degree by Western ethnocentrism, in its reception as well as its production. The reverse of this is also the case: just because something is orientalist doesn't mean it is not true.

To say all this is to begin to discover that the major problem of "Pound and China" criticism is large indeed: nothing less than the question of representation itself, or, more specifically, the ability of representations to seem real while being unreal, or to be unreal while seeming real. While for Eliot this is an ontological problem, for Said it is a political and historical one, but all these—ontology, politics, history—find themselves caught up in the history of "Pound and China." We cannot not represent; "China," in the field of Pound criticism, names a particularly inescapable ethical bind.

As I move on to discuss more specifically Pound's relation to China, and the critical understanding of that relationship, I will be looking at some work that denies the reality of Pound's China, and other work that insists upon it. Rather than issue a final decision on the Chineseness of Pound's Chinese influence—that is, rather than make a difficult ethical decision—I will be exploring the persistent need to pin down and define true Chineseness (or its absence) in Pound's work, a need shared by both Pound and his critics. The terms of such a discussion have already been set, first by Eliot and then by Said, the modernist and postmodernist joined together by a similar sense of the difficulties of representation. In the rest of this chapter, I will be interested both in mapping the limits of that epistemology and in demonstrating its widespread influence, all as part of a larger effort to look at how Pound and the literary academy, through Pound, have understood the East/West binary. One of the primary articulations of such an understanding has come through reaction to Pound's translations, especially *Cathay*, to which I now turn.

Two Translations of Modernism

Cathay was fourteen poems gathered together in a flimsy volume the color of a brown paper bag.[1] It was also, in 1915, a radical example of the new English poetry, a substantial break from traditional Anglo-American poetics and previous translations of Chinese. Its most remarkable aspect today is its endurance. Pound may have been the inventor of Chinese poetry for Eliot's time; he remains in many ways its inventor for our time as well. As Octavio Paz has remarked of Pound's influence: "All of us since who have translated Chinese and Japanese poetry are not only his followers but his debtors. . . . With that small volume of translations Pound, to a great extent, began modern poetry in English. Yet, at the same time, he also began something unique: the modern tradition of classical Chinese poetry in the poetic conscience of the West" (Weinberger and Paz, 46).

Pound, who did not begin studying Chinese until 1936, translated *Cathay* on the basis of notes taken by the American scholar Ernest Fenollosa, who, while living and working in Japan, had transcribed a number of Chinese poems with the help of a Professor Mori and Mr. Ariga. Often following, sometimes deviating from Fenollosa's notes, Pound worked the word-for-word translations into English poetry. Sometimes he guessed at meanings, sometimes he misread Fenollosa's writing, sometimes Fenollosa got things wrong. That Pound's translations are successful has been taken by any number of critics as a literary miracle, by others as a literary fraud.

Such debates revolve around Pound's disruption of then-conventional codes of translation, a disruption through which he granted himself the right to substantially modify any literal or philologically correct reading in order to follow something he might have called the poem "itself." For instance, in *Cathay*'s second poem, "The Beautiful Toilet," Pound simply removed the original's fifth line, making it into the poem's title. "The Beautiful Toilet" is a translation of a poem attributed to Mei Sheng, originally written around 140 B.C. We know that Pound had seen Herbert Giles's version of the poem before he translated it; there is also a version by Arthur Waley, written shortly after Pound's, and another version by Wai-Lim Yip, written in the 1960s. Below are the poem's first four lines in Chinese; I have put Fenollosa's word-for-character transcriptions beneath the characters:

青	青	河	畔	草
blue	blue	river	bank	grass
[green]²	[green]			

鬱	鬱	園	中	柳
luxuriantly spread the willow [dense]	luxuriantly spread the willow [dense]	garden	in [middle]	willow

盈	盈	樓	上	女
fill / full	fill / full	storied house	on	girl
[in the first bloom of youth]				

皎	皎	當	窗	牖
white/brilliant luminous	white/brilliant luminous	just face [at]	window	door [window]

The earliest important English translation is Herbert Giles's. Giles, who served at one point as a British administrator in China, was with James Legge a major influence in turn-of-the-century English sinology. He translated Mei Sheng's opening as

> Green grows the grass upon the bank,
> The willow-shoots are long and lank;
> A lady in a glistening gown
> Opens the casement and looks down.
> (Qtd. in Kenner, *Era,* 194)

Right away one sees some of the problems when translating from Chinese. Metrically, the switch from iambs in the second and third lines to a trochee in the fourth does not stem from any Chinese pattern or, it would seem, from the content of the English poem. Grammatically, Giles cannot retain the ambiguity of the Chinese. The use of "upon" in the first line, for instance, forces a prepositional assumption where the original has none. Syntactically, one of the poem's major problems for an English reader—the double characters that begin each line—has been resolved by Giles's simply cutting them out.

The choices Giles makes raise a number of questions about translation in general: Should the translation reproduce for its readers the experience of a native reader, who can read the poem without experiencing it as culturally "different"? Or should it indicate and display the differences between the poetic traditions of the source and target languages that make translation so difficult?[3] The answer to these questions has a lot to do with how the translations end up. For instance: Giles's use of an AABB rhyme scheme has no source in the original. But the AABB rhymes are familiar to an English reader in the way that the Chinese patterns of rhyme and tone might be familiar to a Chinese reader. Rather than follow the original's difference from English poetry, Giles effectively "translates" not only the Chinese words but also the Chinese poetic form by putting them into their *cultural* near-equivalents in English. This tendency appears more clearly in Giles's use of cultural anachronisms like "lady in a glistening gown" and "casement." In 140 B.C. China has no casements, but has places that function in literature more or less like casements, in that women who look down from them can be understood as occupying a particular cultural position. Giles thus reproduces the archaism of classical China in an English historical vocabulary, translating the experience of a native Chinese reader who would read *storied house* 樓 and understand it as occupying a certain temporal and cultural space. The English reader can then read the poem as if it takes place in medieval England rather than ancient China.

Pound had, when he translated Mei Sheng's poem, seen Giles's version, and it is worth remembering that "The Beautiful Toilet" might have been quite different had Pound not had something to react against.

The Beautiful Toilet

Blue, blue is the grass about the river
And the willows have overfilled the close garden.
And within, the mistress, in the midmost of her youth,
White, white of face, hesitates, passing the door.
Slender, she puts forth a slender hand

And she was a courtezan in the old days,
And she has married a sot,
Who now goes drunkenly out
And leaves her too much alone

Pound is at his cleverest when dealing with the double characters at the beginning of each line—in line 2, for instance, he has substituted aural for syntactic repetition with his use of "ill" sounds in "willows" and "overfilled," and in line 3 he repeats the "mi" of mistress and midmost; in the fifth line he separates two uses of "slender" and repeats its "nd" sound in "hand" at the end of the line.[4]

The problem is, of course, that it is not clear that the poem actually reproduces the *meaning* of the Chinese, which offers no reason to say the mistress is in the midmost of her youth. Pound's version adds ideas that are not "there" in the original, particularly as it opens itself to metaphor— the claustrophobic garden, "close" and "overfilled," traps the mistress as neatly as does her domesticity. And the word "courtezan," traditionally used to refer to a high-class prostitute or a hanger-on at a royal court, brings Pound's own particular sense of cultural anachronism neatly into the poem. At the same time, Pound estranges the poem in ways Giles does not. The repetition of "and" in lines 2 and 3, combined with a meter that shifts with the poem's tone, offered the English reader in 1915 a poetic experience that registered as different and unusual.

So almost immediately after Pound published *Cathay* there arose a chorus of criticism—criticism typical of the reactions to his earlier translations, including those of the Anglo-Saxon poem "The Seafarer" and *Sextus Propertius.* The traditional grievance against Pound was that his poems were not translations but "brilliant paraphrases" (Waley, *Poetry,* 12). As far as the Chinese poems go, the chief early architect of this critique was Arthur Waley, who wrote a version of the poem three years after *Cathay;* Hugh Kenner suggests it was published in "implied rebuke" (*Era,* 195):

> Green, green,
> The grass by the river bank,
> Thick, thick,
> The willow trees in the garden.
> Sad, sad,
> The lady in the tower.
> (*Translations,* 38)

Looking at the first lines of all three poems, we see instantly that the first prepositional interpolation—Waley's "by," Giles's "upon," Pound's "about"—marks the difference between English and Chinese grammar, as well as, for many critics, the difficulty of reproducing the apparent "spareness" of Chinese poetry in English. That said, Waley uses almost all of Fenollosa's key words, and retains—perhaps at the cost of poetry—the pattern of double characters at the beginning of each line. He makes changes, too: his "Sad, sad," in the fifth line marks an important departure from the poem's other versions, since it bluntly foregrounds the emotional state of the woman in the tower. Pound had left the tower (the "storied house" of Fenollosa's notes) out of things entirely: "And within, the mistress, in the midmost of her youth." Pound's "within" suggests an interior space, but refers most immediately to the garden in the second line. His translation forgoes the specific interiority of the tower in favor of a generalized "within," a space complicated by Pound's choice of "midmost" to place the mistress's youth; she is "within" her youth in the same way that she is "within" the garden. Pound's version metaphorizes as interior the woman's place in both space and time.

It is difficult to know how to take Waley's translation, since it allegedly corrects Pound's. Like the differences between Pound's version and Giles's, the differences between Waley and Pound may depend as much on Waley's felt obligation to criticize his predecessor as an obligation to accurately translate Mei Sheng. But one way to understand the differences between Pound and Waley would simply consider Waley's version more literal. As far as the word is concerned, Waley's poem actually has "Thick, thick," at the beginning of the second line, a match closer to the Chinese than Pound's repetition of "ill" sounds, and through the rest of the poem, Waley's translation quite tirelessly follows Fenollosa's notes. In an introduction to one of his books of translations, Waley wrote that he "tried to produce regular rhythmic effects similar to those in the original. Each character in the Chinese is represented by a stress in the English; but between the stresses unstressed syllables are of course interposed" (*Hundred*, 19). Pound never articulated any rules, and that difference more or less enacts the larger argument between the two men: Pound simply went farther and changed more.[5]

The differences between Pound's versions and Waley's have constituted the necessary guise of any discussion of Pound's Chinese translations for most of their history. This happens because where they differ marks a kind of epistemological fault-line between literature and science, poetics and sinology. The most common form of this debate before, say,

1970, involves a speaker of Chinese on one side, defending Waley for having gotten the details correct, and a literary critic on the other, defending Pound on the grounds that he, at least, wrote good poetry. From the point of view of the literary critics, Waley's reply seems both "lamentable" (Kenner, *Era,* 195) and "insipid" (Yip, 134). And Hugh Kenner comments, on Waley: "This is a resourceless man's verse; the resourceless man wrote but did not transmute; it is hard to wring song from philology" (*Era,* 195).[6]

The literary critics have won the argument. To give a measure of Pound's influence on Chinese translation, it is worth looking at a 1969 version of the same poem done by Wai-Lim Yip, which he published in his book on *Cathay:*

> Green beyond green, the grass along the river.
>> Leaves on leaves, the willows in the garden.
>> Bloom of bloom, the girl up in the tower.
>> A ball of brightness at the window-sill
>> A flash of fairness is her rouged face.
>> Slender, she puts forth a slender white hand.
>> She was a singing girl before,
>> Now wife of a playboy.
>> The playboy went and never returned.
>> Empty bed! Alone! How hard it is to keep.
>
>> (134)

Comparing the latter half of his poem to Pound's, Yip finds "The Beautiful Toilet" *too* literal, saying that it fails to preserve "the ironical play of the original" (136). Yip criticizes Pound for setting off the poem's final four lines and thereby missing the poem's centripetal force by dichotomizing it emotionally and visually. The strength of the emotional outburst in Pound's final lines is not matched, Yip says, by the Chinese poem, which more subtly moves between the woman's beauty and her loss. Yip essentially suggests that Pound's reconstruction of the poem's message suffers from a certain cultural blindness, remarking on Pound's inability to translate the poem's culturally Chinese tendency toward a pleasurable ambiguity of meaning. Certainly Pound shifts tone dramatically toward the end of his version with the hard endings of "sot" and "out," and the way he lets the "and" at the beginning of three of the four final lines catapult the reader out of the poem.

Despite this overall criticism, however, Yip is full of praise for Pound's version, which he calls "subtler music" and "quite satisfactory" at "keeping intact the natural breath of the English language" (134, 135). Looking at Yip's poem, one sees moments in which he seems to return to Pound's version for answers, most obviously in his sixth line, which virtually copies Pound's own "Slender, she puts forth a slender hand." However Yip translates the poem, he does so well within the frame of Pound's modernism, not outside or beyond it.

And so the anxiety of Pound's influence makes it hard to say what a good translation ought to look like. But the vitriol spilled over the Pound versus Waley debate, focused mainly on how much one ought to change, and the difference between a so-called literal translation and a something else—something like a "transmutation" or a "translucency"—obscures the infinitely greater distance between Pound, Waley, and Yip on one hand and Herbert Giles on the other. Reading Waley and Pound, one senses that the poetic ground has shifted away from Giles, that both Waley and Pound are writing "specimens of XXth century poetry," differing in degree from one another but in kind or genre from Giles.[7] Pound's influence on what we today consider to be good translations of Chinese poetry has modified the technologies of reading and writing such that most translators no longer recognize Giles as part of our poetic world. Octavio Paz has written, for instance, that Pound was "the first to attempt to make English poems out of Chinese originals" (Weinberger and Paz, 46); Eliot Weinberger writes of a Giles-like translation by W. J. B. Fletcher that it is "typical of those written before the general recognition" of *Cathay* (Weinberger and Paz, 9).

In that sense, Eliot was right all along: Pound did invent Chinese poetry for our time. But what that means is tricky. As Kern points out, many critics who quote Eliot on Pound leave out what Eliot says immediately afterward: "I predict that in three hundred years Pound's *Cathay* will be a 'Windsor Translation' as Chapman and North are now 'Tudor Translations': it will be called (and justly) a 'magnificent specimen of XXth Century poetry' rather than a 'translation'" (14–15). What Eliot understands, then, is that Pound's translations are spectacular not necessarily because of their accurate translation of Chineseness but because of their participation in a new mode of twentieth-century English poetry. At the same time, however, Eliot remarks—and this is where the whole thing gets complicated and interesting—that Pound's translations, more than anyone else's, produce *in our time* the sense that we are close to the Chinese; they produce the sense that through the translation "we really at last get the original."

What this means is that one might read Pound's translations not as instances of a certain style of translation, but rather in the context of a developing modernism. Or rather—since they have been read both ways at different times—that one has to read both of these things simultaneously, the Chineseness and modernism intertwined, not as coincidental but as causal. In what follows I attempt to see that intertwining, and to think about what it means for our understanding of translation, of Chineseness, and of modernity.

Translation itself is a domesticating art, and bears the burden of strangeness only by rendering it familiar. In 1916, a *Times Literary Supplement* review of Pound's Chinese translations commented, "The Chinese poems are full of content and of a content interesting to every one. 'The River Merchant's Wife,' for instance, reminds one of a story by Tolstoy" ("The Poems of Mr. Ezra Pound," 545). In comparing "The River Merchant's Wife" to Tolstoy, the author signals that the pleasure of reading the Chinese approximates the pleasure a reader might have gotten from a story he or she had already read—a story already marked as a kind of capital-L literature. All this is simply a way of saying that Pound's translations conformed in one way or another—by "being full of content," for instance—to the expectations the *TLS* writer had for what he thought of as literary language or literary work. But it is not just *universal* literature. The comparison to a Russian author is telling: Russia's position on the eastern edge of Europe (and the western edge of Asia) already makes it a culturally mixed location; the author may be inviting Chinese, different and yet vaguely familiar, to take up a similar position on the margins of the West. *Cathay*'s pleasurable difference is effectively contained within its similarity to Tolstoy, who is almost European, but not quite.

From the first the reception of *Cathay* seems to have understood that its pleasures were connected in some way to an Eastern "translation," so that the East might offer up a literary experience full of interesting content in an idiom unfamiliar in just the right ways. One of *Cathay*'s great successes is that it managed to translate in a manner that seemed entirely culturally authentic—this despite Pound's absolute ignorance of Chinese. But then knowledge of a certain kind can only get in the way of translation. As another early reviewer of *Cathay* remarked, it was hard to know if Pound had actually translated directly from the Chinese. But maybe that made no difference: "for those who, like ourselves, know no Chinese, it does not matter much. The result, however produced, is well worth having, and it seems to us very Chinese" ("Poems from Cathay," 144).

How do things come to seem Chinese? George Steiner attributes Pound's ability to call forth the Chinese original for his Western readers without breaks for explanation to "a general phenomenon of hermeneutic trust" (359). By this he means that Pound's adoption of certain conventional associations (bowmen, blue grass, mountains, and so on) effectively reproduces an absence of knowledge he and the reader share: "Pound can imitate and persuade with utmost economy not because he or his reader knows so much but because both concur in knowing so little" (359). In other words, Pound translated via a kind of cultural shorthand, in which elements easily recognizable as "Chinese" established the authenticity of the Eastern setting.

Edward Baker, picking up on Steiner, says that Pound "forces the reader to pay strict attention to form, rather than to any cultural content the poems may have originally possessed" (76). Baker writes, "The actual contents of the poems, the bowmen and willows and husbands off to war, will come to strike the Western reader as the necessary accoutrements of any Chinese poem" (76). Such a structure establishes a sort of reality-code, and by reproducing the elements of the code, the poet (or the scholar) can reproduce the sense that one really gets at China through the text. Crucially, the tense of Baker's "will come" reveals the dual motion of the hermeneutic trust, which not only depends on what most Western readers already (do not) know, but also *creates* the new shared (lack of) knowledge that will structure future *chinoiseries*.

To some extent, then, this kind of knowledge produces a self-fulfilling prophecy. Since Pound invents Chinese poetry for our time, everything after him has to look like his work to seem "Chinese." Ming Xie argues that "for the better half of the twentieth century the movement begun by Fenollosa and Pound . . . to mold the Western reader with a quite different expectation of what Chinese poetry is, has been so successful and become so preponderant a tradition in itself that it may be said to have redefined the nature of classical Chinese poetry" (224). In fact, as Robert Kern notes, "to the extent that any translation deviates from these [Pound's] conventions, it runs the risk of violating our sense of what Chinese poetry has in fact come to be" (181). With "come to be," Kern captures well Pound's seminal role in creating Chinese poetry for the West, and points to that creation as part of a *process*—one that, as we have seen, engages writers, readers, translators, and scholars in a set of arguments over culture and beauty, translation and truth. When, one day, we read Pound's poems the way we read Giles's, we will be in another era.

But in 1915 we were still at the beginning of what Hugh Kenner calls the Pound Era. The sense of genuine foreignness produced by Chinese translations then depended on an economy of almost-knowledge shared by the author and the reader. Edward Baker gives an instructive counterexample to Pound, a few lines from a translation by James Liu: "West of the bbyang gate no old acquaintance / will you meet again?" (77). Here the reader trips over "bbyang gate," which causes a focus on the "content" of the poem rather than its "formal otherness," says Baker. Annotating the line to explain the history of the bbyang gate (whatever it is) would presumably send the reader off in the wrong direction entirely, breaking up the poetic experience.

Pound himself had addressed the issue of notes and annotations on *Cathay*'s final page. Noting that he had translated only fourteen of Fenollosa's poems, he wrote:

> There are also other poems. . . . But if I give them, with the necessary breaks for explanation, and a tedium of notes, it is quite certain that the personal hatred in which I am held by many, and the *invidia* which is directed against me because I have dared openly to declare my belief in certain young artists, will be brought to bear first on the flaws of such translation, and will then be merged into depreciation of the whole book of translations. Therefore I give only these unquestionable poems. (32)

Given the paucity of his knowledge about China or Chinese in 1915, Pound was right to worry that an attack on *Cathay* would become an attack on his scholarly credentials. By insisting that any critical attack on the translations was not the product of a desire for knowledge but rather "the personal hatred in which I am held by many," Pound attempted to disrupt the critical process before it began. Considering the vast differences between China and England, and Chinese and English poetry, Pound certainly could have chosen to give his readers some explanatory material. By choosing to reject explanation as a mode of translation in favor of the aesthetic production of poetic experience, however, Pound chose to define the best, least "questionable" translations as those that give the reader a sense of the self-evidence of cultural differences by making them intelligible, without notes, in a language whose strangeness needed no explanation.

All this would be well and good if none of Pound's *Cathay* poems had annotations. But it cannot account for *Cathay*'s "The Jewel Stairs' Grievance," which has an annotation that is longer than the poem itself. In his discussion of "breaks for explanation," Pound nowhere mentions "Grievance":

> The jewelled steps are already quite white with dew,
> It is so late that the dew soaks my gauze stockings,
> And I let down the crystal curtain
> And watch the moon through the clear autumn.
>
> *By Rihaku (Li T'ai Po)*

Note: Jewel stairs, therefore a palace. Grievance, therefore there is something to complain of. Gauze stockings, therefore a court lady, not a servant who complains. Clear autumn, therefore he has no excuse on account of the weather. Also she has come early, for the dew has not merely whitened the stairs, but has soaked her stockings. The poem is especially prized because she utters no direct reproach. (55)

The original of this poem has no clear subjective presence; the "my" and "I" in the translation do not appear in the original poem. In Pound's version, this absence of subjectivity appears to be displaced onto the annotation, which while elaborating on the poem's references makes no acknowledgment of its own being-written. The writing subject of the annotation is nowhere to be found, and its disappearance is nowhere more visible than in the referentially bizarre passive voice of the last sentence: "The poem is especially prized because she utters no direct reproach." I am guessing that the sentence means to inform the reader that the poem is especially prized *by the Chinese*. In so saying the annotation attempts to instruct the reader in a culturally appropriate reaction to the poem.

If Pound's explanation of the woman's silence is a necessary step in the appreciation of the poem as Chinese, though, the problem is that in order to show that the lady deserves praise for uttering no reproach—and hence to provide a culturally richer understanding of the poem—Pound must drown out her silence with an annotation, which in stating that she has cause for a "grievance" utters her reproach for her. It is as though the annotation retranslates the poem, so that the reader can return to it a second time and appreciate it for the same reason Pound and the Chinese do. The annotation, unlike the poem, is not meant to be read twice, but having given up its information, effectively dissipates into the realm of "knowledge," leaving a new aesthetic experience in its wake.

But while the annotation's final line instructs the reader on how to *culturally* appreciate the poem, the rest of the annotation seems more concerned in teaching the reader how to discern the poem's *literary* motivations. Pound takes five sentences to explain the poem's inexpressive images, in each case laying out the larger context implicit in his terse language: "Jewel stairs, therefore a palace. Grievance, therefore there is something to complain of," and so on.

For the most part, then, the poem's annotation has less to do with Chinese writing than with Pound's. Five of its six sentences explain not the poem's Chineseness but the poetics that make the poem different from conventional English poetry. In doing so the annotation shows the reader how to extend the subtleties of Poundian images into larger themes and narratives. Pound is teaching the reader to read modernism, to take each line as the miniature and concatenated version of some larger idea, or a clearer and more specific referent. Or, as Anne Chapple says, "The prose gloss appended to the poem is intended to compensate for the cultural differences which prevent our appreciation of the poem" (18).

By "cultural differences," Chapple means to refer to the distances among different readers of English poetry, not the differences between English readers and Chinese ones. Her specific frame of reference is Imagism, a poetic movement Pound developed with several friends in the years before *Cathay;* her general claim is that Pound wrote *Cathay* specifically to exemplify Imagist poetry. But "Grievance," Chapple writes, is even more subtle, even more Imagistic, than Pound's other Imagist poems and his other Chinese translations. The annotation is therefore especially necessary because the poem's images are unusually hard to decipher: "I would claim that [the poem] manages to 'convey an emotion by presenting the object and circumstance of that emotion without comment' as other Imagist poems do, but with a difference: the 'object' and 'circumstance' of the emotion are themselves so subtly conveyed that we might easily overlook them" (19).

And in fact they might be overlooked if not for the annotation. If the poem is like other Imagist poems, only subtler, it is so not only by virtue of the poem itself but also through Pound's unsubtle note. Like an appreciation of the lady's uttering no direct reproach, an admiration of the poem's subtlety becomes predicated on being able to forget the annotation and return to the poem as though for the first time. The reader might then admire the incredible artfulness of Pound's images, but the admiration has been constructed quite literally by the annotation. This, combined with Pound's invective against annotations, is what makes "Grievance" fundamentally ironic: the rules by which the prose gloss produces meaning are basically opposed to the poem's rules, and yet are vitally necessary to the creation of its meaning.

If one thinks about "cultural difference" as the difference between China and the West—that is the way we most commonly think about cultural difference today in any case—one may be surprised by Chapple's description of "cultural differences." But Chapple is right that the poem's *other* (or perhaps original) cultural difference is what separates it as a literary text from the vast majority of English readers in 1915—its modernism.

From this perspective, the poem is translated twice. The reader, untrained in new English or ancient Chinese poetry, uses the annotation to "translate" the poem's two strangenesses—its cultural Chineseness, and its Imagist poetics. By virtue of this double movement, "The Jewel Stairs' Grievance" associates Imagism with a Chinese mind-set, producing the "original" for Imagism *avant la lettre:* what Imagism is in 1915, Chinese poetry seems to have been all along. But only if it is translated the way Pound translates it—a translation by Giles does not make, can never make—the same literary argument.

Where Steiner and Baker focused on the development of "hermeneutic trust" that allowed the reader to imagine Pound's poems as Chinese, Chapple's interest in other cultural differences shows that such trust extends to literary style as well. In its clear explication of its own multifaceted "cultural differences," Pound's "Grievance" reveals the mechanism that produces comfortable knowledge about China in every *Cathay* poem. Where the reader was not explicitly instructed in her reading enjoyment, there developed nonetheless an overall impression of both China and Imagism, an impression that has stayed with us well past Pound's death as the marker of good Chinese translations. So while "The Jewel Stairs' Grievance" is the only *Cathay* poem with an annotation, it is not for all that so exceptional. The hermeneutic trust that it makes explicit is simply the same process that drives the other poems in the volume. What the annotation does make clear, however, is the degree to which that hermeneutic trust involved not only Chineseness but also modernism itself. The poem's difference—the part that needs translating—lies just as much with Pound's adoption of new aesthetic techniques that shaped themselves to the strangeness of his language as it does with the fact that it was originally written in Chinese.

Perhaps this literary strangeness is easy to forget, trained as we are in a literary criticism whose major insights and reading styles owe their origins to many of modernism's discoveries about language—today, modernism needs no real translation. But in 1915, the awkward relationship between Pound's language and the language of Chinese presented a clear enough problem. In an anonymous review of *Cathay* published in the *Times Literary Supplement,* the writer warned his readers not to be angry or surprised at its strange use of language, and asked the following remarkable question: "is the Chinese language, we wonder, as unusual as Mr. Pound's?" If not, the writer continued, maybe Pound "does misrepresent the effect upon a Chinese reader, though he may deliberately do that so as to enable us to understand the Chinese method" ("Poems from Cathay," 144).

Is the Chinese language as unusual as Mr. Pound's? Probably not to Chinese people, but actual China is only marginally implicated here, as a shadow to the infinitely realer "China" whose presence Pound's *Cathay* produced so vividly. As Saussy remarks, echoing Eliot, "China has always been, is always still, in the process of being invented"—both for us and the Chinese (*Problem,* 4). Modernism, too, had to be invented; Pound was there for that as well. The differences in translation between Pound and Waley on one side and Giles on the other speak not simply to a difference in style but to a radical change in literary epistemology—a change in the way we know what we know in the text, the way in which we express that knowledge to approximate the presence of the real, if that's what we want to do with writing in any case.

Inasmuch as the *Cathay* poems produce the feeling that—in Eliot's phrase—"we really at last get the original," the epistemology of its style is especially effective: *Cathay* seems to know, and to allow us to know, the thing that is impossible to know in translation: the original text. This feeling that we are at last at the original is the most important product of modernism's two translations. It is not just that *Cathay*'s translation of aesthetic otherness into English happens at the same time as its translation of Chinese cultural otherness into England. Rather, at some level, the second translation is part of what makes the first translation possible. That is, the guarantor of these almost-perfect translations is not simply Pound's poetic genius but something in the felt "Chineseness" of the Chinese poetry. This dialectical relationship differs fundamentally from the one Qian ascribes to Pound's Imagism in *Orientalism and Modernism*. Speaking of the presence of "Chinese" poems in the original Imagist collection, *Des imagistes* (1914), he writes: "By bringing in the Chinese poems in the first Imagist volume, Pound had actually pointed out to the Imagist movement a new direction and a new possibility—the possibility of drawing on the robust Imagistic tradition of the Chinese" (54–55). Qian's capitalization of "Imagistic" indicates that he sees "Imagism" as a natively Chinese phenomenon—that is, Pound's Imagism, for Qian, simply draws on the "Imagistic" tradition already there in China. I am arguing, instead, that Pound's Imagism produces itself simultaneously through a reference to China and a new modernist poetics that may have had nothing to do with actual China, in other words, that Imagism's modernism draws on its association with Chineseness just as its Chineseness secures the historio-cultural legitimacy of its modernist aesthetic. The relation is dialectical and graphic (that is, produced by its own being-written), and not simply a question of cross-cultural influence. It is, in the end, the ineffable presence of this (legitimate?) Chineseness, which appears to precede the translation itself by centuries, even though it is produced in exactly the same moment as the translation—it is in fact *part* of the translation—it is this presence that authorizes and enables the spectacular poetic gesture through which Pound, reaching Eastward for the unquestionable translation, grasps the poetic voice of his own modernity.[8]

27

Unveiling the Universal AROUND CATHAY

In the years surrounding *Cathay*'s publication, Pound seemed to be laying the foundations for the presence of this poetic Chineseness in his original poetry and his other translations. In 1911, Pound wrote his best-known poem, "In a Station of the Metro." The poem, which he later called "hokku-like," was printed as follows:

In a Station of the Metro

The apparition   of these faces   in the crowd;
Petals   on a wet, black bough.

The stark play of black on white, both in the poem and in the spacing on the page, reminiscent of Chinese or Japanese painting, reflect a "tacit orientalism . . . superimposed upon metropolitan displacement" (Xie, 63). The petals and the bough work against the title's mechanical Metro, staging the clash between a "natural" culture and an "industrial" one, East and West, that establishes and contextualizes the poem's form. "Station" occasions its meaning by juxtaposing well-known opposites, allowing each half of the binary (industrial West/natural East) to create new knowledge about its counterpart. At the same time, the momentary appearance of the East in the West here points to the possibility of an Eastern understanding of Western experience, a vision of the smoke-and-steel West mediated by an Eastern emphasis on the colors and shapes of nature.

In the years between 1911 and 1915, Pound was, with H. D., Richard Aldington, and others, developing the doctrine of poetic Imagism. In 1913, F. S. Flint published an interview with Pound in *Poetry*, laying out Imagism's principles. Pound followed Flint's article with a six-page piece called "A Few Don'ts by an Imagist," in which he wrote: "An 'Image' is that which presents an intellectual and emotional complex in an instant of time. . . . the natural object is always the *adequate* symbol."

That was in March 1913. Later that year,[9] Pound wrote "Fan-Piece, for Her Imperial Lord," based on a Chinese translation by Giles:

Fan-Piece, for Her Imperial Lord

O fan of white silk,
      Clear as frost on the grass-blade,
You are also laid aside.

Giles's version had gone like this:

O fair white silk, fresh from the weaver's loom,
Clear as the frost, bright as the winter snow—
See! Friendship fashions out of thee a fan,
Round as the round moon shines in heaven's above,
At home, abroad, a close companion thou,
Stirring at every move the grateful gale.
And yet I fear, ah me! that autumn chills,
Cooling the dying summer's torrid rage,
Will see thee laid neglected on the shelf,
All thoughts of bygone days, like them bygone.

Pound's condensation of Giles's narrative into three sharp images demonstrates the effect of combining Imagist principles with Chinese material. The long, resonant vowels of Pound's opening and his final line come up against the precision of detail in the images, as if he were demonstrating in practice the difference between the phonetic and the visual, the English alphabet and the Chinese character. And yet, of course, the original Chinese poem is not three lines long. The innovations of Pound's poetics justify themselves by reference to a style that does not exist as such in the original.[10]

In September of that same year, *Poetry* contained a sequence of poems called "Scented Leaves—from a Chinese Jar," written by Allen Upward. In late September, Pound went to visit Upward, who told Pound that he had "made it [the poem sequence] up out of his head, using a certain amount of Chinese reminiscence" (Carpenter, 218).[11] While at Upward's, Pound also met Mary Fenollosa, Ernest Fenollosa's widow. On October 2 Pound wrote to his future wife, Dorothy Shakespear, "I seem to be getting orient from all quarters. . . . I'm stocked up with K'ung fu Tsze [Confucius], and Men Tsze [Mencius], etc. I suppose they'll keep me calm for a week or so" (Pound and Shakespear, 264). Some short time later, Mary Fenollosa handed Pound the manuscripts of her dead husband's work: preliminary translations of a great many Chinese poems and some Japanese No plays, to edit and publish as he saw fit. Pound was delighted; he wrote to Shakespear, "There is *no* long poem in chinese. . . . THE period was 4th cent. B.C.—Chu Yüan, Imagiste" (Pound and Shakspear, 267).[12]

Alongside the creative work that became *Cathay* was an essay by Ernest Fenollosa that Pound did not publish until 1918. Fenollosa's "The Chinese Written Character as a Medium for Poetry" is a primer for reading *Cathay,* since it contains many of the poetic principles that inspired

Pound's translations. The essay lays out Fenollosa's premise that Chinese writing as a visual text and Chinese grammar as an epistemological system are more suited to the progress of Western poetry than phonetic writing and Latinate grammar. Writing, for instance, that Chinese "exactly corresponds to this universal form of action in nature," and that it "brings language close to *things,* and . . . erects all speech into a kind of dramatic poetry" (63), Fenollosa found in the Chinese written character a perfect foil for the inadequacies of Western alphabetic representation. As Pound wrote in 1934's *Make It New,* "Fenollosa's work was given me in manuscript when I was ready for it. It saved me a great deal of time" (8).

For Fenollosa, the fundamental evil of Western languages springs from the verb *to be,* which makes existence a state rather than an action: "Fancy picking up a man and telling him that he is a noun, a dead thing rather than a bundle of functions!" (66). Chinese, on the other hand, is "alive and plastic, because *thing* and *action* are not formally separated" (67). Importantly, Fenollosa believed that Western languages were once very much like Chinese, but that they had slipped away from their roots through a combination of overcivilized medieval logic and a general referential sloppiness. Accordingly, Chinese worked for Fenollosa like a window on the Western past, revealing the prehistory of Western language in all its expressive, natural glory. "In Chinese the chief verb for 'is' not only means actively 'to have,' but shows by its derivation that it expresses something even more concrete, namely 'to snatch the moon from the hand.' 有 Here the baldest symbol of prosaic analysis is transformed by magic into a splendid flash of concrete poetry" (65).

And because the Chinese character is visual, not phonetic, it allows the trained (and sometimes the untrained) reader to *see* history in its brushstrokes: "Its etymology is constantly visible. . . . After thousands of years the lines of metaphoric advance are still shown, and in many cases actually retained in the meaning" (75). Fenollosa's emphasis on the purely visual nature of Chinese characters allowed him to treat them like Poundian images: when you learn that the combination of the *sun* 日 seen through *wood* (a tree) 木 makes *east* 東, you know all you need to know to grasp not just the word-image *east* but also the unornamented true *idea* behind it.[13] While Fenollosa was aware that most scholars (in the West and in China) see elements of most complicated characters as phonetic, not visual, he disagreed: "I find it incredible that any such minute subdivision of the idea could ever have existed alone as abstract sound without the concrete character. It contradicts the law of evolution" (80).[14] In a footnote to Fenollosa's insistence that Chinese characters that seem phonetic to linguists were at some point in time purely pictorial, Pound reports that his friend, the sculptor Henri Gaudier, could read Chinese characters after only two weeks' study, sheerly by dint of the pictures. "He was amazed at the stupidity of lexicographers who could not, for all their learning, discern the pictorial values which were to him perfectly obvious and apparent" (80–81).

For Fenollosa, the "visibility of the metaphor" lay at the heart of all signification: "the very soil of Chinese life seems entangled in the roots of its speech," and the "ideographs are like blood-stained battle-flags to an old campaigner" (75). Fenollosa imbued the Chinese written character with the high materiality of earth and battle—elements readers of *Cathay* would come to associate with China itself—to stress the importance of its status as a grounded metaphor. Fenollosa's character embodies materiality, retaining a fossil record traced in pictures: concept-metaphors that allow the reader literally to see the march of history.[15] Chinese thus becomes available to anyone attuned to visual metaphor, even someone who had not studied Chinese (as Pound did not until 1936).

Before he published Fenollosa's essay, Pound had already been expressing in English a visualness substantially different from anything in ordinary poetic language at the time. While the Imagist aesthetic behind *Cathay*, "Fan-Piece," or "In a Station of the Metro," may have been understood for a while as a quirk of Pound's language, the publication of Fenollosa's essay allowed Pound to answer the *Times Literary Supplement*'s question, "Is the Chinese language as unusual as Mr. Pound's?" with an emphatic and expert "yes." He seemed, unlike any other translator of Chinese, to be bringing the heart of Chinese poetry into English, giving his readers the experience of real China unmediated by English rhyme schemes or metrical conventions; his China was exciting, fresh, and new, both in content and in form. Even though parts of Pound's Imagism preceded his reading of Fenollosa, once he published Fenollosa's essay, it fell under the compelling aura of Fenollosa's ontological aesthetics.

Throughout his life, Pound's sense of what China and the Chinese language could mean for the West relied on the principles Fenollosa had laid out in his essay. In an appendix to his 1964 anthology, *Confucius to Cummings,* he wrote that while "Fenollosa was an oriental scholar and this is an essay on the Chinese language . . . it defines what poetry is and how it operates, if you want to know" (Pound and Spann, 334). Besides the enduring presence of Fenollosa for Pound, this sentence testifies to Pound's continuing belief in the ability of the Chinese *language* (rather than just its poetry) to establish a model for all poetry. This sense of the universal value of Chinese—that it could define how *all* poetry worked— was typical of his general project to mine global history for the universal principles of human expression. He was, as Hugh Witemeyer puts it, "determined always to deal with world literature as a single body of material with certain artistic and spiritual unities which transcend differences in time or place of origin" (151).

As with his "invention" of China, Pound tended to find the spiritual unities in ancient and unfamiliar texts rather than contemporary ones, whose familiarity with few exceptions bred in him a withering contempt. In the years before *Cathay* he translated poems from ancient Italian and Provençal, bringing noncanonical and ignored poets into an idiom available to his contemporaries. Indeed, Pound's general investment in the past was such that he often simply amalgamated it into an undifferentiated mass of truth—his Chinese translations sometimes call on Greek mythology, and in his Cantos, Greece and China occasionally fall into one another, both representatives for the lessons of time gone by, equally distant from and equally pertinent to the present.

As for *Cathay,* its readers in 1915 might have been surprised to find, squarely in the middle of the book, one poem that was not at all Chinese. In between two poems by the Chinese poet Li Po appeared a reprint of Pound's 1911 translation of the Anglo-Saxon poem *The Seafarer.* Pound's reasoning appeared at the front of the book: "Rihaku [the Chinese poet Li Po] flourished in the eighth century of our era. The Anglo-Saxon Seafarer is of about this period" (4). As it turns out, *The Seafarer* shares with several of the other *Cathay* poems a certain thematic unity. Ming Xie writes that "'The Seafarer' and 'The Exile's Letter' share a similarity of attitude and value in their respective personae—a recognizable type of individual predicament (seafarer and exile) and a defiance through indifference to conventional attitudes" (104). The question is, what does this similarity demonstrate? By putting *The Seafarer* and Li Po together,

Pound was reminding his readers that the value in Li Po lay not in his Chineseness, but in his universality, in the fact that his poems revealed a shared history of ideas across time and space. And yet the mechanism by which this insight was revealed could not, in 1915, be separated from the fact of its Chineseness—it was as though something in the Chinese permitted, or gave birth to, the Poundian unveiling of the universal.[16]

Cathay, English or Chinese?

Following Pound's canonization in the 1950s, the definitive position on *Cathay*'s national identity was laid out by Hugh Kenner. Kenner's 1950 declaration that "*Cathay* is notable, considered as an English rather than a Chinese product" (*Poetry*, 154) exorcised the critiques of those who, like Waley, had read *Cathay* primarily as a failure of translation, or who, like Achilles Fang, noted Pound's errors without comment.[17] Such a position produced for Kenner an entire reading of *Cathay* as an English product, which appeared in *The Pound Era* in 1971. In a chapter called "The Invention of China," Kenner writes that *Cathay* "inaugurated the long tradition of Pound the inspired but unreliable translator. In the subsequent half-century's sniffling and squabbling [over the correctness of translations] its real achievement went virtually unnoticed" (199). The real achievement, Kenner says, lay in *Cathay*'s "effort to rethink the nature of an English poem" (199).[18]

The difference between Kenner and Eliot comes out in the contrast between Kenner's "The Invention of China" and Eliot's "Pound is the inventor of Chinese poetry for our time." The change from Eliot's version to Kenner's not only grants Pound's work a larger breadth of influence (not just poetry but the whole country, and not just "for our time") but also reflects a different critical moment in Pound scholarship. Eliot's more modest claim for Pound's abilities indicates a different sense not only of Pound as a person but also of Pound's place in the history of Western literature. It would probably have been as difficult for Eliot to imagine that Pound invented China wholesale as it was for Kenner to imagine he hadn't.[19]

Kenner's defense of *Cathay* in *The Pound Era* insists that it is good poetry rather than bad translation. He does so by noting the impossibility of ever translating to perfection, and declares that Pound has done the best he could with often-difficult source material: "from 'Yellow dog useless lament,' which is all [Fenollosa's] text provides, nothing intelligible can be done for an occidental. . . . every detail [in Pound's version] feels intelligible without notes" (206). At the same time, Kenner throws down the gauntlet to other translators who might criticize Pound, including native Chinese. He quotes, for instance, several lines from Pound's Canto 80, chock-full of references to European artists and poets, and asks: "What might some translator in China do with that?" (207). Against those who might see Pound as a hapless or ignorant translator, Kenner describes a poet who brilliantly develops a theory that allows him to translate the essentials of Chinese poetry without notes or detailed explanations, doing the best possible job with the material he had. Kenner stresses that many of Pound's "mistranslations" occur intentionally, according to his sense of what the poem needed: "These are normally what are called mistranslations, in one case grotesque mistranslation. Let us be quite clear that they are deflections taken with open eyes. There is no question of seduction by half-understood ideograms" (213).[20]

Kenner's position is, at some level, uncomplicated: Pound did the best he could with what he had, and the poems are brilliant in English in any case. But one gets the occasional sense that Kenner believes that Pound's translations nonetheless manage to move closer to the Chinese originals than Waley's or Giles's, that despite their philological inaccuracy they *are* in some way Chinese products, not just English ones. Nowhere does Kenner say this explicitly about Pound, but at the end of a chapter titled "The Persistent East," he does say something similar about Fenollosa: "If so, then Fenollosa's sinological mistakes, rectifying 17th-century sinological mistakes, owed their right intuitions (brought with him from Massachusetts) originally after all to China: as though the east, with centuries-long deliberation, were writing the macro-history of western thought" (231). Fenollosa's mistakes point toward genuine China not because he knew what China was, but because he had an idea of what it was not; the "intuition" that provokes him away from his predecessors' mistakes is owed, somehow, to China itself, as though Fenollosa were the beneficiary of some kind of magical connection that allowed him to be right even when he was wrong.

While Kenner, not an expert in Chinese, did not say outright that Pound's translations were, despite their mistakes, accurate and intuitively

correct representations of their originals, several Chinese scholars working in the United States have said so. First among these is Wai-Lim Yip,
who published *Ezra Pound's "Cathay"* in 1969, two years before Kenner's *The Pound Era* (though Yip thanks Kenner for being allowed to
read an early draft of "The Invention of China"). Following his meticulous comparison of Pound's poems, Fenollosa's notes (when available),
and the Chinese originals, Yip concludes,

> Considered as a translation, *Cathay* ought to be viewed as a kind of re-cre-
> ation. In these pieces, we cannot expect to find reproduction of all the
> details. . . . Instead, we find the "essential poems" preserved in luminous
> details. As such, they are bound to differ from the originals in the sense that
> certain literal details are either eliminated or violated; local taste is modified
> or even altered to suit the English audience and certain allusions are sup-
> pressed in order to relieve the readers from the burden of footnotes. And yet,
> in the examples we have examined, the "cuts and turns" of the mind in the
> originals are largely preserved, although Pound's ignorance of the Chinese
> language and Fenollosa's crippled texts occasionally led him into blind
> alleys. (164)

Yip contrasts two types of information that come across in translation, a
difference perhaps clearest between the second and third sentences,
which differentiate "all the details" from "luminous details." Yip says that
while Pound could not get "all the details," he reproduced the ones that
were "luminous," that is to say, the ones that "illuminate" the "essential
poems." Yip puts "essential poems" in scare quotes, as if to warn the
reader against taking that idea too seriously. But "essential" seems to be
exactly what Yip means when he says that Pound preserves the "'cuts
and turns' of the mind in the originals." He is claiming that Pound, while
not following the exact letter (all the details) of the Chinese poems, has
nonetheless seen enough to illuminate their spirit. Both "essence" and
"cuts and turns" suggest that Pound in fact reaches the heart of the Chinese originals *as such* and not simply as he knew them, that he manages to
retain the crux of the original even though he misses out on some of the
details. Like Tiresias, whose blindness produces a heightened ability to
"see" into the unknown and there discern the truth of things, Pound as
translator appears to know China with an understanding epistemologically beyond book-learning, beyond his own ignorance or Fenollosa's
mistakes.

Gyung-Ryul Jang, in "*Cathay* Reconsidered: Pound as Inventor of Chinese Poetry," goes even further than Yip in finding Chinese authenticity in *Cathay*. Jang writes that we "can tentatively, but safely, conclude that Pound could invent *Cathay—not in spite of* his ignorance of the Chinese language, *but because of* his ignorance of the Chinese language" (353). For Jang, ignorance allows Pound to avoid being trapped by a desire for a literal or accurate translation. Freed from knowledge, Pound can discern the spirit of the original Chinese, leading Jang to conclude that "Pound is truly 'an inventor of Chinese poetry,' even though he may be a 'devious' translator, as far as *Cathay* is concerned" (362).[21]

Jang's claim that Pound is a "devious" translator would appear to acknowledge that the carrying over of the Chinese originals to Europe does not happen without distortion. Following an early Pound essay on translation, Jang declares that Pound might have adequately translated the visual quality and logic of the Chinese originals, but that reproducing their rhythm or their music would be well-nigh impossible. And yet Jang's Pound displays an uncanny ability to reproduce the music of the original Chinese. While translations from Waley, William Acker, and James Hightower do not sound "natural" to the "mind's ears" of the English reader (352), Pound's somehow sound just right.

Jang quotes a section of Pound's "Separation on the River Kiang" to explain:

> Ko-jin goes west from Ko-kaku-ro,
> The smoke-flowers are blurred over the river.
> His lone sail blots the far sky.
> And now I see only the river,
>   The long Kiang, reaching heaven.

Jang comments: "The above translation, in spite of its naturalness of rhythm and language and its precision in producing original mood and images, contains some errors. Errors? Yes, if this poem be a translation at all" (357).[22] As it turns out, Pound's "errors" are not really errors at all. Pound "must have known," Jang writes, that "Ko-jin" was not a person's proper name, and "Ko-kaku-ro would be far more desirable than any naive word-to-word translations" of "Yellow Crane Tower" (358). Pound's errors become sound poetic choices, and Jang notes that the first line of the poem—the source of all three errors—allows the reader to "sense waves of pleasant 'recurring sounds'" (358).[23]

Pound's fortuitous errors lead therefore to a "better" translation, if only in the context of an English "mind's ear." The emphasis on the sounds of Pound's poetry gives the lie to Jang's claim that Pound could not translate the Chinese music into English. For Jang, Pound's unconscious brilliance at the musical level leads him to make "errors" that improve rather than detract from his translation and are therefore not "wrong" in the poetic sense. This focus on Pound's errors-that-are-not-errors leads to the conclusion that Pound, while translating with Europe in mind, has actually done a better job translating China than others who may speak or read Chinese. Pound's lack of knowledge about China as such thus allows him to present it better, *as such,* to his European readers, via a translation that "deviously" takes a circuitous route to the truth.

Jang's position on Pound raises interesting questions about *Cathay*'s place as a Chinese or English product. While Kenner and other Pound scholars who were not experts in Chinese[24] had accepted and even emphasized Eliot's judgment that *Cathay*'s China revolved largely if not entirely around the needs of twentieth-century English poetry, Jang insists instead on *Cathay*'s Chineseness. Jang's position stems, as I suggested above, from a well-worked notion of Pound's genius. But its major effect is to reposition China at the center of *Cathay,* and therefore to reveal China's effect on Pound (rather than Pound's effect on China "as we know it").

It may be only in light of work like Zhaoming Qian's, where such a position is most clearly articulated, that one can look backwards to Jang and Yip and see how they open the move toward seeing *Cathay* as fundamentally Chinese. In *Orientalism and Modernism,* Qian insists that the East can genuinely influence the West. This position leads him to claim that Pound did very little "inventing" when translating Fenollosa's notes:

> Ever since T. S. Eliot made the influential remark that "Pound is the inventor of Chinese poetry for our time" . . . Pound criticism has shown a tendency to praise his *Cathay* as an invention rather than a translation. Most critics, it seems, agree that *Cathay* has a freshness, elegance, and simplicity that are rarely seen in English and American poetry. Yet, surprisingly, few will acknowledge that *Cathay* is first and foremost a beautiful translation of excellent Chinese poems that exhibit freshness, elegance, and simplicity. (65)

With "acknowledge," Qian implies that the people who see *Cathay* as an English product do so out of a certain stubbornness, a refusal to admit something they do not want to admit. In declaring that the book is "first and foremost" a translation of *Chinese* poems, Qian criticizes those who would see *Cathay* as purely—or even primarily—Pound's. Instead, he is concerned to restore China to its proper place as a major influence on modernism. Zhang Longxi's quotation on the book's back cover concisely testifies to that mission: "*Orientalism and Modernism* clearly *sets the record straight* by addressing the issue of how Chinese poetry and culture helped to precipitate the transition of Pound and Williams toward high Modernism" (emphasis added).

Qian's claim that "*Cathay* is first and foremost a beautiful translation of excellent Chinese poems" expresses most clearly his reading of *Cathay* as Chinese, a reading that depends on seeing China as actively influencing the West rather than as the passive object of its fixations. Accordingly, in his specific readings of Pound's *Cathay* poems, Qian goes much farther than Jang in emphasizing that Pound's "errors" actually improve his translations by bringing them closer to the Chinese originals. On several occasions, for instance, Qian notes that Pound's "errors" suggest interpretations supported by current Chinese scholarship: "Ironically, Pound's merging of images from Chinese and Greek myths in 'After Ch'u Yuan,' which is generally seen as a disruptive endeavor, will find support in current Qu Yuan criticism" (34). In another case involving disagreement over whether Pound's "Song of the Bowmen of Shu," an antiwar poem in its English version, mistranslates the stirring call to arms of the Chinese original, Qian reveals that Pound's translation brilliantly anticipates later scholarship on the poem: "It is amazing that Pound, who knew nothing about the debate, should form an opinion so close to twentieth-century *Shi jing* scholarship" (75).

At another point in "Song of the Bowmen of Shu," Pound had rewritten Fenollosa's "Those four horses are *tied*" as "Horses, his horses even, are *tired*" (emphasis added). Kenner says of this change that "it is hard to know whether his [Pound's] eye failed or his dramatic sense prompted an improvement; presumably the latter" (*Era*, 219), while Yip sees it as evidence of Pound's attempt to exaggerate the sorrow of the poem. Qian, on the other hand, suggests that Pound's change brings the light of day to the Chinese original as it existed *before* it was modified to suit the ancient emperor for whom it was written down: "It is probable that by making these ingenious changes, Pound has cut the decoration and restored the consistent tone of the ancient Chinese folk song" (76).

Pound's most remarkable ability involves his seeing beyond Fenollosa's notes to the intention of the original Chinese. Writing, for instance, of a case where the "artistic emphasis" of the original has been lost in Fenollosa's notes, Qian says: "Pound, with his keen sensibility . . . must have perceived from the context the intensification of the poet's sense of loss in the concluding line" (71). Sometimes, Pound learns not merely from the context, but from the original poet's consciousness: "Pound is able to catch Liu Che's vivid imagery precisely because he and the Chinese emperor-poet see things from the same point of view" (41). And on the subject of Ronald Bush's praise for Pound's "inventions," Qian writes: "Amusingly, to my mind what Bush calls fine 'inventions' represent some of Pound's most admirable practices, in which he pierces beneath Fenollosa's crippled notes to Li Bo's original consciousness" (84). While Kenner's justification of Pound's "errors" works on the strength of the poetry's value in Europe, Qian's explaining them instead as instances of Pound's genius for China requires a belief in the accessibility of a truth that offers itself only to those gifted with a kind of second sight.

That Qian understands Pound's deviations as ultimately leading back to their original source, and thus producing a China in Europe, rather than a Europeanized China, makes it clear why he must reject the work of Edward Said. In a book that seeks to redress the failed acknowledgment of China's influence on Anglo-American poetry, Qian cannot see Pound's use of China as negative, distorting, or as an extension of European cultural imperialism. If Pound admired something under the name of "China," then Qian's project might be understood as linking that "China" to real China, and then insisting that what Pound admired, what influenced him, and what he translated were all genuinely Chinese, thus restoring China's influence on modernism to its proper place.[25]

So Qian opens *Orientalism and Modernism* by sharply differentiating his use of "orientalism" from Said's: "For Said the Orient is specifically the Muslim Orient. For me it is the Far East, particularly China. . . . For Said 'Orientalism is a cultural and a political fact . . .' . . . For me the concept is primarily a literary one" (1). Qian's literary, Chinese orientalism, as it plays out in his analysis of Pound's and William Carlos Williams's use of Chinese poetry, refers to the positive influences of China and Japan on Euro-American modernism. Qian explains that Said's model has its shortcomings when applied to Williams and Pound: "First, Pound and Williams did not seem to believe in Western cultural superiority. Second, what attracted the two poets toward the Orient was really the affinities (the Self in the Other) rather than the differences (the Otherness in the Other)" (2). Qian goes on to suggest that it is the Far East, rather than the Middle East, that has most influenced the twentieth-century West. Accordingly, he believes that "a study of the Far East's impact on Modernism indisputably has greater significance" than a study of Middle Eastern influence (1), and says that "it would be a gross insensibility not to perceive the Oriental contribution to [modernism's] growth" (5). While Said's Orient is weak and debased, Qian's Orient exerts a powerful, almost-magical influence on Western authors: "Little wonder that the early Imagists . . . soon fell under the spell of the Orient" (3). Qian goes on to identify Chinese as a sort of ur-model for all world poetry: "In the Chinese models provided by Giles . . . Pound found an art more objective than the Greek, more suggestive than the Provençal, more precise than the modern French, and more brilliant and resourceful than the medieval Japanese" (51–52).

Qian's critique of both Said and canonical *Cathay* criticism thus stem from the same ground, namely that neither acknowledges, though for different reasons, the importance of China for Western modernism. In Said's case, Qian criticizes what he sees as an inadequate and unfair stereotype of the Orient as the weak and passive subject of the West's literary musings. For *Cathay,* Qian seems to suggest that a certain Eurocentric bias has led to a general acceptance, following some version of Eliot, of the idea that China had little to do with *Cathay.* Qian upends the Eliot-Said assumption that any Western take on the East was mostly "invented," insisting instead that Pound's poetry *translates* (rather than paraphrases or invents) Chinese poetry. In other words, Qian believes in the possibility of knowing the matter as such across the East/West cultural divide, a feeling he makes clearest in his epilogue: "Things non-Western can, therefore, be converted into part of a Western literary heritage" (167). It is a sentence that Fenollosa would not have disagreed with, and yet it represents for Qian a strongly pro-China stance that was simply not possible for Fenollosa (or Pound).[26]

Apotheosis: Chineseness and Modernism in The Cantos

Shortly after he published *Cathay,* Pound began work on *The Cantos,* a series of long poems that attempt to retell the history of world civilization and offer a prescription for its future. The project would take the rest of his life. China's first appearance in *The Cantos* comes in Canto 13, which Pound wrote in 1922 and once described as the "backbone moral" of *The Cantos* (Brooker, *Guide,* 157). While Canto 12 ends with a joke about a sailor who has anal sex with a "rich merchant from Stambouli," the beginning of Canto 13 presents an East sharply differentiated from Turkish Istanbul in both tone and subject matter:

> Kung walked
> > by the dynastic temple
> > and into the cedar grove,
> > > and then out by the lower river
> > > > (13/58)

As in *Cathay, The Cantos* quickly structure the reader's knowledge of the East via a shared set of historical prejudices: here, Pound gives the reader the Arab East as mercantile and sodomitic, the Chinese as contemplative and natural.

Canto 13 consists of a series of episodes from the life of Confucius, strung together to create an overall sense of Confucian philosophy. Pound had taken the episodes from a French translation of the four primary books of Confucian philosophy by M. G. Pauthier. The stories Pound retells about Confucius establish guidelines for moral living:

> And Kung said, and wrote on the bo leaves:
> > If a man have not order within him
> He can not spread order about him;
> And if a man have not order within him
> his family will not act with due order.
> > (13/59)

Pound's repetition of the word "order" is all the more striking when one considers the relative disorder that surrounds this Canto. In Canto 12, nature is turned upside down as a man imagines he is his son's mother;

Cantos 14 and 15, known as the "Hell Cantos," present a vision of Europe in chaotic and excremental upheaval.

While most of the Canto reflects episodes from the life of Confucius, however, the final three lines are Pound's own:

> The blossoms of the apricot
>> blow from the east to the west,
> And I have tried to keep them from falling.

As John Nolde notes in his *Blossoms from the East,* Pound might have learned from Pauthier that Confucius often lectured from a small pavilion called the Apricot Altar (18). The title of Nolde's book suggests his identification and pleasure in Pound's image of Eastern blossoms blowing westward, an image that, like so much in Pound, depends on a notion of the East as bringing a true understanding of nature to the West.

In many ways, Canto 13 seems to replicate *Cathay*'s relation to China, in which the presentation of strange, foreign images (apricot blossoms) or names (Kung, Yuan Jang, and so on) establishes China via the minutiae of "Chinese-seeming" historical details. *Cathay*'s treatment of China had relied on the presentation of juxtaposed images as part of a new aesthetics. But Canto 13 asks the reader to follow its images into moral philosophy, and to find in China a principle of thematic but also moral order in *The Cantos.* This change reflects the assimilation of the style first developed in *Cathay* into Pound's general political project. Seven years after *Cathay,* Pound in this Canto seems to be extending the aesthetic principles that made things new in *Cathay* to include a broad range of human behavior.

In the years between the composition of Canto 13 and China's next major appearance in *The Cantos,* Pound spent a good deal of time developing the politics that would eventually get him tried for treason after World War II. Driven by his sense that an international conspiracy of Jewish bankers and armsmakers had caused the decline of Western civilization, Pound was in those years becoming more and more aggressive, more pro-fascist, more anti-Semitic. Like Canto 13, however, Canto 49, from 1937, seemed to offer its readers a break from Pound's difficult and uncomfortable positions, a chance to breathe freely before another mad plunge into *The Cantos'* wild mixture of history, poetry, and politics (Canto 50 opens with John Adams on government and tales of the English industrial revolution).

Kenner, for instance, calls Canto 49 "one of the pivots of the poem: the emotional still point of *The Cantos*" (*Poetry*, 326). William Cookson agrees, referring to Canto 49 as "The still centre of *The Cantos*: the images speak with quiet power, expressing the repose and harmony with the universe of Pound's Confucianism" (53). In the context of Pound's other writing, the "emotional still point" is as political as it is poetic. John Nolde remarks uncomfortably on Pound's turn in the 1930s toward political and economic themes: "Essays on these subjects, often shrill and strident, poured out: essays on Social Credit; the virtues of Mussolini's economic policy; the ever-expanding evil of usury; diatribes against the Jews, the banks, against Roosevelt and the American establishment. . . . Only in 'The Seven Lakes' [Canto 49] do we feel a moment of calm" (20). Nolde's "poured" indicates his sense of Pound's loss of control, and his use of "we" in the final sentence presumes a general readership that finds Pound's political and economic turn embarrassing as well; the "moment of calm" provides a retreat to a moment removed philosophically and politically from the Canto's present.

The poem produces that calmness by a complete absence of subjectivity. It opens:

> For the seven lakes, and by no man these verses:
>> Rain; empty river; a voyage,
>> Fire from frozen cloud, heavy rain in the twilight
>> Under the cabin roof was one lantern
>
> (49/244)

The phrase "no man" is literally true, as Pound composed Canto 49 on the basis of a screen book of anonymously composed Chinese and Japanese poems and paintings he received from his parents in 1928.[27] Robert Kern remarks on Pound's presentation of "a world almost devoid of human activity, a world on the point of fading into or being absorbed by its several gradations of qualities of light," and the effect of his monosyllabic style, which places its nouns "in an indeterminate space in which time seems all but suspended" (207).[28]

As the Canto progresses, however, Pound inserts signs of life, with lines like "And at San Yin / they are a people of leisure" and "where the young boys prod stones for shrimp" (49/244–45). And then this:

> State by creating riches shd. thereby get into debt?
> This is infamy; this is Geryon.

The interruption for a further attack on usury affirms Pound's interest in connecting the peaceful stillness of the Chinese scene with his political and economic themes. Stylistically, these lines act out the two thrusts of their content: while the absence of articles here recalls the Chinese style of the rest of the Canto, the use of "shd." can be read as a deliberate gesture toward Pound's typewriter and modern industrial culture. The Canto's search for "the dimension of stillness" that Pound refers to in its penultimate line culminates not in its review of an idyllic and unavailable past, but as a need for that dimension's appearance in the present.

Much more explicitly than Canto 13, Canto 49 extends the principles of Chinese aesthetics Pound found in *Cathay* and Fenollosa to the political realm. As Kern points out, the Canto is "a Western critique, by *means* of the East, of the West, both in itself and in the context of *The Cantos* as a whole" (209). Nolde's sense that the Canto allows for an escape from Pound's unpleasant political views depends on missing this point, on believing that the Eastern alternative remains in some sense outside the purview of Pound's other interests; Cookson's "repose and harmony with the universe of Pound's Confucianism" seems equally misguided, since it misses the acid concentration of anger in Pound's line, "This is infamy; this is Geryon."[29]

Canto 49 is a sort of watershed for Pound's treatment of China in *The Cantos,* since it immediately precedes the virtual explosion of Chinese characters onto his pages, and comes shortly before the "Chinese History Cantos," an incredibly hard-to-follow exposition of Chinese history from 5000 B.C.E. through 1700. Kern calls Canto 49 Pound's "culminating attempt to invent Chinese for his English reader," and says that it "builds upon and surpasses the achievement of *Cathay*" (206). He goes on to suggest that "Pound's language seems situated at the furthest limit of what is possible in English before it slips over into ideograms themselves" (207). It is, in other words, the apotheosis of this difficult relationship between modernism and Chineseness, a moment in which Pound's unusual language finds itself inextricable from the apparently Chinese stillness that determines both its politics and its poetics.

Style and Chineseness after Canto 49

In 1928, Pound published his version of the Confucian *Ta Hio (Da Xue,* The Great Learning). His "Immediate Need of Confucius" (and Canto

49) appeared in 1937, his essays "Kung" in *Guide to Kulchur* and "Mang Tze" in 1938, the "Chinese History Cantos" in 1940, the Confucian translation *The Unwobbling Pivot and The Great Digest* (a retranslation of the *Da Xue*) in 1947, his translation of *The Classic Anthology Defined by Confucius* in 1954, the *Confucius to Cummings* anthology he edited with Marcella Spann in 1964, and *Confucius* in 1967. In the meantime he placed hundreds of Chinese characters into *The Cantos*.

And yet, critically speaking, Canto 49 is also the furthest limit of a certain moment in the discourse of Pound and China, one that does not follow exactly the trajectory of Pound's own relationship to China or Chinese texts. Mary Paterson Cheadle has remarked extensively on the relative lack of critical interest in Pound's later Chinese translations. In *Ezra Pound's Confucian Translations,* Cheadle notes that Pound's several volumes of Confucian translations constitute a major portion of his lifetime literary output, and attributes the lack of attention to two factors: first, Pound scholars are "generally concerned more with poetry than with prose," and second, "relatively few Pound scholars are also sinologists" (3). And yet, she argues, without an understanding of the Confucian translations, "it is impossible to arrive at a clear and comprehensive understanding of Pound's long, metamorphic career or of *The Cantos* that are its achievement" (7).

Cheadle goes on to read Pound's translations largely in the light of his politics, showing how his various translations and retranslations reflected proto-totalitarian, totalitarian, and post-totalitarian stages in his own political development. Cheadle is concerned to demonstrate, then, that the driving force behind the production of Pound's translations was both personal and European—focused at all times on his particular relationship to fascism and World War II. When she does criticize Pound's understanding of the Confucian texts, she does so in order to point out his mistakes: "Confucianism does not advocate the kind of aggressive colonization or imperialism that was practiced by Germany in Europe or by Italy in Africa in the 1930s and early 1940s" (232).[30] This corrective, in which the true and original meaning of the Chinese is made to work against Pound's Eurocentric distortion, reads the translations essentially as a Kennerian "English product."

In this, Cheadle's book is typical of work done on Pound's relation to China after Canto 49. The issues that so dominated reactions to *Cathay*—

aesthetic theories of Imagism, the development of a modernist style, the question of Chinese reality, and the possibilities of cross-cultural influence—simply do not surface in the same way.[31] This is true even for scholars like Kern and Qian, who despite an overt interest in orientalism and modernism do not carry that approach into Pound's later work. Kern at one point writes, "After *Cathay* and World War I, Pound's work with Chinese seems to trail off, or at least to become less visible and, at best, intermittent" (202). Measured by the number of pages written or translated, this is simply not true. But in Kern's main chapter on Pound, only three pages of about sixty-five are devoted to Pound's work on China after Canto 49. Similarly, Qian's *Orientalism and Modernism* contains five chapters on Pound and China up to and including *Cathay,* and one on work after 1915. Though he spends a few pages on *The Cantos* (and mentions Cantos 13 and 49), he says nothing about Pound's use of Chinese characters or his vast outpouring of prose work on China or Confucian translations. They do not seem to fit with his interest in Pound's "Modernist style for *The Cantos*" (109) in *Orientalism and Modernism.*[32]

Oddly, this shift of emphasis—in which the Chineseness of Chinese drops out of the critical picture—mirrors Pound's own sense of what he was doing after World War I. In "Mang Tze" (1938) he wrote, "Serious approach to Chinese doctrines must start with wiping off any idea that they are merely Chinese" (*Selected Prose,* 83). He went on to offer a rare acknowledgment of China's ongoing existence:

> It may quite well be that Confucius and Mencius are a hormone that could be more vitally effective in the West today than in a China busily engaged in livening up the business of the Acceptance Houses. Apropos of which I understand that a living Kung [a descendant of Confucius] has stated in private conversation that his Most Illustrious Ancestor is now more regarded here than in Pekin. Foreign loans for munitions do not enter the Analects. (92)

Pound's disdain for China's state of affairs[33]—governmental loans and arms sales being two of his least favorite things—appears to allow him to imagine himself (and the West) as the true inheritor of China's ideas. For Pound, real China—the China that mattered—could always be found in the past, in the days when emperors ruled with velvet fists and Confucius walked among the apricot blossoms. China's potential in the present stemmed, in turn, from its writing system and its philosophy, which *The*

Cantos showed could be applied, with work, to the West, "wiping off the idea that they are merely Chinese." In other words, as Pound's interest in China became more political, he more clearly stated his case that Confucian thought and ideographic writing could be separated from China so that he could call for the modification of the contemporary West by the East.[34] And as Pound learned more and more about Chinese—he began studying the language in 1936, shortly before the appearance of characters in *The Cantos* and his essay "Mang Tze"—he was able to claim more and more of his insights about China as his own.

Why do the Chinese characters that appear in *The Cantos* seem marginal—at least for Kern and Qian, at least in the mid-1990s—to the question of a "Modernist style"? Part of this may have to do with the fact that for readers who do not know Chinese the characters are simply unreadable. For such readers, every particular instance of Chinese writing in *The Cantos* means roughly the same thing: Chinese characters represent a higher truth than alphabetic ones. Every character in *The Cantos* works, then, as a sort of prosthesis for Fenollosa's essay, reminding the reader that being representable in Chinese is the ultimate validation of an idea. Kern, following this line of thought, writes that Chinese characters "are an intermediary for Pound between ordinary or alphabetical scripts and the world, and he tends to use them in this way, as a means of anchoring his discourse to what it represents, appealing to the characters as a kind of evidence, an authoritative and nearly absolute representation of what they refer to" (204). What is an interesting theoretical idea, however, ends up making the characters boring, since they all mean the same thing, namely that an English idea finds its authoritative and absolute representation in Chinese. Pound himself noted at the end of Canto 85, "Meaning of ideograms is usually given in the English text," as though the Chinese were merely a mirror of the English (85/579).

The Cantos' first character, *xin* 信, is typical of this mirror effect.[35] *Xin,* whose meanings include "trust" and "confidence" but also "letter" and "message," appears next to "Constans proposito . . . . / Justum et Tenacem" (34/171). The quotation is from Horace and translates "Constant in purpose . . . / Just and enduring" (Cookson, 39). Pound's sense of the meaning of *xin* came from its two components; on the left, *ren* 人, a person, and on the right, *yan,* 言, word; a man standing by his word (*Selected Prose,* 85). Seen from this perspective, the character reflects and repeats the Latin phrase to its right, emphasizing the common ideal of "trust" (or constancy in meaning) across world and time. And yet without knowing about the two halves of the character, the average reader is left wishing he or she could be more like Henri Gaudier, who learned to read Chinese simply by looking at the pictures. In any case, however, *xin* 信 is not, like a jeweled stair, something that *feels* Chinese. It would seem to be genuinely Chinese, working for most Western readers at a level outside speech itself. Much work on *The Cantos* seems happy to take this view, treating the characters as more or less unmediated emanations of real China, which at some level of course they are.[36] It is difficult to imagine claims that Pound's characters are only a "brilliant paraphrase" of their originals, because the characters seem accurately and directly to represent themselves. It is as though Fenollosa's sense of the ontological force of Chinese writing had actually come true, as though *The Cantos'* Chinese writing had an absolute and perfect relationship to its referent.[37]

What such a view leaves behind is Pound's own peculiar reading of Chinese characters. Kenner, striving always to see things as Pound did, remarks that Pound's reading of *xian* (to display) in Canto 74 separates the sun 日 (top left) from silk 絲 (bottom left) to produce the lines "plowed in the sacred field and unwound the silk worms early / in tensile 顯 / in the light of the light is the *virtù*" (74/449; Kenner, *Era,* 459). That is, Pound has taken apart the character, which is made up separately of the characters for sun 日, silk 絲, and leaf or page 頁, and repeated those first two elements in the poem via references to "silk worms" and "the light of the light." In paying a close attention of his own to Pound's close attention to Chinese, Kenner is, here too, seeing Pound's work as an English rather than a Chinese product. In so doing, he recaptures the strangeness of Pound's understanding of Chinese writing, an understanding that was in fact quite a good distance from how Chinese is used or spoken "on the ground" in China. The average Chinese person does not, for instance, experience 信 as a "man standing next to his word," much in the same way an English speaker rarely considers that *monster* comes from the Latin "to warn" or remembers that *breakfast* comes from "breaking fast."[38] Having such an awareness of the history of signs is the mark, in English as in Chinese, of a literary or philological mind, and often of a faith in critical reading's ability to access deep meaning via historical, connotative, or philological close-up. Kenner, by reproducing this critical methodology, shows that Pound's Chinese characters are as mediated by Pound's experience as any of *Cathay*'s distant friends or gardened mistresses.

Such a reading of *xian* 顯 suggests that *The Cantos*' Chinese characters *could* be read within the same framework as the poems in *Cathay*. Like *Cathay*'s bowmen, the characters participate in a phenomenon of "hermeneutic trust" in which they create a sense of genuine Chineseness while performing a "devious" reading of the original Chinese material. As in *Cathay*, this sense of Chineseness participates in the development of Pound's own poetic voice, such that both in the production (the "silk worms early / in tensile 顯 / light of the light") and the reception (for the reader who sees that line on the page) what counts as poetry for Pound is inevitably intertwined with something "Chinese."

In *Orientalism, Modernism, and the American Poem* Kern writes that *Cathay*'s most important residue is not its representation of English aesthetics or Chinese reality, but in the development of something he calls "English-as-Chinese." Kern identifies "English-as-Chinese" as the development in English of a style of writing drawn from the structure and form of the Chinese language (or at least from a Western sense of that structure). Accordingly, Kern treats *Cathay* as revealing the origins of a general Poundian *style*, a style inflected by the onto-epistemology of the Chinese character itself, but with its share of universal relevance: "ideogrammatic writing as I am describing it here may be regarded as a possibility inherent in all verse—a sort of deep structure or primitive substratum of poetic utterance that is prelogical, pregrammatical, and prior to what Fenollosa would see as the dubious refinements of civilized, rational discourse" (216). The proof of English-as-Chinese's importance lies not with Pound's Chinese translations but with his non-Chinese material, which reveals English-as-Chinese to be a style of writing applicable to any type of content, not just for translating Chinese poetry. Kern's teleological reading of English-as-Chinese's development does eventually carry him into *The Cantos,* but not to read the Chinese characters. There he finds Pound using English-as-Chinese to make poems about ancient Greece. This reading allows Kern to conclude his chapter on Pound by declaring a "style" disconnected from explicitly Chinese content to be the most important product of Pound's encounter with China: "Pound's approximation of Chinese is also, finally, an effort to fashion a modernist style, one informed by primitive modes of speech still linked, for him, to the reality they represent" (220).[39]

Kern's interest in Pound's "effort to fashion a modernist style" recalls Qian's characterization of Pound's "Modernist style for *The Cantos*" (*Orientalism,* 109). In his newest book, *The Modernist Response to Chinese Art* (2003), Qian spends a chapter discussing the Chinese characters in the later Cantos in a manner that illuminates once again the contrast between the critical challenge produced by *Cathay* and the question of Chineseness more broadly. While much of Qian's chapter focuses on Kennerian analyses of the characters' pictographic dimensions, his discussion of Canto 99, in which the vast majority of Chinese words appear as phonetic transliterations, suggests that something else may be going on: a phonetic rather than semantic or visual transfer between Chinese and English.

> Chou saw it, my SIRE also,
> With splendour,
>   Catholicity,
> Woven in order,
>   As on cords in the loom
> cognome, indirizo (pien^1 hu^4
> sincerity, simplicity, red: South, and naïveté
> meng^2, the people, the many, the menée,
>   the perishing.
>
> (99/715)

As Qian points out, the tonal marks on the Chinese words (the numbers in superscript) allow Pound not only to generate differences in meaning but also to signal "Chinese cadence" (*Modernist,* 217). What we end up with is not so much English-as-Chinese as it is Chinese-as-English, a Chinese whose phonetic properties allow Pound to play with rhythm and alliteration ("meng"/"many"/"menée") across languages, demonstrating what Qian calls his "passionate rejection of a prolonged indifference to *melopoeia* in Chinese" (218).

The implications of this shift for the question of Poundian style remain unclear, and Qian does not address them. Speculatively, then, one might wonder if the Chinese-as-English of Canto 99 does not revise in some vital way Pound's own Fenollosan tradition by reducing the importance of visual perception, and especially of Chinese as the site of that form of

perception, in the production of poetic meaning (even as the vital geographic and cultural reference to China is retained). And if this is so, then
might not Pound's later work be considered not simply an extension of a
Chinese (or English-as-Chinese) style developed in *Cathay* (whatever the
valence of its orientalism), but also a more relaxed, broader elaboration of
that style? If *Cathay* is the crucible of Pound's style, the place where the
spirit of Pound's modernism calcines into a dry and demanding hardness, then Canto 99 might figure another process: an opening up, an
efflorescence, in which Pound's Chinese takes its place among the languages rather than outside them.

It cannot be in doubt that whatever "China" might have been getting
written in Canto 99 happens, historically, too late for it to substantially
affect the broader topic of what Pound did to or with Chinese poetry, culture, and language. And if Pound owes his modernist style to something
in *Cathay*, then the degree to which *Cathay*'s Chineseness is genuine or
fantasized makes a real difference in how one understands modernism—
especially if one takes Pound as an avatar of the era. Is the Chinese language as unusual as Mr. Pound's? Asked in 1915, the question bares with
a pellucid clarity the dual translation that *Cathay* undergoes, first from
the Chinese into English, and second from an expected poetic English to
the English of Pound's modernism. However critics come to understand
Pound later on—as English or Chinese—there can be little doubt that the
reception of Pound's new poetics in the second decade of the century was
mediated by *Cathay*'s connection to a Chineseness that may or may not
have had much to do with actual China itself. Following the critical history from Kenner through Yip, to Kern and Qian, one sees that any subsequent understanding of the meaning and value of Pound's modernism
is predicated at least partially on a reading of that Chineseness in relation
to authenticity. And these readings in turn justify larger theories of translation, or modernity, of orientalism, or even of the relationships among
those three things. The stakes are high: if through Pound we really do at
last get the original (following Qian, contra Eliot), then what is "original"
about Pound?

Toward Brecht and Tel quel

Within Western poetry, Pound's "invention" of China was both aston-
ishingly and wonderfully new (his "real achievement"). But at another

level the ideas it sprang from were completely ordinary, part of the commonly accepted framework for European thinking about China in the years around 1915. The critical discourse on Pound and China gives life to both of these understandings of Pound. In doing so, it extends the ideas originally framed by *Cathay* and Pound's other work with China and Chinese, allowing them to endure beyond the specifics of an actual China or an actual Pound, continuing to define the Western perception of China in terms at once extraordinary and banal. Kept alive in criticism, this special version of "China" continues to name a Western limit and a Western possibility, encompassing both the thrill of at last getting the original and the denial of that extraordinary circumstance.

At this point we are some way toward a preliminary sense of what Chineseness might mean in relation to modernism. Around *Cathay,* it can work, at its most extraordinary, as a sort of philosopher's stone, the long-sought catalyst for an epistemological or linguistic process outside the ken of the Western mind. From the point of view of critics like Qian, but also for Pound and Fenollosa, and even—though only "for our time"—Eliot, Chineseness allows for the possibility of pure translation, translation undeviated from the original in ways that either are, or seem to be, magical. For others, Chinese writing might grant us a style—what Kern calls "English-as-Chinese"—that pierces the veil of signification, giving us words and phrases that not only point us toward the world, but reveal it in its originary, prelinguistic state. As it articulates these visions, Chineseness in Pound moves inexorably along an axis of authenticity, marked in the critical discourse at one pole by Kenner's "English product" and at the other by Qian's "first and foremost a beautiful translation of excellent Chinese poems."

Attached, finally, to these competing notions of Chineseness are two ideas worth carrying over into the next chapters. First, there is a persistent tendency in criticism to want Pound to have seen through to the original Chinese, notwithstanding his well-documented ignorance on historical and linguistic matters (and contra both Eliot and Said). That tendency, whether motivated by a belief in the intensity of genius or a desire to strengthen a claim that China truly influenced the West, merits attention on the one hand as a remnant of an older view of literary production and on the other as a newer theoretical take on, and resistance to, orientalism. It is in fact the simultaneous presentation of those ideas that seems most interesting—whether at its boldest in Qian's work, or in its less direct manifestations elsewhere.

Second, regardless of the reality-status of Pound's China, it remains clear that he was influenced by something he and lots of other people were willing to understand as Chinese. I am not especially concerned to explore the differences between Pound's China and actual China; I do not dispute that they are not the same thing. The project here is to trace the presence of Chineseness in crucial moments of Western modernity and postmodernity. Reading for "China," one sees that the critical discourse that surrounds Pound not only extends his own version of China into the present but also reshapes it according to particular critical and global concerns, including broader themes of orientalism, modernism, and translation.

That same critical discourse cannot be said to surround the other authors in this book, whose own encounters with China and Chineseness have not received the critical attention of Pound's. There have been, here and there, attempts to decide the meaning of Brecht's relation to China, or *Tel quel*'s, but the material is sufficiently scarce to prevent any large-scale sense of critical history. The end of this chapter thus marks the end of a certain kind of critical work—that of linking the Poundian story and its critical metanarrative. As a result, the framing narrative for Brecht and for *Tel quel* will continue to be in many ways Pound's own, as though in fact he were truly the inventor of a relation to China for our time. How that invention looks in the light of other creative imaginations is the subject of the next two chapters.

Chapter Two BRECHT

*O*n January 28, 1934, Ezra Pound answered T. S. Eliot's standing question, "What does Mr. Pound believe?" with "I believe the *Ta Hio*," the Confucian *Da Xue,* which Pound had translated in 1928 as *The Great Learning.* Such a moment justifies and gives reason to a project on "Pound and China" by affirming the intensity and depth of Pound's commitment to a certain version of Chinese thought.

That Bertolt Brecht never uttered or wrote any sentence that so clearly articulated not only an interest but a *faith* in China—and that Pound did—constitutes a major problem for anyone writing on Brecht's relationship to China. Brecht wrote much in his lifetime about China, and about Chinese philosophers and poets, often repeating things he had learned from Arthur Waley's books on Chinese poetry. But Brecht never wrote about what it meant to be interested in China. He made no major statements about the relation he had—epistemologically, aesthetically— to the Chinese poems he translated. Even when remarking with approval a Chinese poet's use of simple words and clear writing ("Seine Gedichte sind in einfachen Worten, jedoch sehr sorgfältig geschrieben" [*Gesammelte Werke,* 19:424–25]) Brecht does not then come out and say, "Our poetry needs to be more like this Chinese poetry." As a result, there surrounds "Brecht and China" a very particular silence, produced by the fact that while Brecht frequently wrote *about* Chinese things, he never tried to justify or explain his own relationship to China or Chineseness.

Reading Brecht with an eye toward China, one might be forgiven for simply connecting willy-nilly Brecht's multiplicity of short references to, facts about, names hinting at, and disguised borrowings from China. A list purporting to do just that might begin: in Brecht's flat in East Berlin hung a portrait of Confucius, beside a scroll of Mao Zedong's poem "Snow," across from a picture of a (Japanese) Kabuki actor and

three No theater masks; his poetry demonstrates the well-known conci-
sion of Japanese and Chinese poetic forms. But it is hard to make such
lists into convincing arguments. There exists no metadiscourse on
China with which to begin to think about not only Brecht's relation to
China, but his own understanding of that relation. Unlike in Pound's
work—or, as we shall see, *Tel quel*'s—where China ravels itself into the
very nature of thought, Brecht's China skates, as it were, on the surfaces
of his text.

Reading other critics on Brecht and China, one sees them confronting
this same silence. Taking up the critical challenge of Brecht's China has
required developing, through detailed archival and interview work, the
theory of China that Brecht never elaborated for himself. The two major
studies of Brecht and China in English both attempt to develop such a
theory. Antony Tatlow's *Mask of Evil: Brecht's Response to the Poetry,
Theatre, and Thought of China and Japan* (1977), the generally recognized masterwork on the subject, shows that Brecht's Chinese moments
imbricate themselves fully into his life and texts. Tatlow at times hints at
the presence of a Chinese (or more generally Eastern) Brecht in the
shadow of the Western one, a Brecht whose private library at his death
contained scores of Chinese books, both by classical philosophers and
Mao Zedong, and who wrote most of his work in the presence of a Chinese painting he called "The Doubter." The second major study, Renata
Berg-Pan's 1979 *Bertolt Brecht and China,* adopts a more biographical
approach, arguing that "Brecht studied Chinese literature, art, and philosophy in order to find a viable relationship between his political views,
his literary talent, his integrity as an artist and his physical survival as a
man" (ix).

Despite the large amount of writing Brecht produced about China and
Chinese art, both books have trouble connecting Brecht to China in a
meaningful way. Berg-Pan mentions her struggle against the notion that
Brecht's interest in the far East was "merely a passing fad" (xi). Tatlow
opens *Mask of Evil* by quoting another critic on Brecht's relation to China
and other exotic places:

> Unlike the Brechtians, Brecht knew very well how little his plays had to do
> with countries which he used as background. The India of *A Man is a Man*
> and the Russia of the *Mother,* the London of the *Threepenny Opera* and the

> Chicago of *St. Joan of the Stockyards*—considered carefully, we see that
> these are all fairy-tale worlds, poetic fictions. Geographical concepts prove
> always to be mere provocations with the modish (and usually so cheap) chic
> of the exotic. The town Mahagonny no more lies in the USA than Szechuan
> in China. (Reich-Ranicki, qtd. in Tatlow, 3)

The argument Reich-Ranicki makes about the cheap modishness of the
exotic suggests that the appearances of China in Brecht's work are no
more than *chinoiseries,* vaguely participating in some very general ideology of the exotic without developing a substantial or even interesting new
idea about China. Such a view, Tatlow remarks, is

> so unexceptional, so obviously correct on a certain level that, were it not for
> the tone of the language, one almost passes over the unmistakable insinua-
> tion: Brecht and China—modish frippery, cheap trivialities. Brecht's
> Szechuan certainly does not lie "in" China. Neither does it stand in the same
> relation to China as Mahagonny to the USA or Kilkoa to India. The quota-
> tion betrays a provincial concept of the exotic. (3)

In response to Reich-Ranicki, Tatlow argues for specificity: Brecht's
Szechuan does not "stand in the same relation to China as Mahagonny to
the USA." For Tatlow, Reich-Ranicki's concept of the exotic is provin-
cial because it imagines all exotic things are the same, and believes that
the overdetermining characteristic of exotic things is their exoticness. But
not all exoticisms are equal.

In responding to critics who argue that Brecht's China was never more
than a vaguely orientalist, easily discarded fantasy, writers who wish to
emphasize the relationship between Brecht and China most often begin
by turning to Brecht's translations of Chinese poetry—since Pound the
most evident mark of a Chinese interest. Brecht's first six translations,
based not on Chinese originals but translated from Waley's English versions in *A Hundred and Seventy Chinese Poems,* appeared in a 1938 issue
of the Moscow-based journal *Das Wort.* They made nothing like the
splash of Pound's *Cathay* and have been more or less ignored by scholars
not working specifically on Brecht and China. The English edition of
Brecht's poems, for instance, does not retranslate Brecht's Chinese translations into English, presumably out of a sense that Waley's versions are
adequate representations of what Brecht was up to.

That is not the case. The first poem in the sequence "Sechs chinesische Gedichte" (Six Chinese poems) treats the subject of unexpectedly

meeting a friend on the road. Waley's original, published in *A Hundred and Seventy Chinese Poems* and titled "Oaths of Friendship," reads:

If you were riding a coach
And I were wearing a "li,"[1]
And one day we met in the road,
You would get down and bow.
If you were carrying a "teng,"[2]
And I were riding on a horse,
And one day we met in the road
I would get down for you.

Brecht's German version, called "Die Freunde" (The friends) reads as follows:

Wenn du in einer Kutsche gefahren kämst
Und ich trüge eines Bauern Rock
Und wir träfen uns eines Tages so auf der Straße
Würdest du aussteigen und dich verbeugen.
Und wenn du Wasser verkauftest
Und ich käme spazieren geritten auf einem Pferd
Und wir träfen uns eines Tages so auf der Straße
Würde ich absteigen vor dir.

(Tatlow, *Brechts,* 33)

As far as I know no translation exists of the German version back into English. But the two most obvious changes Brecht made are clear even if one does not speak German: he has removed the Chinese transliterations "li" and "teng" and replaced them with German words. His second line reads "And I were wearing a peasant's coat," which more or less literally interprets Waley's footnote. Line 5, however, reads, "And if you were selling water," which adds something that appears nowhere in Waley's version, nor in the original Chinese.

In *Brechts chinesische Gedichte* (Brecht's Chinese poems), Tatlow has a lengthy comment on Brecht's change:

Waley's poem is an unusually clear example of the weaknesses of a completely literal translation. Here he tries to get around the problem when he simply leaves two words untranslated. This considerably damages his version. He reminds the reader of the difficulty of his task, and that this is a Chinese poem being translated here. Leaving the words in Chinese effectively constitutes an admission of defeat. It irritates the reader, who has to perform the work of the translator on his own. . . . Instead he [Brecht] introduces something completely new, which nonetheless preserves the essential meaning of the original: the two friends' difference in rank. The water-seller preserves the Chinese milieu and will be immediately understood. (37)[3]

Brecht's use of "water-seller" rather than a Chinese word, even though it moves further from the letter of the original, has for Tatlow two major virtues: it enables readers to *enjoy* the poem without tripping over something they do not recognize, and it maintains the spirit of the original (the idea that the two friends may have different social status). The use of the commonly known *chinoiserie* enables a smooth understanding; Waley's too-literal approach has made him unable to pass on the experience of the Chinese original.

The argument here recalls Edward Baker's remark, made about Pound's *Cathay* translations, that "[t]he actual contents of the poems, the bowmen and willows and husbands off to war, will come to strike the Western reader as the necessary accoutrements of any Chinese poem" (76). Baker had gone on to say that the phrase "bbyang gate" in a translation by James Liu caused a focus on the poem's form rather than its content, thereby distracting the reader. Presumably a reader of Waley's would be distracted from the poetic experience by the footnotes, which interrupt reading through the poem. The question turns, as it did with Pound, on authenticity: the presence of the Chinese word offers too much of it, the water-seller just enough.

Tatlow also praises the natural flow of Brecht's rhythm, which breaks with Waley's insistence on one stressed syllable for every Chinese character (*Hundred,* 33). In general Brecht's translations move much of Waley's relatively formal language into the realm of daily speech, as in the second of the *Das Wort* poems, "Die große Decke" (The big blanket):

Der Gouverneur, von mir befragt, was nötig wäre
Den Frierenden in unsrer Stadt zu helfen
Antwortete: Eine Decke, zehntausend Fuß lang
Die die ganzen Vorstädte einfach zudeckt.

The governor, when I asked what was needed
To help those freezing in our city
Answered: A blanket, ten thousand feet long,
To simply cover over the slums.[4]

Unlike many of his other translations, Waley's "The Big Rug" substantially modifies the original, which is a fourteen-line poem (by Tang dynasty writer Po Chü-yi [Bo Juyi]) that discusses at greater length how the poet's pleasure in his new jacket fades when he considers the plight of the poor. Waley's version reads:

> That so many of the poor should suffer from the cold
> > what can we do to prevent
> To bring warmth to a single body is not much use.
> I wish I had a big rug ten thousand feet long,
> Which at one time would cover up every inch of the city.

Brecht's introduction of the governor and quoted speech makes the poem far more dramatic, and injects a political sensibility into Waley's more empathetic version. Brecht replaces the awkwardness of Waley's "what can we do to prevent" with a dynamic speech act, in which the question asked of the governor takes on a distinctly dialogic and social tone. As Tatlow points out, the governor's response can be read as either sympathetic or cynical, giving the poem a social and political dimension appropriate to Brecht's general interests (*Brechts,* 45).[5]

Brecht was not beyond adding to Waley's versions where he felt they were inadequate. In his retranslation of Waley's "Resignation," Brecht added two final lines to a poem generally urging the reader toward apathy. Waley's version ends simply: "When food comes open your mouth; / When sleep comes, then close your eyes." Brecht finishes with: "Ist's das Essen: auf das Maul! / Ist's der Schlaf: zu die Augen! / Hockst du im Wagen, schafft's der Gaul; / Muß zu etwas taugen" [Time to eat: open your mouth! / Time to sleep: close your eyes! / Slump in the wagon, the nag will pull; / It's got to be good for something]. The rhythm and tone of Brecht's verses, with their exclamation points, suggests an almost Dionysian enjoyment of animal laziness, rather than the affected lassitude of Waley's version. Brecht's version also rhymes throughout, giving it more energy and verve than Waley's, making the poem more like a song.

Brecht's addition of two more lines suggest an alternative to the poem's apathy as well as an entire social world of work that simply never enters Waley's version. As Tatlow points out, the lines open the possibility of movement and change, if only through the work of the horse (*Brechts,* 110). And it turns out that Waley had cut the final two lines of the original Chinese poem by Bo Juyi. The lines, with Tatlow's translations, read:

更	若	有	興	來
in addition	if	there is	interest	coming
außerdem	*wenn*	*es gibt*	*Neigung*	*erwachend*

狂	歌	酒	—	盞
wildly	sing	wine	one	glass
wild	*singen*	*Wein*	*ein*	*Glas*

Tatlow comments: "Though we can see that Brecht's attitude is analogous to that of the Chinese poet, he must have thought that he was altering him since he changed Waley's translation without knowing that it was partial or misleading" (*Mask*, 142). Nonetheless, one can argue, as Tatlow does, that Brecht's final twist on Waley's version restores something like the spirit of the original, if not its letter. (Of course it is also easy to argue that it does not.)[6]

Part of what provoked such changes was, Tatlow argues, Brecht's feeling that he resembled Bo Juyi, whose poetic didacticism and political outlook he admired.[7] Brecht's "restoration" of an original sense both of social and political space and of a certain hopefulness thus jibed with his own sense of who Bo Juyi might have been and what he might have thought. Waley, on the other hand, knew of Bo Juyi's stated interest in both didactic and political verse and found it inappropriate material for art: "Like Confucius, he [Bo Juyi] regarded art solely as a method of conveying instruction. He is not the only great artist who has advanced this untenable theory. He accordingly valued his didactic poems far above his other work; but it is obvious that much of his best poetry contains no moral whatsoever" (*Hundred*, 166). Waley's attitude frustrated Brecht, who called him a "donkey" and wrote: "This excellent sinologist cannot get used to the idea that for Po Chü-yi there is no distinction between didacticism and amusement" (*Über Lyrik*, 48, trans. Berg-Pan, 226).

Brecht's surprising affinity for the spirit of the Chinese poem—an affinity particularly sharpened via its contrast to Waley—recalls structures of affiliation familiar from the chapter on Pound. Let me try to make that recollection more explicit by comparing the following two quotations, the first from Zhaoming Qian on Pound: "Amusingly, to my mind what Bush calls fine 'inventions' represent some of Pound's most admirable practices, in which he pierces beneath Fenollosa's crippled notes to Li Bo's original consciousness" (*Orientalism*, 84). The sentiment expressed bears a striking resemblance to Tatlow's claim, "In Brecht's versions the Chinese poems come to life again, because of his *sympathetic understanding* of Po Chü-yi and because he was prepared to interpret Waley's more literal versions" (*Mask*, 130; emphasis added). For both Qian and Tatlow, the artist manages to produce better translations via an access to the mind of the original author, either through a piercing vision (Qian) or a sympathetic understanding (Tatlow), both beyond the reach of rational explanation.

In *Bertolt Brecht and China,* Berg-Pan is far more tentative than Tatlow on the subject of Brecht's affinity with the Chinese poets. She writes that Brecht's intuitive translations likely had to do as much with his freedom from the restrictions of a literal translation as any ability to delve into the past's exotic reaches. Yet she accedes to some version of Tatlow's "sympathetic understanding" in a long, extraordinary paragraph:

> Very likely, the best explanation regarding the success of Brecht's translations is that Brecht profoundly agreed with the world view expressed in all the poems he translated. Most of the twelve poems reveal attitudes and opinions which Brecht himself cherished all his life and which echo Marxist-Socialist thought. This is the raison d'être of his "Chinese" poems, and this explains why Brecht succeeded in penetrating through the medium of the foreign language in order to empathize with the poet's state of mind, his anger perhaps, or his great pity—whatever mental process was necessary to generate the poem before it was actually written down. (231)

The reason that Brecht's "Chinese" poems translate the spirit of the originals has to do, then, with a sort of a priori psychological affinity with the Chinese poets. The fact that the poems "reveal attitudes and opinions which Brecht himself cherished all his life" allows him to succeed "in penetrating through the medium of the foreign language in order to empathize with the poet's state of mind." Brecht thus comes to Waley's poems with their basic emotions or ideas *already* inside him; the process whereby Brecht comes to "profoundly agree" with their worldview occurs *before* he encounters their poetry. This agreement in turn allows him to translate the poems well, because they essentially express what he already knows.

As Berg-Pan goes on, she moves from a notion of sheer psychological affinity to one that centers on Brecht's self-recognition:

> Having found ideas and opinions resembling his own in monuments of a culture as distant, exotic and ancient as that of China must have thrilled Brecht

with a shock of recognition and a sense of self-justification. This thrill obliterated the barriers imposed by two foreign languages and many centuries of history, and congealed into a poetic form that was appropriate to his great anger. (231)

Berg-Pan appears to be arguing that Brecht's initial appreciation of or resemblance to the Chinese poets—established both *before* and *outside* of any relation to Chinese poetry—allowed him to literally see better and further than Waley, whose book-learning could only take him so far.

Let me be clear: reading Tatlow and Berg-Pan on Brecht and China, one finds oneself approaching the limits of a notion of genius or of coincidence that is hard to take as an article of faith. One can imagine two conflicting responses to the notion of the penetrating, cross-cultural reading. On one hand, it seems important to see it *as though it could be true,* out of a sense that there may be mysteries in the darknesses unloved by a rational, scientific reading of literary production. On the other, the claim that Brecht (or Pound) somehow pierced through to the original emotional state of Bo Juyi (or Li Po) via an emotional affinity is so clearly unprovable that it must be the product of an intense critical wish.[8] One might consider, then, that one confronts in such a claim two disconnected truths or realities. The first revolves around whether Pound or Brecht *actually* saw through the shroud of language and into the Chinese. The second turns on the stakes in claiming that they did.

Waley has a vital role to play in the argument about Brechtian (or Poundian) genius. For both Pound and Brecht, there exists an object called "Waley's China," which pretends—far more than either of theirs— to a literal presentation of China in which the author/translator insulates the original text from his own influence. But one sees this only from the critical perspective of our time. As Tatlow argues in *The Mask of Evil,* Waley appears to have had a profoundly radicalizing influence on Brecht, if one considers the differences between English and German poetry between the wars.

In Germany, the most popular Chinese translations in the early twentieth century were those by Klabund (Alfred Henschke), who produced two volumes of especially loose translations that proved quite successful. Klabund did not call his translations *übersetzungen,* "translations," but *nachdichtungen,* a word that literally means "after-poems" and refers to a relatively free paraphrase or rendering of a poem. Tatlow, who considers the *nachdichtungen* execrable, writes that Klabund's popularity at the time depended on his offering readers a conventionally exotic China, full of mysterious princesses and dissipated young noblemen, all framed by a poetic form appropriate to late-nineteenth-century romanticism.

From such a perspective, Waley looked much more like the avant-gardist Pound than the retrograde Klabund. Chinese poetry as romanticized doggerel was exactly what both Pound and Waley worked against, trying to capture in English something of the original's apparent austerity and visual focus. Against translations that made all Chinese verse sound like Western poetry, both Waley and Pound tried to bring the formal and experiential qualities of the Chinese poem—including its arresting visual images and its end-stopped lines—into English. Such a commitment, Tatlow argues, carries with it both a theory of translation and the formal concerns appropriate to an aesthetic avant-garde. The formal innovations (including the use of unrhymed lines and irregular meters) of the "English" style had no correlates in Germany. As a result, Chinese poetry there did not signify culturally in the same way as it did in England, and it did not offer itself up, as it had with Pound and the Imagists, as the medium of a liberal avant-garde. When Brecht became interested in Chinese poetry, Tatlow writes, he almost had to do so through English rather than German translations: "Because of the impact of Pound's methods, Chinese poetry was brought much closer to the English- than to the German- or French-speaking world. In Germany it remained at the edge, remote, suspect and exotic. . . . It is hardly surprising that Brecht approached Chinese poetry, when he became really interested in it, through the medium of English" (*Mask,* 111).[9]

Ironically, however, from such a perspective Brecht finds himself in the same position, relative to Waley, that Pound was: someone whose ignorance of Chinese allowed him to make "mistakes" that apparently brought his versions closer to the originals in feeling and tone. Whatever closeness Tatlow posits between Pound and Waley (and the "English style") fades in light of his ultimate critical judgment of Brecht's translations. Brecht, translating Waley into German, could not trump his sinology. But he could write better poetry, and it is precisely in returning the poetic to the poetry that he moves closer, some argue, to the original Chinese. Fredric Jameson, summarizing Tatlow's *Brechts chinesische Gedichte,* writes: "It turns out that without any knowledge of Chinese,

Brecht's versions are more faithful to their originals than Waley's, since he instinctively restored to them the social dimensions and details that (equally instinctively, no doubt) Waley omitted" (32). Jameson's use of "instinctively" with regards not only to Brecht but also to Waley judges the situation more fairly than most. Waley's translations differ not necessarily because he was (as Brecht said) a "donkey," but because his entire aesthetic approach was alien to the ideologies of modernism.

To what extent is Brecht's relationship to China in these translations produced by the "example" of Pound? There are two major factors here: the history of primary texts, and the critical history.[10] Though both men published their first "Chinese" material in the same year—1915, the year of Pound's *Cathay* and Brecht's "Der Tschingtausoldat"[11]—Pound's relation to China became an important part of his self-presentation and his critical history well before anyone wondered about Brecht and China. Similarly, the critical history of "Pound and China"—established as early as Waley's poetic response—comes far earlier than work on "Brecht and China." The first four major texts in the field—Tatlow's *Brechts chinesische Gedichte* and *The Mask of Evil*, Berg-Pan's *Brecht and China*, and Yun-Yeop Song's *Bertolt Brecht und die chinesische Philosophie*—were all published in the 1970s (though, inspired perhaps by a more general interest in East-West comparative literature, several new studies in German appeared in the 1990s, including Tatlow's *Brechts Ost Asien* [Brecht's East Asia], a beautifully produced book that echoes *The Mask of Evil* and *Brechts chinesische Gedichte*, and adds essays on Brecht and Foucault, Brecht and Barthes, and Brecht and Derrida).[12] Tatlow quite explicitly in both *Mask of Evil* and *Brechts chinesische Gedichte* compares Brecht's relation to China to Pound's, sometimes quoting Kenner; it is not unfair to say that both of his books model themselves to some extent on the already-existing discursive field of "Pound and China."[13] Tatlow remarks that he has no evidence of a direct connection between Brecht and Pound. He goes on to say that "an indirect connection is in itself perhaps more interesting than any proof of direct influence, since it underlines the importance of conclusions, in this case concerning the translation of Chinese poetry, which were arrived at independently" (*Mask*, 113).

Whatever Brecht's China was, or is, then, it was and is to a large extent by virtue of two things: First, the framework provided Brecht (and Brecht scholars) by both Pound and Waley; second, the extent to which both

Brecht and Pound *(avant la lettre)* reacted against an essentially conservative take on the truth-possibilities of the aesthetic form. This is truest for the poetry, where despite differences between Brecht and Pound, the major similarity remains: the sense that for reasons rooted in a sympathetic understanding of the Chinese poets, Brecht produced translations of Chinese poetry that transcended his total ignorance of the Chinese language and got back to the spirit of the originals. Whatever similarity one might identify between Pound and Waley along the lines of an "English" style of translation is surpassed by the more fundamental resemblance between Pound and Brecht: that of the artist.[14]

In that sense, one might say that they both "invented" Chinese poetry for our time. But "inventing" Chinese poetry implies—as Kenner suggests with his chapter title in *The Pound Era*—an invention of "China," as well. It is in fact possible to go farther and say that every translation of Chinese poetry—including Waley's—takes part in an invention of a China that justifies its own theory of translation. When critics read Brecht or Pound against Waley, they essentially invent China *twice*. In its initial version, "China" is a highly realistic, geopolitical object—the thing most people mean when they say "China." This is Waley's China, best approached by the standards of rationality—knowledge, scholarship, direct experience. While this China may appear initially to be reasonable, its major function is to be eventually shown to be inadequate, unimaginative, even wrong. Essentially, it serves as a foil for the China eventually shown to be Brecht's or Pound's: a "China" accessible through nonscientific, mystical affinities and understandings that reach truths unavailable to purely scientific investigation. These two Chinas are constructed, then, out of two fundamentally incompatible epistemologies: "science" and "romantic mysticism."

That these opposing terms—science and mysticism—are commonly associated with the West and the East respectively simply reinforces the difference between Waley's philological translations and Pound's or Brecht's poetic ones (Kenner on Waley's translations: "it is hard to wring song from philology"). In a postromantic world in which the poetic is already opposed to the rational, in which truths available through literature are deemed to be fundamentally different at the epistemological level from truths given by science, it makes a certain binary sense that an imaginary East would have an affinity with Western artists. Part of what is pro-

duced, or reproduced, by these readings of Pound's and Brecht's translations as closer to their originals in spirit—even if it turns out to be factually true that they are—is therefore a certain binary understanding of the
relationship between East and West. It is not clear if the relationship
between mystical East and scientific West creates these readings or rather
is simply reinforced by them.

What we learn, then, from Brecht's China in the poetry, is something
about the reach of a particular theory of China across cultural and literary
boundaries, and its use as a general model for a certain kind of relation to
China—as well as to a certain kind of China. The critical issues surrounding Pound's China are *transportable,* pointing not only to a specific
theory produced by Pound but to a more general theory of how one
might come to know China at all, as well as a sense of the cultural and ideological stakes of such a knowing. As with Pound, what we see with
Brecht is that his ability to know this mystical China seems to justify his
relationship to a certain kind of nonscientific (and nonetheless accurate)
translation, as well as his relationship to a certain aesthetic modernity (as
against, for instance, Klabund and other German translators of Chinese
in the romantic tradition).

But if everything Brecht does simply reproduces the relatively banal
mystical East/scientific West divide that one saw in Pound, then there
would not be much point in moving further. The fact remains that there
are major differences between the ways Pound and Brecht dealt with
China, primarily in terms of the degree to which they spoke their interest.
As critics have struggled to show that Brecht truly was interested in
China, they have tried to fill in the gaps left by Brecht's silence by discovering Chinese elements in his later work. These attempts demonstrate
some of the pitfalls of such an approach, and ultimately point the way
toward a purely Brechtian relationship to China and Chineseness.

Beyond Pound: Authenticity and Brecht

In setting forth to demonstrate the influence of China on Pound's work,
Robert Kern in *Orientalism, Modernism, and the American Poem* settles
on "English-as-Chinese" as a name for Pound's language as it looks when
most inflected by Fenollosa's theory of the Chinese ideogram. For Kern,
as for other Pound and China scholars, one of the major tasks of criticism
is to pursue Pound's China beyond its simple referents in Pound's trans-

lations and into Pound's other work, searching for and defining the effects of Pound's China encounter. The influence so defined stands as proof of the endurance of Pound's China, which thus reaches in some way into Pound's (Western) self.

Likewise, many critics have searched for a recognizable Chinese influence on Brecht's other poetry, arguing that such influence would indicate the depths of Brecht's genuine interest in China. Hans Mayer has famously written, "Die späten Gedichte sind ohne das chinesische Vorbild nicht zu denken" [The later poems are unthinkable without the Chinese example] (qtd. in Tatlow, *Mask,* 11). As Tatlow comments, the remark would certainly be true of Pound, but is it really true of Brecht?

Patrick Bridgewater's article "Arthur Waley and Brecht" makes this case most forcefully. Bridgewater opens his essay by asserting that "not only did Pound almost certainly have some influence on Brecht (though this has yet to be proved), but in the case of both poets Chinese and Japanese poetry provided the model for their own best work" (216). He goes on to remark, "It is therefore probably true to say that Brecht will have found in these four ways of thought in ancient China some of the main tenets of his private and public philosophies" (218), before eventually claiming that "[i]t is therefore probably true to say that Brecht's ideas on unrhymed verse with irregular rhythms were further clarified, modified and strengthened when he came across Waley's translations from the Chinese and Japanese" (220).[15] In both cases "probably true" excuses Bridgewater's saying what he believes but cannot prove; since Brecht never said anything about the issue, any such claims remain undecidable.

Part of Bridgewater's sense of Brecht's adoption of Chinese ideas—about the didacticism of poetry, for instance—stems from his belief that Brecht already believed many of these things. He writes, for instance, that the poem "Meiner Mutter" (My mother) shows "that right from the beginning Brecht's own style as a lyric poet possessed the same sort of austere beauty that we associate with Chinese and Japanese poetry" (221). He goes on to remark that "in Chinese and Japanese poetry it will have been above all the austerity and economical beauty—the features of his own private poetry right from the beginning—that appealed to this highly emotional but emotionally reserved poet" (221). Here Bridgewater follows both Berg-Pan and Tatlow in arguing that Brecht's poetry resembled "right from the beginning" the work of the Chinese, and only later came to be influenced by it.

Lane Jennings, in "Chinese Literature and Thought in the Poetry and Prose of Bertolt Brecht," has a more reserved approach to the question of Chinese style in Brecht's poetry. Jennings, like Bridgewater, is working under the misconception that Brecht did not see the Waley translations until 1938, when in fact Brecht saw them first in 1929. His argument that "while Brecht's early poetry makes use of images common in Chinese verse, there is little evidence that Brecht was influenced by Chinese attitudes or Chinese verse forms until much later" would surely be reshaped in light of that new information (211). As it is, Jennings must argue, like Bridgewater and Berg-Pan, for an affinity for Chinese verse that was there in Brecht before he ever saw Waley's work.

Jennings goes on to posit a Chinese influence on Brecht's later poems, but his attempt to prove this shows some of the difficulties of doing so. He quotes this poem: "Die Oberen sagen: Es geht in den Ruhm. / Die Unteren sagen: Es geht ins Grab" [Those at the top say: / This way to glory. / Those down below say: / This way to the grave] (*Gesammelte Werke*, 9:637; *Poems*, 288). Jennings writes that the poem bears a remarkable resemblance to a Chinese poem:

> "*Die Oberen sagen . . .*" is a perfect parallel couplet of the sort found in many Chinese poems. If written out in two lines instead of four this poem could even stand as a translation of a Chinese couplet with five characters per line. Literally rendered into English such a couplet would read: "Leader say this way fame; Subject say this way grave." (216)

If, in the first sentence, Jennings is content to remark a similarity between two verse forms, by the second he is engaging in something of reverse translation, a translation of Brecht's work back into an "original" Chinese. By pointing out that the poem might be structured differently—as though it were itself a translation from Chinese—and then retranslating that imaginary, original poem back into English, Jennings effectively imagines into being the Chinese original that he believes could have been there.

The English into which Jennings translates is, of course, not really English at all, but something like Chinglish, Chinese grammar rendered in English words. In remarking on this kind of "translation" from Chinese, Haun Saussy has written, "Word-for-word translation aims at a surpassing *nearness,* a one-for-one correspondence between signs of the original and of the rendition. . . . The more convincingly the translator observes the protocols of 'nearness,' the more exquisite the reader's sense of strangeness, of distance from the original text" (*Great Walls,* 2). Particularly when it comes to Chinese, Saussy remarks, the word-for-word translation provides a compelling, delicate sense of primitiveness by offering itself up in a "me Tarzan, you Jane" format. For example: with "Leader say this way fame" instead of "The leader says fame lies this way," the first instance reflects accurately certain facts about Chinese grammar and sentence structure while giving a sense of Chinese as fundamentally ungrammatical, or pregrammatical. In any number of translations from Chinese into English, the new English version exists as a kind of *double* translation, in which the "literal" Chinese (in English) is not so much Chinese as it is a new kind of English, designed specifically to illustrate the strangeness of Chinese.

Saussy is, of course, talking about actual translations of Chinese, and Jennings's translation of Brecht's "Die Oberen sagen" does not literally translate Chinese. Jennings's sense that the poem resembles Chinese verse depends on his ability first to "translate" it into some imaginary and unseen version of Chinese, and then *back* into pidgin English ("Leader say this way fame"), whose lack of articles or conjugations any number of Western readers have learned to recognize as literal "Chinese."[16]

The "translation" into "Chinese" and back into English shows how easily the process of looking for Chinese influences on Brecht can forget or ignore the consequences of its own theorization of China. A more subtle example of the same process can be found in Jennings's reading of Brecht's "Frühling 1938" (*Gesammelte Werke,* 9:815–16, trans. as "Spring 1938," *Poems,* 303). Chinese poetry, Jennings writes, "is related to painting as well as to music—a connection suggested no doubt by the calligraphic nature of Chinese writing—and it is more often pictorial than dramatic" (220). Here Jennings recalls Pound's early relation to Chinese writing, which itself comes out of a lengthy European tradition of considering the pictographic function of Chinese characters to be the dominant characteristic not only of Chinese writing but of Chinese thought. Jennings continues: "Brecht sounds like a Chinese poet most when . . . painting a picture with words" (220). He goes on to quote from "Spring 1938" (*Poems,* 303):

Above the Sound hang rainclouds, but the garden is
Gilded still by the sun. The pear trees
Have green leaves and no blossom yet, the cherries
Blossom and no leaves yet. The white clusters
Seem to sprout from the withered branches.
Across the wrinkled waters of the sound
Goes a little boat with a patched sail.

Jennings comments: "The scene described is essentially static, but its significance unrolls like a Chinese scroll. First the sky, then the trees, then the boat on the water are brought to the reader's attention. The entire scene is set in the very first line where water *(Sund)*, sky *(Regenewölke)*, and trees *(Garten)* are all mentioned" (220). In saying the poem's significance unrolls like a Chinese scroll, Jennings once again establishes the meaning of "seeming Chinese" via a comparison to a known fact about China—namely that its calligraphers and artists sometimes paint on scrolls. He also implies without proof that the unrolling of such a scroll constitutes part of a Chinese aesthetic of representation—that something like "gradually making visible" is a characteristic of Chinese art in general. Such a theory may not be wrong, but the text seems not to be aware that in theorizing Chinese aesthetics in that way, it essentially repeats the same maneuver of the "Leader say this way fame" translation, which is to invent a China in *reverse,* as it were, by positing the original that must have been there for Brecht to crib from. As a corollary to this problem, Jennings never addresses the question of whether Brecht felt the same way about pictographs or the unrolling of scrolls as Jennings himself does, and thus never makes a connection between his own theory of "China" and Brecht's. About the same poem Tatlow remarks: "Pear and cherry trees do not amount to a Chinese spring" (141).

Of the critics who write on Brecht and China, Tatlow is by far the most aware of the problem of inventing China, and develops a careful theory not only of what "China" means but of what it could have meant to Brecht, given what he had seen.[17] In doing so, he most clearly differentiates between the later work of Brecht and Pound. Quoting a section of Pound's Canto 49, Tatlow writes that "Pound's imagery, the diction, even the rhythm, and the direction of his thought, the evocation of a condition of being through the direct presentation of natural image and landscape—everything here is completely Chinese" *(Mask,*133). Tatlow's theory of what counts as aesthetically "Chinese" contains a clearly articulated sense of Chinese *style* (diction, rhythm) and *thought*. He goes on to distinguish between the use of Chinese poetry as a "model," in which the author makes a conscious attempt to adopt the perceived style of Chinese (like Pound, he says), and as an "example," in which the author finds affinities in Chinese style or content and pursues those issues in his or her own writing (like Brecht). The distinction is crucial, particularly as it plays out against the claim that Brecht's later poetry is unthinkable without the Chinese.

Tatlow writes that we "should first ask whether the late poems can all be defined in terms of certain qualities, whether formal characteristics or similarities in tone and intention. . . . There are, in reality, many different forms of verse in the late poetry, some of which clearly have no connection whatsoever with Chinese poetry, either as model or example" (139). The poems that do resemble the ones Brecht translated from Waley are of two types, Tatlow writes, "'censorial' poems and poems of personal observation, often elegiac in mood" (141). Of the second type, Tatlow remarks that the "sometimes mitigated sorrows in the intimations of mortality are not, I think, a prerogative of Chinese poets" (141). About the "censorial" poems, however, Tatlow is willing to recognize the affinity between Brecht and Bo Juyi, whose role as a social critic Brecht so admired. As I have suggested above, such a claim must proceed to some extent along the lines of "sympathetic understanding," whose theory of the relation between Brecht and China echoes the one developed in Pound criticism.[18]

The problem of discerning Chinese influences on Brecht can be illustrated with another example. Brecht's 1938 poem, "Legend of the Origin of the Book Tao-te-ching on Lao-tsu's Road into Exile," tells the story of how Chinese thinker Lao Zi came to write down his wisdom. According to legend, Lao Zi, on his way into exile, was asked by a customs official to write down what he had learned before leaving. He complied, and the result is the book that gives its name to Taoism. Brecht first referred to this anecdote in a newspaper article, "The Polite Chinese" ("Die höflichen Chinesen"), published in the 1920s. The poem changes the story slightly, most notably by making the customs official of legend a lowly border guard, whose request that Lao Zi write down his knowledge does not stem from a sense that it might be culturally important but rather that it might be personally useful. The encounter begins when the man asks what Lao Zi taught. The boy leading the philosopher's ox replies: "He learnt how quite soft water, by attrition / Over the years will grind strong rocks away. / In other words, that hardness must lose the day." The teacher and the boy make to move on, and the border guard holds them up: " 'What was that you said about the water?' / Old man pauses: 'Do you want to know?' / Man replies: 'I'm not at all important / Who wins or loses interests me, though. / If you've found out, say so.' " The philosopher thinks about it: "Turning round, the old man looks in sorrow / At the man. Worn tunic. Got no shoes. / And his forehead just a single furrow. / Ah, no winner this he's talking to. / And he softly says: 'You too?' " (*Poems*, 315).

With these verses Brecht makes the border guard's question stem not from an intellectual interest, but a social one. The emphasis on the guard's worn clothes, his concern with who wins or loses—particularly his use of "interests," with its fiscal connotations—justify the guard's request in terms of suffering, particularly economic suffering (he cannot afford shoes, for instance). Brecht closes the poem by remarking the politeness of Lao Zi and his boy, who stayed a week to write, and then adding this final postscript: "But the honour should not be restricted / To the sage whose name is clearly writ. / For a wise man's wisdom needs to be extracted. / So the customs man deserves his bit. / It was he who called for it" (*Poems*, 315-16). The poem thus ends with a thoroughly Brechtian critique of bourgeois intellectual production, which gives all credit to the thinker and none to those who ask for thought, and use it.

In her reading of the poem, Berg-Pan concludes, typically for her, that Brecht's relation to Taoism and Lao Zi had to do with his own personal position at the time—in 1938 Brecht had been living in exile in Denmark for five years, having fled Nazi Germany. She writes:

> The emphasis of the poem, however, is on the dialectic according to which soft water breaks down the hard stone. In many ways this is a typical Chinese idea, because it preaches something the Chinese value very highly: patience. Patience is precisely what Brecht must have needed at the time when he wrote this poem, because he had just been forced to emigrate by the evil though mighty forces in Germany, the National Socialists. The Taoist dialectic predicts victory from a moment which looked like defeat, and hence reinforced hope and optimism not only for Brecht personally, but for the success of socialism generally. (81)

Tatlow offers a similar argument, noting the poem's role in developing a more or less "Chinese" concept of *freundlichkeit* (friendliness) in Brecht's work: "In the calmer frustration of exile Brecht had more leisure to reflect. It was then that the clarity and undiminished confidence of the Chinese philosophers made such an impression on him" (*Mask*, 378).

The overwhelming concern in both cases is with explaining *how* and *why* Brecht came to write the poem. Additionally both Tatlow and Berg-Pan want to argue that the poem is not merely, as Tatlow would put it, a *chinoiserie*—something that partakes of an undifferentiated exoticism. Berg-Pan points out the coincidence between the Chinese conception of patience—particularly as it applies to intellectuals and the state—and Brecht's personal circumstance. Tatlow gives a nod to biography, then goes on to argue that Brecht's sense of Lao Zi's worth stemmed from his relatively extensive readings of Chinese philosophy, including the work of Confucius, Mencius (Mo Zi), and the *Tao te ching* (all in German translation). The critical emphasis lies entirely on convincing the reader that the poem has some connection to China that runs deeper than its surface content. Berg-Pan, for instance, argues this two ways: first by suggesting that the poem's representation of Taoism (in the line about the water and the stone) is both accurate and representative of a general Chineseness, and second by arguing that the ideas behind that representation corresponded to Brecht's personal state of mind at the time. Tatlow adopts the same arguments but weights them differently, focusing more on the way that Brecht's representation of Lao Zi's friendliness pointed toward deeper influences from Chinese philosophy.

So why do both texts seem to be trying too hard? First, there is the difference between the poem's reference to a Chinese legend and its political and aesthetic ideologies. While the superficial content of "Legend of the Origin" has clearly to do with China, its major idea—stemming from the change Brecht made to the original story—is undeniably Brecht's and not so clearly the original's. Second, the poem's formal properties have no apparent relation to Chinese poetic style; neither Tatlow nor Berg-Pan makes that argument. The claim that China influenced Brecht proceeds, then, on the basis of unprovable biographical coincidences, and Tatlow's especially fine reading around the concept of "friendliness," about which Brecht never said anything directly. Comparing this situation to Pound's, one sees that whatever relation Brecht had to China was of an epistemological order fundamentally unlike Pound's. Not only did Brecht know China differently than Pound, but critics have also come to know Brecht's China differently, using a critical approach that cannot take the relationship for granted.

Following Said's definition of orientalism as "the enormously systematic discipline by which European culture was able to manage—and even produce—the Orient" (3), I discussed in the previous chapter the ways in which Pound produced a China for his readers that was not only believable but compelling. Can Brecht be said to have managed, or even produced, a coherent vision of China? The fact that no one has yet asked that question suggests the answer is no. Brecht's China does not lend itself to the kind of analysis one normally accords the cross-cultural reference: Is it culturally accurate? What is its relation to history, to geopolitics? A study of Brecht and China answers such queries most often by being factually inaccurate and philosophically vague; the object "China" in Brecht's work is neither "a kitsch stereotype nor any concretely historical one" (Jameson, 13).

This chapter began by looking at the place where Brecht most resembles Pound, namely in his translations of Chinese poetry, in order to produce a clearer understanding of the limits of both Brecht and Pound (and their critics) when it comes to constructing China. For Pound, that debate centered precisely around whether his China was kitschy or historical (genuine). There the question of representation was always a question of accuracy (in a broad sense). And in many cases the notion of accuracy itself came under question, with such critics as Kenner, Jang, and Qian acknowledging small factual inaccuracies while pointing to larger, almost-magical accuracies produced by sympathetic understanding. As far as Brecht's translations are concerned, following the Poundian model was, for purposes of exposition, both natural and useful. It allowed me to show that the questions it produced did not simply belong to Pound but rather constituted a more general paradigm—if not a sine qua non—for discussing translations of Chinese.

But what one sees in the later work, and what comes to a particularly sharp point in Jameson's sense of Brecht's China as neither kitsch nor historical, is that despite the many similarities produced by the earlier reading, there exist nonetheless some vital differences between Brecht's

China and Pound's. Unlike Pound's representations of Chinese poetry, which pretended to historical correctness, Brecht's China never claims for itself that degree of accuracy. And yet it is not, as Jameson points out, merely a kitsch stereotype: the intensity of Brecht's interest, the degree to which he seems to have sometimes gotten things right, belie a dismissive critique.

What then is Brecht's China? Any reading that attempts to get beyond the kitsch/history division must confront the extraordinary problem of Brecht's very particular silence around the China question. Some have argued that Brecht never wrote about China in Pound's particular, self-aware way because he had nothing to say about it, was not really interested in it, did not really care. But one could also—and this is where Brecht's silence might be understood most actively as a challenge to the ways we have of understanding what it has meant to represent China—try to understand Brecht's silence not simply as the result of his having nothing to say, or taking his relation to China for granted, but rather as an *active* and *willful* position on what it means to represent China in the West. In other words as a kind of refusal of the position already there in Pound.

Alienation and Estrangement

For a map of this refusal I turn to Brecht's 1936 essay, "Verfremdungseffekte in der chinesischen Schauspielkunst," his only sustained articulation of a specifically formal interest in Chinese art. The essay, translated by John Willett as "Alienation Effects in Chinese Acting," has given its name to Brecht's best-known theoretical concept, that of the alienation- or A-effect.[19] "Alienation Effects" was written some time after Brecht's visit to Moscow in 1935, during which he saw several performances by the Peking Opera actor Mei Lanfang in the company of Russian friends, including the young director Sergei Tretyakov (author of the 1926 anti-imperialist play *Roar China*), the film director Sergei Eisenstein, and the theorist of formalism, Viktor Shklovsky. Brecht's concept of the A-effect may owe something to those Russian avant-gardists, though as Peter Brooker argues, "Brecht's conception and use of *Verfremdung* . . . entailed a degree of political insight which thoroughly radicalised the formalist device of 'making strange.' Whereas, therefore, in a telling contrast, Shklovsky spoke of art's 'laying bare of the device' as the sign of its

75

defining self-reflexivity, Brecht spoke of art's 'laying bare society's causal network'" ("Key Words," 192).

Brecht's essay begins with the following paragraph:

> The following is intended to refer briefly to the use of the alienation effect in traditional Chinese acting. This method was most recently used in Germany for plays of a non-aristotelian (not dependent on empathy) type as part of the attempts being made to evolve an epic theater. The efforts in question were directed to playing in such a way that the audience was hindered from simply identifying itself with the characters in the play. (*Theatre,* 91)

The "attempts" Brecht mentions in the second sentence are his own; he is referring to his experiments in German theater, particularly around his "learning plays," which were performed for working-class audiences in the late 1920s and early 1930s. While acknowledging that the A-effect exists in Chinese theater, Brecht does not want to mark it as fully Chinese; rather the effect has an unconnected development in Germany and China.

In his next paragraph Brecht stresses again that separate development, writing that the "effort to make the incidents represented appear strange to the public can be seen in a primitive form in the theatrical and pictorial displays at the old [German] popular fairs" (91). What the popular fair and China have in common lies in their being not at all bourgeois. While the former offers a "primitive" form of the A-effect, the latter "applies it most subtly" (91). Brecht goes on to describe the subtlety of various effects—the flags worn on a general's back to represent armies, the characters' painted faces. Before going on to describe *how* the alienation effect occurs in Chinese theater, he writes: "All this has long been known, and cannot very well be exported" (91).[20] The claim that Chinese theater techniques cannot be "exported"[21] emphasizes the gap between German and Chinese uses of the A-effect; though they resemble one another, the Chinese technique cannot simply be carried into German theater. The cultural ownership of the A-effect is thus somewhat muddy—though it is more "subtle" in China, it exists in a native form in Germany; the Chinese version cannot simply be transferred there. All this Brecht establishes before beginning to discuss the particulars of Chinese theater.

Throughout the essay Brecht explains how the A-effect works by describing its alteration of the actors' relation to the audience. He opens his discussion of how the Chinese actor produces the A-effect by writing that "he expresses his awareness of being watched. . . . The audience can no longer have the illusion of being the unseen spectator at an event which is really taking place" (92). The watching goes both ways: not only does the actor know he is being watched, but the audience itself can no longer be "unseen." The gazes of the audience and the actor can meet, as when the actor "will occasionally look at the audience as if to say: isn't it just like that?" (92). And above all, the actor sees himself as an actor acting out a part, in order to "appear strange and even surprising to the audience. He achieves this by looking strangely at himself and his work" (92). Such an act is not without its effect on the audience, which "identifies itself with the actor as being an observer, and accordingly develops his attitude of observing or looking on" (93).

For Brecht, who aimed to produce not only a new theater but a new audience, the Chinese actor's apparent relationship to his audience constitutes both parties in a fully social, historical mode, as "conscious" observers who are drawn into the issues of the theatrical presentation rather than into identification and empathy. For this reason, Brecht writes, the "Chinese artist's performance often strikes the Western actor as cold" (93). The unemotional presentation of emotion does not, however, negate emotion altogether. Brecht gives an example: "At those points where the character portrayed is deeply excited the performer takes a lock of hair between his lips and chews it. But this is like a ritual, there is nothing eruptive about it. It is quite clearly somebody else's repetition of the incident: a representation, even though an artistic one" (93). The ritualistic representation of emotion marks itself as a sign—the hair between the teeth takes on a purely symbolic meaning, with no emotional content; as in ritual the symbol dissociates itself from a "realistic" representation. Or rather its representationality is already *recognized* as such, and so while it represents genuine emotion it does not reproduce it.

For such a gesture to work, it must be shown to an audience that is ready for it; actors not only get the audiences they expect, but the ones they establish or create. When it comes to European theater, Brecht describes actors and audiences fully caught up in a theater of empathy whose major sensibility is bourgeois. As he writes against European theater, Brecht develops a clear critique of the aesthetic of the bourgeoisie; by describing Chinese actors (on the basis of having seen Mei Lanfang's troupe perform) he also simultaneously develops (as a by-product of that description) a theory of Chinese audiences, on the assumption that the technique of theater produces not only a different kind of actor but also a different kind of public.

Thus the discussion of Chinese theater carries with it, piggyback, a more general theory of China itself. The discussion of the Chinese actor's "coldness" is therefore of particular interest. As Brecht takes pains to say, the actor only *seems* cold, because he presents emotional and psychological states as *signs* rather than as *states:* "lack of control is decorously expressed, or if not decorously at any rate decorously for the stage. Among all the possible signs certain particular ones are picked out, with careful and visible consideration" (93). The Chinese actor thus externalizes emotion by making it into a discrete sign, and by making visible not only that sign (through his action) but also his consideration of which sign to use. He thus alienates himself from the presentation that he invites the audience to read, as it were, on his body, which remains visible as *his* body throughout his presentation. What is achieved is a kind of superrealism, in which, as Brecht puts it, "there is of course a creative process at work; but it is a higher one, because it is raised to the conscious level" (95).

For Brecht, the major problem with Western acting lies in its attempt to present the unconscious truth of the characters it portrays (he reserves special criticism for methods like Stanislavsky's, which are designed to help actors overcome the barriers to becoming one with their characters). Brecht asks:

> What Western actor of the old sort (apart from one or two comedians) could demonstrate the elements of his art like the Chinese actor Mei Lan-fang, without special lighting and wearing a dinner jacket in an ordinary room full of specialists? It would be like the magician at a fair giving away his tricks, so that nobody ever wanted to see the act again. (94)

Where the Western actor might attribute success to an ability to "get inside" a character, for Mei Lanfang all that matters is technique; it can therefore be demonstrated without shame or embarrassment. And unlike a trick, it cannot be copied; the technique can only be learned through work. The differences here point to the relative lack of sophistication of bourgeois Western theater technique, which not only thrives on illusion but requires it.

In a short essay labeled in his complete works "On the Theater of the Chinese," Brecht elaborated on Western audiences' reaction to Mei Lanfang:

> Doubtless on the strength of the bad experiences at Western guest performances or from Western audience members in China, the great Chinese actor found it necessary to repeat reassuringly through his interpreter that though he played women on stage, he was not a female impersonator. The press was informed that Dr. Mei Lanfang was a completely manly person, a good father, even a banker. We know that it's required in certain primitive areas, in order to avoid insults, to let the audience know that the actor playing the villain is not actually a villain. This necessity stems naturally not only from the primitiveness of the viewer, but also from the primitiveness of Western acting. (*Gesammelte Werke*, 15:426–27)[22]

Faced with the sophisticated technique of Chinese theater, the Western audience needs an instruction normally only given "in certain primitive areas." The Western assumption that for a man to play a woman necessarily requires impersonation—to get inside the person of the character—for Brecht evinces the sorry intellectual state of Western theater. As far as he is concerned, acting like a woman does not mean becoming like one.

The primitiveness of the Western audience affects its experience during the performance as well. Brecht writes in "Alienation Effects" that when Mei Lanfang "was playing a death scene a spectator sitting next [to] me exclaimed with astonishment at one of his gestures. One or two people sitting in front of us turned round indignantly and sshhh'd. Possibly their attitude would have been all right for a European production, but for a Chinese it was unspeakably ridiculous. In their case the A-effect had misfired" (*Theatre*, 95). Brecht's use of "misfired" (*verfehlt*, to miss out or fail) indicates the gap between the demands made by the performer and the expectations of the audience; those who hush demonstrate the degree to which they, at least, have entered emotionally into the scene. The A-effect cannot therefore be produced entirely by the acting but must come about as a sort of agreement between the actors and the audience—a mutual recognition that remains impossible for the bourgeois spectator. The A-effect itself cannot be an estranged gesture, but must be familiar and expected by the audience.

As many scholars have pointed out, however, part of what produced the Chinese theater's strange effect may have been its being Chinese.

Western spectators witnessing possibly the only Peking Opera performances of their lifetime (as was Brecht) could be expected to find the production at least strange, if not downright bizarre. Brecht comments: "When one sees the Chinese acting it is at first very hard to discount the feeling of estrangement [*Befremdung*] which they produce in us as Europeans. One has to be able to imagine them achieving an A-effect among their Chinese spectators too" (96). Willett here uses "estrangement" to translate *Befremdung*, a word that can also be translated as "alienation." Both Brecht and Willett therefore differentiate this use of *Befremdung* from the word *Verfremdung*, which names the A-effect. (Willett's decision to translate *Verfremdung* as "alienation" causes him to do this backwards, as it were.) One might then ask, what is the difference between the estrangement *(Befremdung)* produced by seeing Chinese people and the alienation *(Verfremdung)* that occurs in Chinese acting?

When Brecht talks about alienation, as he does for most of the essay, he refers to the process of Chinese acting in general *(chinesischen Schauspielkunst)* as well as the Chinese actor in particular *(der chinesische Artist)*. "Chinese" as an adjective names a style or culture of acting, whose ideas Brecht comfortably understands. In this moment, however, discussing estrangement, Brecht shifts the discussion to "the Chinese" *(Chinesen,* Chinese people), highlighting for the first time his own awareness of Chinese otherness: "When one sees *the Chinese* acting it is at first very hard to discount the feeling of estrangement which they produce in us as Europeans" (96; emphasis added).

That feeling of estrangement *(Befremdung)* is immediately turned, however, to understanding the vicissitudes of the A-effect in China, about which Brecht writes that one "has to be able to imagine them [the Chinese actors] achieving an A-effect among their Chinese spectators too" (96). That is, one must not confuse the experience produced by seeing Chinese people acting with the effects intended by their theater. In order to see the A-effect in Chinese acting, Brecht must imagine that the feeling of strangeness he experiences does not stem simply from racial or cultural difference, but rather that the A-effect works on those who do not experience Chinese people as strange: other Chinese people. In imagining the experience of the Chinese audience, Brecht imagines himself as a kind of Chinese spectator, someone for whom the only estrangement *(Befremdung)* produced by Chinese acting is alienation *(Verfremdung)*.

Berg-Pan among others has argued that Brecht simply misunderstands the experience of the Chinese audience. She writes that while, for instance, the biting of hair might work as an A-effect for Western audiences, Chinese audiences are well aware of the ritualistic or symbolic codes of Peking Opera and therefore find them quite natural. She writes: "The mere fact that Mei's performance was taken out of the context of China's national theater scene . . . endowed it with a certain mysteriousness and glamour, a strangeness which it might not have possessed for the western observer witnessing a performance in China" (165). A page later, she adds, "It is important to remember that Chinese audiences know all these gestures or are expected to know them, and hence, they do not really provide an alienation effect" (166). The "strangeness" Berg-Pan refers to in the first quote is the same strangeness that Brecht describes with *Befremdung*, namely the strangeness of seeing something new or unusual. Where Brecht has taken pains specifically to distinguish that strangeness from the process of the A-effect, Berg-Pan argues instead that Brecht's construction of the Chinese audience's experience—on which his differentiation depends—is mistaken and produced by his desire "to find his own ideas confirmed" in the theater of the Chinese (164). In other words she argues that Brecht mistakes his feeling of *Befremdung* for a general principle of *Verfremdung*.

Both points of view—Brecht's and Berg-Pan's, which is its opposite—depend on a sense of what the Chinese audience experiences when it watches Peking Opera. For Brecht, the A-effect is created at least partly by the audience, which shares the *look* of the actor (looking at the actor, seeing the actor looking at the audience, observing the actor looking at himself). And so he must imagine that A-effect as it appears in Chinese acting *in Moscow* happens at least partly because somewhere in China there are Chinese audiences who understand the A-effect and share the actor's regard for it—even if some Europeans watching the play don't get it. Brecht thus imagines a Chinese audience attuned to the A-effect in the same way that he is. Berg-Pan, on the other hand, imagines a Chinese audience that finds Chinese acting familiar and even dull. She remarks acerbically that the "fact that the traditional Chinese theater experienced a rapid and drastic decline immediately after the advent of the communist regime, suggests that for China's revolutionary government it was not exactly revolutionary" (175–76). In both cases the ground for judging whether or not the A-effect exists in Chinese acting in China remains the Chinese audience; both Brecht and Berg-Pan measure the truth of Brecht's analysis against conditions in Chinese theater's native space.[23]

Brecht's sense of the role of the Chinese audience is immediately followed by a longer description of Chinese actors.

> [The Chinese actor] makes his own mystery from the mysteries of nature (especially human nature): he allows nobody to examine how he produces the natural phenomenon, *nor does nature allow him to understand as he produces it.* We have here the artistic counterpart of a primitive technology, a rudimentary science. The Chinese performer gets his A-effect by association with magic. "How it's done" remains hidden; knowledge is a matter of knowing the tricks and is in the hand of a few men who guard it jealously and profit from their secrets. (96; emphasis added)

It is hard to know what to make of this claim, in particular since it directly contradicts Brecht's earlier praise of Mei Lanfang's tuxedoed performance. In that instance Brecht compared the *Western* actor to a magician unwilling to give away his tricks, and remarked the ease with which Mei performed with no special lighting or costumes. Here instead not only does the Chinese actor associate himself with magic, but he does so in order to profit. And whereas in "On the Theater of the Chinese" Brecht had pointed to the "primitiveness" of Western audiences, here he suggests that the Chinese actor—who does not really understand how he produces the A-effect (!)—operates on the basis of "primitive technology."

Factually, one might respond that while training of Peking Opera actors in the early twentieth century involved creating a sharp distinction between professionals and the large communities of amateurs, reserving certain knowledge for the former, the audience was nonetheless privy to the repertoire of gestures and codes the actors used to produce reality-effects.[24]

But that misses the point. Brecht's claim here is rhetorical, not informational. He is not interested in the radical possibilities of Chinese acting *in China.* His denigration of the Chinese actor's magic is immediately followed by this argument:

> In point of fact the only people who can profitably study a piece of technique like Chinese acting's A-effect are those who need such a technique for quite definite social purposes.
>
> The experiments conducted by modern German theatre led to a wholly

independent development of the A-effect. So far Asiatic acting has exerted
no influence. (96)

With these three sentences Brecht turns his back on the Chinese A-effect.
He does so in two ways. The first sentence picks up on the claims he has
just been making about the primitiveness and magic of the Chinese A-
effect, whose techniques are kept secret so that the actors can continue to
profit ("aus ihren Geheimnissen Gewinn ziehen"). He contrasts the
profit motive in China with the "definite social purposes" of his own theater, arguing that the "only people who can profitably study" [mit
Gewinn studieren] the A-effect now live in Europe. The delicateness of
this rhetorical turn reveals itself most clearly in the uses to which Brecht
puts the word "profit" *(Gewinn):* in the first instance it refers, quite literally, to the Chinese actor's lust for lucre; in the second it points figuratively to the gains of those who fight for social change.[25] Though Brecht
does not name the people who can profitably study the A-effect, the transition in the next paragraph to the "modern German theater" suggests
that it is that theater, at least, which must take up the radical potential of
the A-effect as a technique. In those two sentences, Brecht repeats the
assertion he had made as he opened the essay, namely that the German
development of the A-effect has had historically nothing to do with the
Chinese one.

By the time the reader arrives at the claim that the German theater has
independently developed the A-effect, the relative valuations of German
and Chinese theater have been completely reversed. Whereas earlier the
Chinese acting is sophisticated and subtle, and Western theater primitive
and "hopelessly parsonical" (94), in these last moments of Brecht's discussion the Chinese actor uses primitive technology and only the German theater can truly understand and use the A-effect. Brecht's sense of
Chinese acting as ritualistic and primitive—and of the Chinese A-effect as
being produced *by nature* through the actor ("nor does nature allow him
to understand as he produces it")—repeats the well-known structure
whereby the West gives sense, meaning, and theory to an East whose
innovations would otherwise remain irrational or primitive. Having made
this judgment, Brecht turns to a discussion of the problems and history of
German rather than Chinese theater. The essay's remaining pages never
again mention Chinese theater, or China.

How can one read this classically orientalist reconstruction of Chinese acting (and through it, China) in light of the rest of the essay? It would be unwise, I think, to read backward into the first half of the essay the orientalism of the second half, or to excuse the latter half by gesturing toward the first one. When Brecht writes that "so far, Asiatic acting has exerted no influence" [es fand bisher keine Beeinflussung durch die asiatische Schauspielkunst statt] (96), the words "so far" *(bisher)* imply that Chinese acting might influence German theater in the future. And yet in the pages that follow, Brecht offers no model for such influence, and instead shows how the independent development of the A-effect in Germany came out of a need to resist a bourgeois theater, giving substance to his claim that only those who need the A-effect for social purposes can profitably study Chinese acting. As I read it, there is something incommensurable in the essay, and it is this incommensurability itself that offers the best sense of Brecht's sense of China.

Later, some of Brecht's plays reminded audience members—including some Chinese ones—of Chinese theater (Tatlow, *Mask,* 323). But, as Tatlow points out, one should not confuse being reminded of the Chinese theater *with* the Chinese theater (323). Whatever Brecht took from Chinese theater—and his admiration for Mei Lanfang seems the clearest instance of potential influence—he did not conceive of it as "Chinese." Brecht's interest in distinguishing precisely the difference between Chinese strangeness *(Befremdung,* Willett's "estrangement") and Chinese acting's alienation *(Verfremdung)* offer a way of reading the latter's technique out of its cultural context. Brecht does so by imagining that in Chinese space, the technique of alienation offers no experience of strangeness. He goes on to adopt a "Chinese" attitude toward Chinese acting, turning, at essay's end, away from Chinese acting and actors and toward the needs of a specifically German theater. This signals the end of Brecht's interest in the Chinese as such (that is, as *strange* or *estranging*) and the beginning of his "profitable study" of the technique's "transportability" (95) in his own world, and his own context. In that world, the reference to Chinese theater exists only as memory, its gestures surfacing in those moments when Brecht's theater reminds its audience of China.

As it is written, the essay has simultaneously nothing and everything to do with China. The manner in which it deals with China strikes me as emblematic of a certain *refusal*—passive or active—of a genuine relation to a space on which it undeniably depends not only for its rhetorical panache but for its *ideas*. Though "Alienation Effects" cannot be conceived without Brecht's Peking Opera experience in Moscow, it also turns its face away from its nominally Chinese inspiration in order to name the A-effect its own (as when Brecht writes of the A-effect's "wholly independent" development in Germany). Brecht does not, like Pound, imagine himself the true inheritor of traditional Chinese techniques; instead he distinguishes clearly and almost violently at times between the uses of the A-effect in the German and Chinese theaters. He remains uninterested in the Chineseness of the technique—he does not want to rely on its strangeness *(Befremdung)* for a certain revolutionary force (as did Pound before him, and the Telquelians after). For Brecht, China never becomes an idea, a desire, a dream. It remains, even when he misunderstands it, a more or less irrelevant fact.

It is via the difference between *Verfremdung* and *Befremdung* in this essay that one might see the beginnings of a Brechtian relationship to China, one that depends on a particular relation to Chinese difference. In "Alienation Effects," Brecht tries to see Mei Lanfang like a Chinese person would—that is, as someone whose Chineseness is simply no big deal. Paradoxically, then, Brecht's attempt to see past Chinese strangeness by seeing Chinese theater as a Chinese person (i.e., as not strange) produces and is produced by a lack of interest in China itself *as different*. So that the name of a certain authenticity (i.e., taking the experience as a Chinese person would) actually depends on *not* noticing the cultural differences at hand, of not treating the A-effect as "Chinese."

This is true from the moment that the essay raises the question of *Befremdung,* when Brecht argues that one must be able to imagine a Chinese audience experiencing Mei Lanfang's performance *in the same way he does*. The discussion is immediately followed by the surprising critique of Chinese actors and their tricks. From that moment on, the essay works both in form and content (and absence of Chinese content) to dissociate the A-effect in Germany with the A-effect in Chinese acting, and to stress differences in both motivation and political context between the two. Brecht's interest in the A-effect technique and its transportability effectively supersede the *Befremdung* of Chinese difference. As with his translations of Chinese poetry Brecht does not claim that his use of Chinese

85

technique borrows formally from Chinese aesthetics; rather Chinese acting (like the poetry) provides a jumping-off point for his own work, which he understands as unrelated (in a cause-effect way) to the Chinese.

In an essay titled "Brecht and the Chinese Other," Shu-hsi Kao takes up the coincidence of *Befremdung* and *Verfremdung* in Brecht in order to argue that the question of China in Brecht "depends obviously on the degree to which one wishes to retain and stress the 'strangeness' of the Chinese fact in the work and thought of the man to whom we owe the concept of the *Verfremdungseffekt*" (89).[26] With this sentence Kao announces her interest in the coincidence of "strangeness" and *Verfremdung,* particularly as they relate to China, by acknowledging the fact of China as "strange." Against Brecht's attempt to dissociate the alienation of the A-effect from the experience of China in the West, Kao wishes to argue for the relevance of Chinese "strangeness" to one's take on "Brecht and China."

Kao's point is that no matter whether Brecht dismisses it or not, "China" continues to mean in "Alienation Effects," if only as an *impression* left on the reader, like a taste in the mouth. China's Chineseness cannot mean nothing, even though the essay wants to ignore it. China remains, in many ways, the *name* of the A-effect, its presumed site of origin, especially for those many readers who only know the essay by its title. And when one remembers China's appearances elsewhere in Brecht, one cannot simply take its presence here as anomalous: it must mean, in a way that depends almost entirely on the very strangeness *(Befremdung)* Brecht wishes to dismiss. China, unlike the German country fair, continues to voice, despite Brecht's intentions, an interesting and obvious strangeness, and Brecht's attempt to ignore that here makes things all the more strange.

As Kao argues, Brecht's attempt to ignore the *Befremdung* of seeing Chinese actors as a European is doomed to failure, because "China" has a history that breaches the confines of Brecht's essay and his thought.

> Basically, the Chinese reference gives Brecht a *dual* benefit: on one hand, the opportunity to draw from the communal well of the European imaginary to find the already "familiar" and recognized figure of the Chinese Other, and on the other hand, the possibility of exploiting that figure's infinite alterity in order to make it the keystone of the *Verfremdungseffekt*'s conceptual structure. (94)[27]

Kao attends to the text's reception by a Europe that already knows its "China." In so doing, she effectively brings "Brecht and China" into the post-Said era, by remarking not on China's role in shaping Brecht's thought but on Brecht's necessary relation to a "China" that is not the same thing as the geopolitical entity with that name. To be interested in China today—or to be interesting *about* China—is to be interested in it *as* strange, to be interested precisely in its Chineseness (its difference, its capacity for *Befremdung*) and not its transportability. Kao's reading depends precisely on that which Brecht wants to ignore: namely that China, for a German writing in 1935, really *is* strange, worth remarking on, talking about in a variety of contexts—contexts that exist prior to Brecht's visit to Moscow and help shape the reception of the "Alienation Effects" essay. Today, such a reading of Brecht and China is not only natural but de rigueur.

But Kao's reading of Brecht as necessarily implicated in the West's "China" does not adequately account for Brecht's resistance to such an implication. Despite bearing many of the signs of such an interest—references to China, translations of Chinese poetry, avid readership of Chinese philosophy, and an awareness of Chinese politics—Brecht does not manifest its primary and most fundamental sign: an interest in China *qua* Chinese, an interest in China as culturally strange or different. Thus the "dual benefit" of the Chinese Other and its "infinite alterity" is one Brecht gains largely via *reception* in a cultural context for which those issues are the sine qua non of a relationship to China. The "Alienation Effects" essay offers the clearest instance of Brecht's direct refusal of such "benefits," and thus his refusal of the culturally preconceived "China" whose presence nonetheless shapes his writing.

To sum up: there exists among readers an expected relation to China that drives most studies of East-West comparative literature. As Saussy has written, "'China' names a country of course, but it more accurately names an international culture; and 'culture' is the identity-tag of a question having, these days in North America at least, a moral as well as an epistemological side" (*Problem,* 4). The major effects of this question, as I see it, are that anyone talking about China will do so within the framework of an ideology that emphasizes China's Chineseness (positively or negatively), that acknowledges its influence as "Chinese" (and its being interesting *because* Chinese).

Chinese Dreams

Brecht, unlike Pound or *Tel quel,* writes about China but is not explicitly interested in it (even though he may gain advantage from Chineseness in his reception, as Kao argues). The tendency to imagine those conditions as identical nonetheless provokes readings of his poetic translation and his philosophy that search for "Chinese" influences on Brecht's work, without understanding that Brecht does not share the reader's sense of what "China" actually means, or does, epistemologically speaking. The "Alienation Effects" essay, by juxtaposing the A-effect with the strangeness of seeing Chinese acting, while claiming that they differ, shows that Brecht understood full well the apparently innate strangeness of the Chinese in Europe, but also that he resisted it. In doing so, he suggests the possibility of another kind of relation to China—one not free of all orientalism or illusion, but rather one whose orientalism and whose illusions configure themselves differently than those of the more traditional (Poundian) model. It is certainly still unclear whether such a "China" is any better or worse than the traditional one, but I am quite sure that it *is,* that is, that it exists, and furthermore that it can teach something about the possibilities of cross-cultural representation beyond the West's most "oriental," dreamed China. Considered in such a context, Brecht's indifference to the Chineseness of Chinese acting (or Chinese poetry) is so extreme as to be literally *beyond* orientalism.

Brecht without Brecht

Toward the end of her article on Brecht, Kao writes,

> In various Chinese philosophical currents, in the traditional forms of Chinese poetry, and especially in the practice of Chinese theater, Brecht was able to find elements that he was able to assimilate to the point of making them his own, *and* that he was able to maintain in their original "strangeness." This constitutes, one might say, a kind of permanent contradiction. (96)[28]

It is precisely this contradiction that fascinates when it comes to Brecht's work on and around China, because it acknowledges and indeed emphasizes the importance of "strangeness" (*étrangeté* can also be "foreignness"). Brecht's antipathy for that strangeness, expressed in the "Alienation Effects" essay, makes it all the more interesting as a way of thinking about the cultural value of his China, and the degree to which Brecht's silence on that same issue might constitute an active refusal of such strangeness rather than simply a lack of interest in it. Such a relation to China is not easily amenable to an admittedly vulgar antiorientalist critique, since that critique proceeds on the assumption that the West's bad desires shape perceptions of the East. Refusal of desire (and I am reading China's "strangeness" as its most visibly desirable aspect) is also, to be sure, a kind of desire. But it is not the same as Pound's.

Kao's quotation also raises the question of intentionality, since it appears to impute to Brecht motivations that are not there "in the text." Kao is less interested in authorship than in reception, and her particular angle of vision—the emphasis on how China's meaning in the West lies well outside Brecht's personal control—clearly affects her sense of both the meaning and value of China in Brecht's work. Contrast this with the attitudes of the vast majority of Brecht critics, most of whom are quite invested in a sense of Brecht as an author and a person (good or bad), and for whom the issue of what exactly Brecht knew and when he knew it is paramount. Whether one considers the issue from the perspective of *China's influence on Brecht* (focus on the author) or *China's influence on Brecht's reception* (focus on reception/reading) clearly makes a difference. A reading focused, as Kao's is, on reception rather than authorship offers the specter of a "Brecht without Brecht," a reading in which the text retains the author's name but little of his original intentions.

The vast majority of work on Brecht's China chooses not to follow such a path, hovering instead somewhere near Brecht the person, confronting and explaining (away) Brecht's odd silences around China. But this focus on authorship has its pitfalls. Recent scholarship on Brecht suggests that parts of his China-centered work were written entirely or partially by his collaborator Elisabeth Hauptmann. For instance, of the twelve translations of Chinese poems Brecht completed in his lifetime, ten were based on Waley's versions, some or all of which Hauptmann first translated into German.[29] While Waley's role in shaping Brecht's China has been critically recognized, Hauptmann's place as Brecht's "silent collaborator" has been slow to be remarked. Recently, however, John Fuegi in *Brecht and Company* (1994) and "The Zelda Syndrome: Brecht and Elisabeth Hauptmann" has forcefully argued for Hauptmann's role not simply as collaborator but as primary author of a good deal of Brecht's work, claiming that Brecht ran a "collective" where he "overwhelmingly collected and where others contributed to his fame and financial welfare" ("Zelda," 114).[30] Even those who do not agree with Fuegi's more extravagant claims, like Brecht's major English translator, John Willett, recognize Hauptmann's role in shaping Brecht's Chinese poems (the English edition of Brecht's *Poems,* which Willett edited with Ralph Manheim, notes that Brecht wrote the Chinese poems with Hauptmann [501]).

Hauptmann's story seems to have gone like this. In 1929, while translating Waley's translation of the Japanese No play *Taniko* into German (that work eventually became Brecht's *Die Massnahme* [The measures taken]), Hauptmann came across Waley's *A Hundred and Seventy Chinese Poems,* which he had published in 1922. In *Elisabeth Hauptmann: Brecht's Silent Collaborator,* Paula Hanssen quotes Hauptmann's enthusiastic response: "Studying these books bowled me over. Here were things that really resembled Brecht. . . . There were some Chinese students who talked about Waley's Chinese translations with me. I worked on or translated about ten poems from English, and showed them to Brecht" (82).[31] While Tatlow would argue in *Mask of Evil* that Brecht approached Chinese "through the medium of English," here Hauptmann's enthusiasm stems from her sense that Chinese approaches Brecht rather than the other way around.[32] Waley's Chinese translations managed to provoke not only a sense that Chinese poetry was interesting but also that Chinese poetry was something like Brecht's. Such a sense remained in effect even as Hauptmann and Brecht made changes to Waley's translations.[33]

But Hauptmann's sense of the affinity between the poetic style of the Chinese and the style of Brecht's earlier work is actually more complicated than it seems. In the years between 1924 and 1929, Hauptmann had not only collaborated with Brecht but had actually written work published under Brecht's name. Fuegi, typically, argues that Hauptmann's role in writing "Brecht's" work was more central than Brecht's himself. But even so moderate a scholar as Willett remarks that for the short stories "Brecht" published in the second half of the 1920s, "the major responsibility was quite likely to be Hauptmann's" (qtd. in Fuegi, "Zelda," 107).

Recall here Berg-Pan's sentence about Brecht's affinity with Chineseness: "Having found ideas and opinions resembling his own in monuments of a culture as distant, exotic and ancient as that of China must have thrilled Brecht with a shock of recognition and a sense of self-justification" (231). Had Berg-Pan known about Hauptmann's role, the sentiment would have been different. But the word "thrilled" captures well the excitement of Hauptmann's feeling "bowled over" [warf mich . . . um] by her encounter with Waley, and Berg-Pan's sense that Brecht found in Chinese poetry things he already felt or knew mirrors Hauptmann's finding in Waley "things that really resembled Brecht." Hauptmann's presence behind the "Brecht" in question merely makes the recognition more complicated, since it adds another layer to the already complex "self" at hand in studies of what the author knew.

Hauptmann's first encounter with Chinese poetry in translation is thus also "Brecht" the author's, though not Brecht the person's. The affinity she felt for Waley's translations would in fact eventually be taken up by Brecht himself; Hanssen quotes a 1934 letter of Hauptmann's responding to a Brecht inquiry about Waley. At the same time, however, Hauptmann's role makes the relation between "Brecht's China" and the eventual publication in 1938 of six German poems from Waley's translations widely assumed to be Brecht's interestingly unclear. Whatever pleasure Brecht eventually gained from his own interest in China, and whatever China he might come to create on his own, the impetus for the translations comes largely if not exclusively from Hauptmann. One might, therefore, think of "Brecht" in "Brecht's China" as something like "the authorial function known as Brecht" rather than the actual person. When it comes to the Chinese translations Hauptmann did most of the work.

It would appear, then, that even a firm sense of authorship can return us to a Brecht without Brecht, a moment in which Brecht the person seems to be less and less at the center of this chapter. Considering that "China" was already laboring under the complications of its reference, it appears that much of the work of the chapter has been to make the entire phrase "Brecht's China" into a catachresis. "Brecht's China" is catachrestic, however, only if one remains committed to the twin realisms of authorship and representation, reading from a perspective that demands that Brecht the author be Brecht the person, and China the represented place be China the geopolitical entity.

There are other perspectives out there. Jameson, writing about Brecht's Chinas (and other places), pointedly notes the limits of a "realistic" perspective: "These settings are no doubt 'unreal' in the sense of being unhistorical: but Brecht always warned us, with annoyance at our inveterate incomprehension, that here we were most often still thinking of naturalism and its photographic ideals of reproduction" (139). Jameson goes a long way toward reminding us that we remain in the realm of the literary, and that the wish for an accurate or true representation (or the dismissal of a text that lacks it) always occurs in relation to "ideals of reproduction." Kao's discussion of Brecht's reception—which is certainly "unreal" in the sense of being unrelated to Brecht's intentions—indicates that there remains plenty to wonder about outside the question of what exactly Brecht meant.

The overwhelming dominance of a naturalistic assumption of representation may in fact explain why no one has yet written about Brecht's China, preferring to concentrate on China's Brecht, the historical Brecht produced out of an encounter with Chinese thought. Such a reading inevitably reads Brecht into a place where he is not, by assuming that whatever representation of China does exist in his work is the dross of a failed or otherwise inefficient attempt to produce a realistic China, or evidence of a powerful and genuine relation to it.

With that in mind I want to turn to Brecht's theater work, and specifically his most "Chinese" play, *The Good Person of Szechwan,* a play whose plotting and performance engage in fun, lively ways the troublesome questions of representation and reproduction. In the play, Shen Teh, a Chinese prostitute, after being rewarded by a trio of visiting gods for being a "good" person, finds herself besieged on all sides by those who want to take advantage of her newfound fortune. At wit's end, Shen Teh transforms herself into Shui Ta, a ruthless, male cousin from out of town, who is able to effectively run her new tobacco shop (in the standard version; at one point Brecht wrote an alternate script where Shen Teh opens an opium den). By moving back and forth between the two roles, Shen Teh discovers that only by being evil can she protect herself and her wish to do good. Eventually those who suffer at Shui Ta's hands report Shen Teh's "disappearance" to the gods, and Shui Ta must reveal herself, telling the gods, "Your order long ago / To be good and yet to live / Tore me like lightning into two halves" (*Collected Plays,* 6:100). The gods, blithely unaware of the difficulties produced by their demand to be good, sail happily back to the heavens, warning Shen Teh to only become Shui Ta once a month.

In 1989 the British National Theatre produced *The Good Person of Sichuan*³⁴ in circumstances that illustrate the ways in which "Brecht and China" opens up in performance. In her highly critical review of the production in *Performing Brecht,* Margaret Eddershaw describes the set as "an open, bleak and urban wasteland of grey concrete, made up of square concrete beams and broken blocks and backed by a huge black wall. . . . The whole effect was that of a dreary city building site. As one of the actors, Bill Paterson, wryly remarked, . . . 'You don't need to go to Hong Kong to see that. The whole of the South Bank [of London] looks like a building site!'" (125). As for a specifically Chinese ambiance, it "was created by the random placing of a number of black-painted bicycles around the set, while the audience was given fleeting glimpses of figures in coolie hats and pyjama-style trousers cycling across the stage" (125). In keeping with director Deborah Warner's interest in making *The Good Person* relevant to contemporary audiences, the play's program "also included pictures of dead bodies lying in Beijing's Tiananmen Square, following the crushing of the student protest in June 1989. Again, the reference seemed to have little connection with the production (except that one picture contained a heap of bicycles)" (128).

Eddershaw is annoyed because Warner does not understand Brecht. What Warner does not understand in particular is that *The Good Person* has almost nothing to do, culturally or politically, with China. For Eddershaw, the play at its most challenging is about the difficulty of being good in a world whose ideological and economic structures force one to be bad to survive; the most exotic idea it offers lies not in its Chinese ambiance but in its assault on the ideological construction of goodness under capitalism (Eddershaw remarks acerbically that Warner "declared that no discussion of the internal politics of the play was necessary" [126]). Contra Eddershaw, Warner's use of various "Chinese" elements, both on stage with the bicycles or the Hong Kong–like buildings, or in the program with the Tiananmen pictures, makes the play exotic *in a familiar way.* Rather than learn anything new (about, for instance, the actual social conditions and poverty in London's South Bank, Eddershaw suggests), the National Theatre production appears to insist on repeating what it already *knows:* that China is a place where people ride bicycles and dress in pajama pants, smoke opium (Warner used the opium shop script), and get murdered by their Communist government. Between the content of the play and the Tiananmen massacre or people on bicycles the spectator can draw no logical connection, except that they are all Chinese.

Eddershaw's critique of Warner's production raises many of the issues covered so far in this chapter. By insisting that the vital impact of the play is to be felt in its antibourgeois politics rather than its Chineseness, Eddershaw makes an argument like the one I made around Brecht's Lao Zi poem: namely that what appears to be truly and originally *Brechtian* about the play has little to do with its Chinese setting or background. For Eddershaw, the production's little hints of China are in fact all *chinoiseries*, distracting from the play's important political message. Eddershaw's argument is made all the more convincing by the relatively banal exoticism of the National Theater production: randomly putting together the disparate and obvious signifiers of "China" (opium, bicycles, and so on) only evokes a China whose differences "we" in the West already know and understand. Rather than pointing to a complex of history and difference in which the audience itself might be implicated, such a superficial exoticism settles for the easy, satisfying aura of worldliness.

And yet Warner's production of *The Good Person*'s Chineseness is at some level so obviously legitimate, so obviously in keeping with the play's own exotic setting, that it is hard to disagree with. Part of the argument of this chapter has been to show that this obvious correctness, this hard-to-disagree-with-ness, is not produced simply by the provincialism of Brecht's "bad" readers, but rather out of the Brecht-China relationship itself.

Let us rehearse this argument once more by looking at Hans Mayer's comparison between *The Good Person*'s Szechwan and another of Brecht's "imaginary" locales, Mahagonny:

> Szechwan is the world of modern, divided, pluralistic society. "Szechwan" is a model, just as "Mahagonny" was a year earlier. Brecht might as well have chosen the title *The Good Person of Mahagonny*. It shouldn't be taken as a chinoiserie, but as the model of a fractured modern society. (Qtd. in Tatlow, *Mask*, 469)[35]

Such a claim is not uncommon in Brecht criticism, and has been made with reference to any number of Brecht's representations of foreign places. (About his *Caucasian Chalk Circle*, which was based on an ancient Chinese story, John Fuegi writes: "It must be stressed that in both milieu and in construction this play is only slightly 'Oriental.' Much of the dramaturgy could have been taken straight from Shakespeare" ["Caucasian," 139–40n].) Ultimately, the argument that the Chineseness of *The Good Person* is either truly related to China (à la National Theatre) or that it is not related to anything genuinely Brechtian (Eddershaw, Mayer) occupy the same ideological position vis-à-vis Brecht's China. In both cases Brecht's "China" has nothing specific about it, and it is taken as a more general instance of either *(a)* all things generically Chinese, or *(b)* all things generically exotic.[36]

Reinhold Grimm, whose *Brecht und die Weltliteratur* inaugurated the current era of "Brecht and China" criticism, has written an article on Brecht and Chicago that responds directly to criticism that treats Brecht's locales as mythic. Referring to the "myth of the myth of" Brecht's Chicago, Grimm argues that any suggestion that Brecht simply made his Chicago up ignores the profound impact the city had on him. Pointing to the content of Brecht's plays (*St. Joan of the Stockyards, In the Jungle of the Cities,* and others) and of his library and reading material, Grimm argues that "the Windy City in his life and work reveals itself as a towering presence, as all but overwhelming. Chicago and the Chicagoans constitute one of Brecht's most frequent as well as most poignant motifs and ideas" ("Bertlot Brecht's Chicago," 229). Grimm goes on to compare Brecht's vision of Chicago with the Chicago-born poet Carl Sandburg, quoting Sandburg's collection *Chicago Poems* (1916) and asking of the verses: "could they not as well have been written by Brecht?" (233).

Grimm's argument about Chicago resembles in most of its particulars the claims made by scholars about Brecht and China, who insist that the sheer volume of reading and writing Brecht did about China indicate a relationship more profound than simple exoticism. In his *Mask of Evil,* Tatlow argues that "we must now show how the universal parable [of *The Good Person*] with its Chinese patina is, in fact, related to fundamental Chinese ideas" (469). Tatlow has a hard time showing exactly why this must be so. He relies on comparisons between the attitudes expressed by Brecht's characters and plotting in *Der gute Mensch* and the work of the Chinese philosopher Mencius. He then goes on to show how various moments in the play repeat (some directly, some less so) words or ideas Brecht found in his reading of Chinese philosophy or poetry (including at one point the story of the Waley translation "The Big Rug"). Unfortunately, conclusions drawn from such work must remain tentative, as Tatlow cannot prove that Brecht, for instance, ever read the work of Mencius: "I do not imply that Brecht read, marked, learned and inwardly digested the words and teachings of this most celebrated if eclectic disciple of Confucius" (471).[37] Nonetheless, Tatlow finds enough similarities to come to the following conclusion: "He [Brecht] responded . . . to Chinese ideas on human potentiality and its institutionalized frustration: that is why we cannot really equate Chicago and Sezuan and that is why his play is rightly entitled *Der gute Mensch von Sezuan,* not *Mahagonny*" (475).

The arguments made by both Tatlow and Grimm as I have presented them here essentially offer two responses to those who believe Brecht's Chicago/China is mythical. First, both Grimm and Tatlow argue that Brecht's intellectual investment in Chicago or China (as evidenced by the amount of reading and writing he did about either place) acts as a prophylactic against his Chicago/China being simply another European myth about strangeness (that is, a *chinoiserie*). Second, both critics compare Brecht's work on Chicago/China to work by native Chicagoans or Chinese, arguing that the similarity between Brecht's work and that of the native shows that Brecht's vision was true to the native experience of that place. But neither argument especially convinces: one could presumably find similarities between the work of any number of French people whose work Brecht owned or read and Brecht's own work which would not convince anyone the play should have been called *The Good Person of Paris.* In any case the whole structure seems odd: it is not clear why the argument that Brecht's China, or his Chicago, are "mythical" (to some extent invented or imagined, disconnected from anything actual) is either dismissive or accusatory. Similarly, it is not clear why the response to that argument must be taken as a *defense* of Brecht, since to do so assumes the potential value of the accusation or dismissal in the first place.

Part of it has to do with intentionality. Did Brecht *mean* to present his China, or Chicago, the way he did, or was he blinded by a European myth? Clearly the former interpretation favors a sense of Brecht as a brilliant author.[38] Another, less stuck reading is Jameson's: by arguing that Brecht *meant* to represent China nonnaturalistically, he neatly rescues both Brecht and China from the critical axe; his accompanying sense of Brecht's "annoyance at our inveterate incomprehension" puts Brecht one step ahead of his readers. Grimm himself seems to come close to something like this idea immediately before he quotes Sandburg, writing that "Brecht knew full well and proclaimed repeatedly that his Chicago albeit *unwirklich* in its presentation (both 'uncanny' and 'non-naturalistic'), was nevertheless *streng wirklichkeitsgetreu* ('essentially true to reality') in its representation" (232). It is precisely the latter half of such a claim—that true representation can stem from an "untrue" presentation—that focuses a good deal of the literary debate around the representation of China in both Brecht and Pound.

But *Der gute Mensch* offers, beyond similarities of thought, quotations from Chinese philosophy, and its ostensibly Chinese setting, a further dimension: that of performance, which offers yet another way of thinking about the Chineseness of Brecht's China. For a European viewer, the play is undeniably "Chinese"—that is, strange or interesting by virtue of its China-like setting—regardless of whether it is in fact Chinese (that is, related in some intellectual or cultural way to actual China). In some productions, the gods appear dressed as figures from Peking Opera (they are shown this way in two photos appearing in Knopf, 84 and 85). Berg-Pan writes that in the productions Brecht directed or helped direct, the actors wore recognizably "Chinese" costumes, except for when Shen Teh appears as the ruthless businessman Shui Ta, who wears Western clothes, and many actors wore masks with "Mongolian features" (191).

Brecht at one point considered the difficulty of balancing the play's Chinese setting with the reception of its Chineseness:

> We are still thinking about the question: bread and milk, or rice and tea, for the "Sezuan parable." Naturally, there are already pilots and still Gods in this Sezuan. I have carefully avoided all folklore. On the other hand, it was not my intention to make jokes about the yellow people who eat white French bread. . . . Should one keep only social anachronisms? Industrialization and the invasion of European customs which are infringing upon the Gods (and upon the morals)—using these [phenomena] I can still remain in the realm of reality. But neither industrialization nor European customs will replace rice with bread . . . that would be using china as a mere disguise, and a ragged disguise at that. (Berg-Pan, 186)

In early written versions of the play the characters did eat bread and drink milk, and Brecht here indicates that the issue was up for discussion. At the same time, this brief note clearly explains the reasoning behind the eventual decision to go with rice and tea. Brecht concerns himself not only with the "realm of reality" in China, but with the realm of Chinese reality produced by the *expectations* of a Western audience. While airplane pilots and European customs (including clothing) might be taken seriously as Chinese (because they fit with the contemporary reality of China), the idea of a Chinese person eating French bread would make people laugh (because it would be incongruous with a general sense of Chinese reality). It is therefore not only a question of Chinese "reality" but of the reality of China as the Western audience knows it, and of balancing the demands of those two (linked) ideas. The presence of the audience—which may not get the quotations from Bo Juyi, or the similarities to Mencius—nonetheless guarantees that the play will be received qua Chinese. And it is that reception that places the play firmly within the dual problems of being *like China* (that is, faithful to Chinese reality) and being "Chinese" (that is, experienced as "strange" and "unusual" by virtue of referring to some idea of China).

The problem of whether the play is generically or specifically Chinese, taken up by Hans Mayer, Tatlow, and many others (around any number of Brecht plays or "imaginary" locations), therefore *disappears* in performance. It is only against the background of a performance in front of a Western audience that already has in mind a "Chinese reality" that the play not only *can be* about China but *must be* about China. And it is "about" China not simply by virtue of seeming "Chinese"—the names, the places, the eating of rice, the Peking Opera–like costumes of the gods, and the "Mongolian" features of the masks—but also because it places its own construction of China in dialogue with its construction of the West, raising the very questions about the construction of China that Brecht himself never directly discusses. If, in performance, the ruthlessly businesslike "cousin," Shui Ta, wears Western clothes, and the good-hearted former prostitute Shen Teh (a European stereotype of the first order) wears Chinese ones, the audience cannot but read that contrast as evoking specifically the difference between a precapitalist China and an aggressive Western imperiousness. Such a reading is mandated, as well, in a performance like Milan's Piccolo Teatro 1981 show, which quite intentionally "Westernized" the setting and script, placing fully within contemporary Europe and removing the "Chinese" elements (Knopf, 217). In both cases attention is called not only to the play's construction of China but also to its construction of the West, to the way in which its

China necessarily returns to the Western audience a vision of the West that exists *relative to* the China of the play.[39]

The audience's experience of the A-effect, then, in which what in its own culture had seemed natural suddenly becomes visible as historical, occurs through its experience of Chinese difference. That is, the *Verfremdung* (alienation, following Willett) occurs specifically via the *Befremdung* (estrangement) of seeing the play's construction of the West *through* China. In performance, the play raises the very question that critics want to answer by reading the script, suggesting that the reception of the suits and trappings of Chineseness must take place within the frame of the audience's understanding of China's *strangeness* (that is, the presumed *difference* of China from the West). In such a framework, the particular accuracy of the play's representation is not at stake, because the action on stage continually calls attention to itself as a representation, and to the manner in which representation gets made cross-culturally. When the gods show up dressed in costumes like those of the Peking Opera, and float past the barbed-wire fence surrounding Shen Teh's tobacco shop, the audience will read both the temporal and cultural incongruity between those things within a framework already constructed out of impressions of what it means to be both "Chinese" and "European" (even or perhaps especially if, as Bill Paterson remarks of the National Theatre production, the play's version of Szechwan looks just like London's South Bank). *Der gute Mensch* does not pretend to be genuinely Chinese (that is, the play does not want to be taken as being "from China"). But the choices it offers to those who perform it make it fully Chinese-*seeming,* and its performance history forces an awareness of the construction of Chineseness onto any production.[40]

To some extent, then, I am arguing that in performance, what happens is precisely what Kao sees in the "Alienation Effects" essay: no matter how much one tries to hide the Chineseness of the play, it remains imbricated in the stagework, not as a reflection of actual historical China but as a representation of a particular European "China."[41] As Roland Barthes puts it, "[T]he originality of the Brechtian sign is that it is *to be read twice over,*" in this case once in China and once in Europe (*Rustle,* 219). *Der gute Mensch*'s attempt to produce the A-effect in its viewers works, paradoxically, by showing them a strangeness with which they are already familiar (the Chinese eating rice), so that the A-effect (which teaches about Europe) is at once unrelated to and dependent on the Chineseness of the play's setting.

When thinking *Der gute Mensch*'s relation to its audience, I too find myself reading into the play an inevitable awareness of its own relation to Chinese strangeness that Brecht may not have wanted there, reading the Brechtian sign twice over, as it were. Reading toward reception rather than authorship—performance rather than script—opens up, for me, the most interesting aspects of Brecht's China. Returning to "Alienation Effects" unburdened (as much as one can ever be) by the question of Brecht's intentions, one more freely sees the text's struggle against confusing Chinese technique with Chinese strangeness, and the difficulty of "transporting" a technique without also bringing over the mark of its "strange" origin, the mark of Chineseness that springs from all the West's receptions and inventions of China. One might, following such a reading, return to Brecht's struggles to separate Chinese strangeness (difference) from the Chinese technique of the A-effect and say, not, "Brecht is contradicting himself," but rather, "Yes, the text articulates precisely the contradiction to which all such representations give voice." The gap between the texts' "Chinas" and "real" China does not have to be disturbing or shameful (and anyway, to whom?); one can read that gap instead as effectively articulating the struggle of representation, particularly the representation of that which is already strange.

It is, finally, in reading Brecht without Brecht, a Brecht whose authorial role in the representation of his China is no longer merely "naturalistic" but willfully "unreal," that one might most clearly see what "China" means in the Brechtian circumstance. One might even say the same thing in reverse: understanding a Brechtian "China" leads one to see more clearly his use of a nonnaturalistic theory of representation. "China" can be a cipher (there may be others) for Brecht's most interesting political and aesthetic ideologies. As with Pound's modernity, Brecht's alienation is predicated both in its reception and its production on the presence of an authorizing Chinese strangeness, even when it is inaccurate or inauthentic.[42]

One of the things that Brecht's China gets past, however, is the question of authenticity. By engaging a China neither kitsch nor historical, neither purely fantastic nor factually accurate, Brecht establishes a problem for critics who read him in those terms. Those who insist on determining the authenticity of his response to China usually end up simply inventing a China whose elements correspond suspiciously to something they see in Brecht, or see something in Brecht that feels like a China they already "know" (Jennings: the poem's significance "unrolls like a Chinese scroll"). One of the stakes in such arguments is not simply the moral value or scientific accuracy of the appropriation or translation, but the very possibility of authenticity itself. When true authenticity appears to be achieved—as when Brecht or Pound translates better than Waley—we have something of magic at work, a confirmation of song's victory over philology. As both the "Alienation Effects" essay and Brecht's own personal history—in which even the author is not authentically himself—suggest, authenticity may be a dead end, not only for Brecht, but for everyone. Brecht's response to this, given with what Jameson calls annoyance at our "inveterate incomprehension," is to remind us that authenticity, too, is an ideology, connected both to moral and political fields (appropriation, orientalism) and aesthetic or literary ones (naturalism, scientific translation). It is perhaps this kind of feeling that has prompted Tatlow to say, in his most recent book on Brecht and East Asia, that Brecht's other "is not a geographical but rather a methodological concept . . . designed to one end: combating the insanity that was the positivist normalization of the actual" (*Shakespeare,* 17).

Whether or not one agrees with Brecht's position on authenticity does not especially matter. I have been trying to show in this chapter that reading Brecht's relation to China clarifies some of the issues around "so-and-so and China" criticism by revealing them as ideological. In so doing, "Brecht and China" points the way to a relationship to China alternative to the one worked out most explicitly around Pound, orientalism, and modernism. This alternative relationship is most explicitly visible around two themes: first, the *Verfremdung/Befremdung* vortex seen in the "Alienation Effects" essay, and second, the emphasis on reception rather than production discussed by Kao, and worked out more explicitly in the discussion of Brecht in performance. Both of these themes, which I will carry over into the next chapter, point to the manner in which China is a figure through which the relation between aesthetics and modernity expresses itself.

In late 1954 the Berliner Ensemble, under Brecht's direction, performed Brecht's *Mother Courage* at the first Festival International d'Art Dramatique in Paris. The play won first prize, and the visit brought Brecht "immediate recognition as a leading figure of the contemporary theater" (Weber, 178). Among those in attendance in Paris was French literary theorist Roland Barthes. Writing in *Le Monde* in 1971, Barthes would remember the performance as able to exhibit simultaneously a materialist awareness and an "ascetic sumptuousness," unfailingly stubborn in both its political and aesthetic commitments. Such a moment was, Barthes wrote, something like a "subtle revolution": "Longing for a political theater enlightened by Marxism and an art which rigorously governs its signs, how could we help being dazzled by the work of the Berliner Ensemble? . . . The product of these two values generated what we can regard as a phenomenon unknown in the West (perhaps precisely because Brecht had learned it from the East): *a theater without hysteria*" (*Rustle*, 157).

Three years later, Barthes, again writing in *Le Monde*, just back from three weeks in China, recalled seeing there in the shops, in the schools, and on the country roads "a people (who in twenty-five years have already constructed a great nation) move, work, drink tea or do gymnastics without theatrics, without commotion, without striking poses, in a word, without hysteria" ("Well, and China," 12). What to make of this moment, where the phrase "without hysteria," which Barthes seems to have learned from Brecht, and Brecht seemed to have learned from the East, returns as a description of what Barthes learned in China? Once again the meaning of "Brecht's China"—a phrase that at this point must be read with the understanding that neither "Brecht" nor "China" is a coherent sign—escapes the boundaries of both its author and its subject. Barthes gives us a certain "Brecht," a certain "China," linked not merely through the possessive's apostrophe, but by virtue of a similarity, a family resemblance: without hysteria. Such a moment performs, if one wishes to see it, a kind of pluralizing reading upon itself, opening up ever more clearly the difficult inseparability of China and "China," the ways in which the knowledge-object "China" twines itself through its authors, its histories, its receptions.

For Barthes, who sustained a brief but intense interest in China as part of his association with the Parisian journal *Tel quel,* the appeal of a certain (unhysterical?) refusal of China was clear. Others, including those who accompanied Barthes to Beijing, found themselves drawn to a China far more violently extravagant than anything found in Brecht. The next chapter tells the story of that difference.

Chapter Three   TEL QUEL

*I*n 1974, a traveler to China came back to Paris with the following description of the peasant village of Huxian:

> Forty kilometers from the former Chinese capital of Xi'an (the first capital of China after it was unified under the emperor Qin Shi Huangdi in the second century B.C., and the great capital of the Tang Dynasty [618–906]) is Huxian, the chief village of an agricultural region. The road we travel to get there is hot; the sun beats down on peasants in broad bamboo hats, on unsupervised children skipping about in quiet games, on a hearse drawn by some men while others, in two parallel lines alongside it, surround it with thin parallel poles carried across their shoulders. Everyone from the village is in the square where we are supposed to attend an exhibit of peasant painting in one of the nearby buildings. An enormous crowd is sitting in the sun: they wait for us wordlessly, perfectly still. Calm eyes, not even curious, but slightly amused or anxious: in any case, piercing, and certain of belonging to a community with which we will never have anything to do. They don't distinguish among us man or woman, blonde or brunette, this or that feature of face or body. As though they were discovering some weird and peculiar animals, harmless but insane. Unaggressive, but on the far side of the abyss of time and space. "A species—what they see in us is a different species," says one of our group. "You are the first foreigners to visit the village," says the interpreter, always sensitive to the least of our tropisms. I don't feel like a foreigner, the way I do in Baghdad or New York. I feel like an ape, a martian, an *other.* Three hours later, when the gates of the exhibit are opened to let our cars pass through, they are still there, sitting in the sun—amused or anxious?—calm, distant, piercing, silent, gently releasing us into our strangeness. (11–12)

This description takes place in two movements, in a vision that can only be called cinematic. First, the long shot of the dirt road, the hot day, the peasants, the children, the ritual of burial, the elaborate historical parenthesis: in these few images the countryside is imbued with all its rhetorical and cultural importance, its timelessness, its endless cycle of life (the children, the dead). Second, however, and more interestingly, the famil-

103

iar vision—familiar even in its unfamiliarity—acquires a shocking new-ness. The observing gaze finds itself not simply reversed but in some sense *refused.*

That refusal takes place in the author's intense awareness of being looked at, not with an anthropomorphic curiosity but rather a dehuman-izing silence: "As though they were discovering some weird and peculiar animals, harmless but insane." Face to face with these strangers, she and her friends are animals, another species; she feels like an ape, a Martian, an other. Even as she remarks that the Chinese "don't distinguish among us man or woman, blonde or brunette, this or that feature of face or body," the author herself does not or perhaps cannot distinguish among the members of the crowd. Her description of the eyes—calm, amused or anxious, piercing—returns in the paragraph's final sentence as a descrip-tion of the crowd itself: "they are still there, sitting in the sun—amused or anxious?—*calm,* distant, *piercing,* silent, gently releasing us into our strangeness." The look—frightening because of what it does *not* see—goes both ways.

A page after this description, the author adds that the Chinese at Hux-ian "did nothing but return the look I gave them without letting them see it, moulded as I am by universalist humanism, proletarian brotherhood, and (why not?) false colonial civility" (13). Few of the traditional metaphors of the anthropological or colonizing gaze work here. Instead, the scene hints at an otherness that goes beyond the merely different or strange, an otherness that blocks all communication or commerce, and does so without anger or malice, hope or desire, or pride in their absence. The author finds herself looked-at-but-not-seen, and in that experience recognizes her own gaze—hidden by "false colonial civility," to be sure—as similarly insensate to that which it falls upon. The result is no civilizing drive, no traditionally exotic curiosity; the strangeness or foreignness the author finds face-to-face with the Huxian peasants has nothing to do with the tourist's banal experience of cultural difference—Baghdad or New York, or even maybe Beijing. The Chinese peasants are not simply strange to her. Rather in facing them she becomes a stranger, perhaps even a stranger to herself.

The "she" in question is French feminist Julia Kristeva. The scene opens *About Chinese Women (Des Chinoises),* a book that is the most intense expression of the French avant-garde's interest in China in the

1970s. The scene is remarkable—in a manner typical of Kristeva—not only for its content but for its literary form and theoretical slant. It is not just what Kristeva describes about China, but how she describes it, and what she learns from it, that make *About Chinese Women* a rich, troubled text. In this opening scene and elsewhere, the text commits itself to a vision of China quite unlike any in Pound or Brecht: Chinese strangeness does not, for Kristeva, arise from some ancient culture, but rather comes out of a modern society that steps into the same ontological and political space as Europe and the West. She writes that China's "strangeness persists . . . through a highly developed civilization which enters without complexes into the modern world" (12). What has happened—and is exciting, even exhilarating, in Kristeva's description of the scene in Huxian—is an experience of a fundamental otherness that is *in the world* and therefore available for thought. In the introduction to *About Chinese Women,* Kristeva writes that her excitement about China has to do precisely with this strangeness that is nonetheless part of the world, since it seems to articulate for her the possibility of making something radically new happen in the West.

Kristeva has for a long time been interested in a notion of strangeness that might bring about liberating change. Her personal relation to that strangeness is complicated and extensive. Kristeva's arrival on the Parisian intellectual scene was heralded by Roland Barthes's 1970 review of her work, entitled "L'Etrangère" (The stranger/foreigner). The first sentence of her *Séméiotiké* (1969) reads: "To work on language, to labor in the *materiality* of that which society regards as a means of contact and understanding, isn't that at one stroke to declare oneself a stranger *(étranger)* to language" (7). In the introduction to *About Chinese Women,* Kristeva writes that women, in monotheistic capitalism, remain "always foreign *(étranger)* to the social order" (14). And in *Strangers to Ourselves* (1988), Kristeva imagines foreignness as an ethics for living: "Henceforth, we know that we are foreigners to ourselves, and it is with the help of that sole support that we can attempt to live with others" (170). All this is mediated in a particular way by China: in her autobiographical novel *The Samurais,* Kristeva writes of the character Olga, a Bulgarian intellectual who, like herself, moves to Paris from Eastern Europe: "For a long time France had been her China: a country of exile can liberate you" (196).

The introductory scene in *About Chinese Women,* with its lush and stylized descriptions, contains both echoes and premonitions of Kristeva's other work, pointing toward what seemed at the time to be a set of new possibilities in social relations, a new way of experiencing and understanding oneself as a stranger face-to-face with one's others—an experience Kristeva had elsewhere identified in Lautréamont and Mallarmé. Throughout Kristeva's career, she has been interested in the ways in which foreignness irrupts inside social orders, and in the radical possibilities in language and politics of such moments. Her presence in France, foreign and yet central to Parisian intellectual circles of the 1970s, might be taken as a living out of her theoretical project.

When it was published, *About Chinese Women* was taken in both France and the United States as a major document of theoretical feminism. Today, a quarter of a century later, the scene at Huxian—or rather Kristeva's description of it—has become the exemplar of a certain kind of bad relation to one's cultural other. This is due in part to an essay by Gayatri Chakravorty Spivak, "French Feminism in an International Frame," which finds in Kristeva's confrontation the expression of a typically self-centered Western interest in the face of the rest of the world. Spivak's major critique focuses on Kristeva's description of the scene in Huxian. Kristeva had concluded that section with the following question: "Who is speaking, then, before the stare of the peasants at Huxian? Whoever on this side is fed up with being a 'dead woman'" (15). This major theoretical question, Spivak remarks, has exclusively to do with the Western self, and nothing to do with China. Spivak goes on to say that Kristeva's concern with her own identity in the face of her cultural other typifies a certain kind of Western interest in the East: "In spite of their occasional interest in touching the other of the West . . . their repeated question is self-centered: if we are not what official history and philosophy say we are, who then are we (not), how are we (not)?" (137).

Considered fully, *About Chinese Women* attempts through an analysis of the conditions of Chinese women to discover and describe an economy of gender and power wholly other to the Western psyche, one in which an original matriarchy and a feminine Taoism continue to produce people who cannot fit into the Western category of "woman" or "man." In *Woman and Chinese Modernity,* Rey Chow argues that in putting forth this argument Kristeva says nothing "that cannot be said without 'China.' What she proposes is not so much learning a lesson from a different culture as a different method of reading from within the West. For, what is claimed to be 'unique' to China is simply understood as the 'negative' or 'repressed' side of Western discourse" (7). In other words, Kristeva's understanding of China simply presents it as the mirror image of the West, so that where the West has gender, China does not, and so on. Such a critique resembles Spivak's in its awareness that Kristeva's imagination of the cultural other is essentially a reversed imagination of her self.

Chow goes on to argue, however, that Kristeva's reversal is not gender-neutral. She does so first by looking at Kristeva's other work on the ontological category of "woman." For Kristeva, "woman" is precisely the name of everything that is "outside" the West—"woman" is *negative to the time of history*" and cannot "be" within the framework of Western metaphysics and history. Chow then remarks that in the same process whereby Kristeva dramatizes "women as totally 'outside,' 'negative,' 'unrepresentable,'" she makes China a place totally outside of or negative to the West. China thus becomes a "woman" to the West's "man," so that the binary oppositions China/West and woman/man come to mean the same thing. Even though Kristeva argues that in China women do not have gender, China as a general concept nonetheless occupies the space of "woman" in a larger world picture. Kristeva's claim that Chinese people have no gender in the Western sense "feminizes" China itself as the West's negative other.

Kristeva's interest in classical China and its history grounds and authorizes her general thesis about Chinese women. In general, in *About Chinese Women* the deep roots of China's ungendered system are revealed to be engendered by classical texts or ancient archaeological sites, which receive the most superficial of readings. Spivak remarks that Kristeva's account of Chinese history suspends itself between a "misty past" and a reportorial present in which "the 'classical' East is studied with primitivistic reverence, even as the 'contemporary' East is treated with realpolitikal contempt" ("French Feminism," 138). Chow, for her part, takes issue with Kristeva's attribution of timeless value to Chinese women, writing that "*About Chinese Women* repeats, in spite of itself, the historical tradition in which China has been thought of in terms of an 'eternal standstill' since the eighteenth century" (*Woman,* 9). In yet another critique, Lisa Lowe comments on Kristeva's inattention to history: "Throughout *Des Chinoises* a historical extravagance, which so easily establishes a correspondence between an ancient modality and a contemporary one, lacks an adequately complex appreciation of the heterogeneous and contradictory forces of history" (147).

These three critiques—from Spivak, Chow, and Lowe—together constituted the critical paradigm for *About Chinese Women* in the 1990s. In each case, Julia Kristeva performs a slightly different function. While for Spivak she is a representative of French feminism (and thus able to introduce Spivak's major question in the essay, which is whether French feminism can apply to conditions in non-Western societies), for Chow Kristeva is a kind of intellectual she describes as a "Maoist," one whose investment in an extremely positive version of some subaltern people or culture (not limited to China) produces a new kind of distortion in the West's visual field. For Lowe, on the other hand, *About Chinese Women* exemplifies a "postcolonial orientalism," one whose positive investments in China reveal the heterogeneous and complicated nature of orientalism itself.

Lowe's phrase "postcolonial orientalism" recalls the legacy of Said. Much work coming out of *Orientalism* has focused on the ways in which Western texts produced their own colonial experiences as part of an attempt to "manage" the colonial situation. These critiques of *About Chinese Women* do not do that. Rather, they look at the ways in which specifically anticolonialist texts experience and contain orientalism— even or perhaps especially when they are trying for a sympathetic, anti-Western reading of the East. In doing so, they raise a number of troubling questions, not the least of which is how the West might ethically talk about the East when even praise can be taken as fundamentally mistaken about its motivations. As I have tried to show throughout this book, the question of praise—the fantasy *in the name of* the other—is central to the Chinese dream.

How did *About Chinese Women* come to be an exemplary text for the orientalism-critique pursued by Spivak, Chow, and Lowe? To understand this one must consider the context of the book's production, and particularly its relation to the Parisian literary journal *Tel quel.* Founded around 1960 by a group of young intellectuals and writers, *Tel quel* became over the next twenty-one years a major force in the French literary and political scene. As Patrick Ffrench writes, *Tel quel* was "not just a review, but also a movement in literature and theory" (3). Its influence should not be measured in sales (the journal's regular issues sold about eight thousand copies) but by those whose major work appeared there: among theorists not only Kristeva, but Roland Barthes, Michel Foucault, Jacques Derrida, Gérard Genette, and translations of Mikhail Bakhtin and the Russian formalists; among novelists and poets Philippe Sollers, Marcelin Pleynet, and Denis Roche (who translated many works by Ezra Pound). *Tel quel* also brought several ignored French authors into contemporary critical awareness, among them Artaud, Bataille, Céline, and Sade. From the beginning, and against the politics and philosophy of Jean-Paul Sartre and others, *Tel quel* advocated an intensely literary, nonpolitical relationship to literature. While the journal was initially touched by the development of the *nouveau roman,* it turned instead toward a lusher, more self-consciously literary and subjective expression in both its poetry and its philosophy.

This is not to say that *Tel quel* had no politics. By the time it dissolved and became *L'Infini* in 1981, *Tel quel* had been involved in intense and often acerbic alliances with the French Communist Party, had made a rallying cry of Maoism and China, and turned, treacherously for some, toward the United States in the late 1970s. At the height of its influence in the early 1970s, *Tel quel* was an important site for the development of the poststructuralist theory that became central in the American academy in the 1980s.

Kristeva's role in all this was anomalous, to say the least. Her progress from *étrangère* in Paris to *Tel quel* insider was remarkably rapid, and proceeded in part thanks to Roland Barthes's "discovery" of her work and her marriage to editor-in-chief Sollers. She was, for most of the journal's existence, the only woman on its editorial committee; of committee members, she remains by far its best-known intellectual, with an international reputation built around her psychoanalytic readings of literary texts and her meditations on love, motherhood, and abjection. Particularly during the 1970s, Kristeva was, with Hélène Cixous and Luce Irigaray, a major force in the development of French feminism and its translation into the American academy.[1] And yet her relations with other French feminists have been strained—erupting in one particular instance around the publication of *About Chinese Women,* which editors of the woman's publishing house *des femmes* felt, Kristeva says in *The Samurais,* did not do enough to praise the women of China. The choice of *About Chinese Women* as a representative text for a certain theoretical relation to China makes it, in such a context, emblematic of a certain historical judgment on both French feminism and the movement around poststructuralist theory in Paris in the 1970s.

In 1974, as part of their engagement with Maoism, several Telquelians decided to arrange a trip to China. On the trip were Barthes, Kristeva, Marcelin Pleynet, Sollers, and François Wahl (the journal's editor at Editions du Seuil). The trip was organized in part by Maria-Antoinetta Macciocchi, an Italian Communist whose book *De la Chine* (On China) had sparked European interest in the Chinese Cultural Revolution. Jacques Lacan, who had originally been scheduled to go with the group, pulled out at the last moment. The group left Paris on April 11 and returned on May 3, having spent some three weeks traveling around China under the direction of Communist Party tour guides and interpreters. The return to Paris produced a flurry of texts: not only *About Chinese Women,* but also articles by Barthes and Wahl in the Paris newspaper *Le Monde,* and a *Tel quel* special issue called "In China." The texts by the members of the editorial committee (Sollers, Pleynet, and Kristeva) praised the Cultural Revolution as the future of Marxism, and named China the potential catalyst for world revolution; Barthes and Wahl were far more reserved.

In the mid-1970s, for reasons having to do both with changes in China and changes in the group's dynamic, *Tel quel* abandoned its Maoism, and late in the decade seemed to find in the United States another possible site of revolution—cultural, not political. These twists and turns in *Tel quel*'s political commitment seemed, after fifteen years of turbulence, finally to convince many readers that the journal's only political interest was an aggressive antagonism—and that moreover that antagonism had been dead wrong vis-à-vis China. Danielle Marx-Scouras:

> [A]s mercurial as *Tel quel* may have been—especially with respect to its political trajectory—the group's infidelities never discouraged journalists from *Le Monde,* Communist militants, and other politicians from incessantly criticizing *Tel quel*'s erratic journey from its so-called apolitical beginnings to its apparently overnight affiliation with the French Communist Party or its deviation from Maoism to the United States. (7)

The "shame" of *Tel quel*'s Maoism continues to influence the general understanding of the group's work, with the political defect of having believed in the Cultural Revolution effectively devolving onto *Tel quel*'s aesthetic theories as well: "In the eyes of most observers, the trip to China works, in the history of *Tel quel,* as the 'damned spot' which nothing can ever erase" (Forest, 483).

Not surprisingly, three recent histories of *Tel quel*—Patrick Ffrench's *The Time of Theory,* Philippe Forest's *Histoire de "Tel quel," 1960–1982,* and Danielle Marx-Scouras's *The Cultural Politics of "Tel quel"*—all take pains to reject this interpretation of the group's project, and indicate a trend toward a reevaluation of *Tel quel*'s presence in the divided heart of theory.[2] The books by Forest and Marx-Scouras in particular reject a criticism that reduces *Tel quel* to its political component. Forest does so out of a sense that the group's mistakes came out of a salutary desire: "The Telquelians believed that China would be for our time what Greece was for the Renaissance: an ignored continent would rise up and completely overturn Western knowledge and thought. How could one reproach anyone for having dreamed that dream?" (484–85). Marx-Scouras, on the other hand, forcefully insists on the value and constancy of *Tel quel*'s aesthetic project, which for her trumps any of the group's variegated political interests: "It is my contention that there has been not only a coherent cultural program operant in *Tel quel* for more than twenty years, but that such a program was already in place in the review's inaugural issue" (8). This position mirrors the one taken by Ffrench, who writes that his book "seeks to rescue *Tel quel* from the largely pejorative images of it in the English-speaking academic world by analysing the history of the review from the perspective of what is identified as a coherent and consistent theory of literature" (2).

I do not especially conceive of this chapter as a "rescue" of *Tel quel,* nor am I interested in exposing the coherence of the group's aesthetic project. I am, however, trying to be as attentive to the Telquelians' aesthetic values as I am to the failures of their political perception. I have tried not to separate aesthetics from politics. Rather, the chapter aims to explore how the aesthetic vision and the political one were produced simultaneously, sometimes complementing, sometimes at odds with one another. It is, after all, precisely this conjunction of aesthetics and politics that is at the center of *Tel quel.* And, as in Kristeva's description of the scene at Huxian, the question of whether the aesthetic vision makes the political one, or vice versa, depends ultimately not on what one looks at, but what one *sees.*

For most American readers, Kristeva's association with *Tel quel* remains shadowy; her individual importance in the American academy has disrupted her immediate link to the context from which she came. Spivak's "French Feminism" essay, for instance, does not mention *Tel quel* at all; Chow's essay refers to "Maoists" in general but does not deal with *Tel quel* in particular. Most strikingly, Lowe's discussion of Barthes and Kristeva in her chapter "Postcolonial Orientalisms" proceeds by separating their work from that of *Tel quel,* so that she is able to write that "the journal *Tel quel* provides another figuration of China—compatible with, but inflected differently from, Kristeva's and Barthes's figurations" (174), as though the impressions Kristeva and Barthes had of China did not occur under the rubric of *Tel quel.* Lowe's position is borne out in the organization of her chapter, which offers separate sections on Barthes, Kristeva, and *Tel quel* as though they were essentially three different—though linked—objects, a claim that might work for Barthes but does not for Kristeva.

One of the goals of the chapter that follows is to put Kristeva back into the context of *Tel quel.* The chapter proceeds on the basis of the following idea: that the moment in which one gains a new critical understanding indicates not only a new ability to see but a new limitation on seeing. That is, the antiorientalist critique of Kristeva depends not only on a theoretical *gain*—the ability to see and explain reverse ethnocentrism—but also a *loss*—the ability to see China as Kristeva saw it the day she followed the road from Xi'an to Huxian. Whatever she felt, we can no longer feel it; when she (and Barthes, and Sollers, and the others) looked at China, she saw something we ourselves can no longer see, even as we recognize and name the *way* that she saw.

Tel quel *Invents Its China: Paris, 1965–74*

Tel quel's interest in China did not appear overnight. Rather, over the years leading up to the group's decision to go to Beijing, *Tel quel* developed the idea of China that would sustain and justify its Chinese interest. This China-idea stemmed from a variety of factors whose importance waxed and waned over time. The major catalytic event was, to be sure, the Chinese Cultural Revolution (1966–76).[3] But *Tel quel*'s reception of the Cultural Revolution was itself conditioned by a number of contexts, both practical and theoretical. It was these contexts that set the stage for *Tel quel*'s eventual embrace of Maoism and the 1974 trip to China.

SOLLERS AND CHINESE WRITING

In interviews and articles published well after the return from China, Sollers claims that his interest in China began well before word of the Cultural Revolution reached the West. His book *Drame* (*Drama,* 1965), he said, was his first Chinese novel, organized by the principles of Taoism. By the time of the publication of his novel *Nombres* (*Numbers,* 1968) Sollers was willing to acknowledge an interest in Chinese both formally and visually; in a strategy reminiscent of Pound's *Cantos,* the novel's pages are interspersed with Chinese characters and quotations in French from Chinese texts. As a narrative, *Nombres* has no identifiable characters or plot; its general project, organized into four sections of one hundred parts each, involves thinking through the narrative relationship between the present and the imperfect tenses. Its back cover, however, announces its intention to mark the "arrival of the dialogue between Occident and Orient" and to raise the "question of the passage from an alienated writing to a tracing one, across war, sex, and the mute and hidden work of transformations."[4] The text carries out this project through an ideology of Chinese writing that strongly resembles Fenollosa's—associating Chinese characters with the material expression of language and alphabetic writing with debased and distracted signification. Like Pound's *Cantos, Nombres* also contains a variety of other visual symbols, usually charts or graphs. These extend the major theoretical interest in Chinese writing to graphs of all types, which also foreground a nonauditory, more material experience of reading.

Unlike in Fenollosa, however, in *Nombres* Chinese works not to reground Western signification but rather to destroy it. Sollers writes: "In the West, the crowd; in the East, the people. In the West, the image; in the East, the stage. In the West, signs without roots, accumulating signs without a hold on the profound axis of the outside. . . . In the East, the invisible force of mutations, complete and without remainders, square writing that disrupts the most assured ground, the inscription common to mud and blood" (36).[5] While the sense of the West as fake and superficial resembles Fenollosa's, here the East's "square writing" *disrupts* the ground rather than strengthens it. Sollers's interest in a "dialogue between Occident and Orient," stated on the book's back cover, produces not a sense of a return to original values but instead the excitement and chaos of new ones.

Like characters into the *Cantos,* however, the Chinese characters in *Nombres* usually reflect or reprise the alphabetic text that immediately precedes them. Whether they "tend to block the reading process and brutally introduce the limits of Western ideology" (Ffrench, 146), depends on how one understands their meaning and value relative to the rest of the text. At some level the characters in *Nombres* simply signify that they are Chinese characters rather than denote any particular meaning. For readers of Chinese, on the other hand, they indicate Sollers's interest in rethinking the West. In one instance, Sollers puts the Chinese character for "seeing" into the middle of a reflection on the phenomenological experience of a murder: "and leaving with her into violence escaped from laws, into the convulsion and the entanglement of the murder climbing back up her legs, her fingers, receiving it also 'through perception'—seeing, hearing— 見 —thus passing through the entire provocative breadth of the play of hands" (93–94).[6] As Pound knew, the character *jian* 見, "to see," arises from a combination of the character for *eye* (目) and a pair of running legs (儿).[7] When Sollers writes "through perception," he is explaining, in some sense, the idea that seeing as an activity could be understood as the movement (running legs) of the eye rather than simply a passive experience.[8] This em-bodied experience of vision, like the entanglement of the murder, climbs up the legs and into the eye of the perceiver: the experience of "seeing" (*jian* 見), coming from an eye and running legs, finds itself doubled in Sollers's description of the woman's experience. Following Ffrench, one might remark that this brutally introduces the limits of Western ideology by indicating a place where "seeing" can mean something radically different than what it has traditionally meant in the West. The name of those limits, however, is China: the new experience of seeing takes place through the pictographical history of Chinese writing. Sollers's invocation of a more *physical* understanding of vision suggests that the overdetermined Western opposition between body and vision can be exploded if one reads Chinese.

This important relation to Chinese writing—so like Pound's culturally, but with such a different political valence—remained strong throughout Sollers's move toward Maoism at the end of the 1960s. His translations of ten poems by Mao in 1970, for instance, while signaling *Tel quel*'s political interest in China, also adopted a theory of translation similar to Pound's. Philippe Forest remarks of Sollers's method that it "consists of creating a new French that can attempt to render the ideogrammatic function of Chinese, aiming toward the same imaged condensation, the same fragmentation" (379). This is exactly what was said in the earliest articles on Pound's *Cathay*, and by Antony Tatlow of Brecht's translations; indeed it may be the most insistent principle of modern translation from Chinese.

The remarkable similarities among responses to translations of Chinese poems by Pound, Brecht, and Sollers suggest that one of the crucial components of the Chinese dream is in fact a notion of translation that not only deforms that language it translates from (the much-lamented topic of many translation studies), but the language it translates *into* as well.[9] The relation between such a theory of translation and the modernist avant-garde has been explored by Steven Yao, and I will not go into it further here, except to note that the particular articulation of this in poetry might be extended, especially for Pound and *Tel quel*, to a general notion that China could be used in some way to reform or deform the West—politically and poetically.

The advent of China's Cultural Revolution played a vital role in the transformation of Sollers's Poundian China into *Tel quel*'s vastly more energetic and political version. It was, in those years, as though China were stepping through a mirror and into the real world. It was precisely this effect, in which China became not only the name of an exotic and remote otherness but also a way of understanding the contemporary world, that produced so much of *Tel quel*'s energy around China. After 1966, the distinction between the cultural dream-object "China" and actual China became less desirable to maintain, since doing so would be to miss out on "the message" China was putting out for the first time (Sollers, "Pourquoi," 14). The sudden breath of revolution *now* from a place that had previously functioned largely as an exotic utopia in the past pushed *Tel quel* toward an increasing sense that China was the literal place of world revolution, and toward a greater sense of the material and intellectual value of China. Sollers in 1968 and 1969 began debates among the *Tel quel* editorial committee designed to move the journal toward a Maoist politics—politics that would only surface fully in 1971, after the final break with the French Communist Party (PCF). As Sollers stated in 1966, the historical possibilities of that year could be summed up by one word: *China* (Forest, 275).

THE POLITICAL TURN

In his history of *Tel quel* Forest remarks that events in Asia in the late 1960s occupied a good deal of the French imagination: "On one side, the Vietnam War is perceived as an ignominy, a savage butchery; on the other, the Chinese situation seems to announce the possibility of a revolution inside the revolution itself. French intellectual history unfolds itself from afar on this real and mythical background" (273).[10] Forest's perspective captures well the events that made "China" for *Tel quel* in the years before their trip. The combination of real and mythical space was to produce an enormous outpouring of intellectual work, all predicated on a China whose name indicated a growing complexity of ideas, people, events, and histories. "China" at this moment included both aspects of China at once, a mythical and utopian version laid on top of the actual one, in a kind of dual topography of attention and desire. It was as though "mythical Asia, invented by Pound and Artaud, wrote itself once again into the history of peoples" (Forest, 272).[11]

It was in such a context that *Tel quel* turned openly to Maoism in 1971. The move came about partly because of the journal's deteriorating relationship with the French Communist Party. Between 1966 and 1971, as *Tel quel* began publishing texts on China, the journal and the PCF stood together in the field of French politics, a stance that remained largely true even during the student revolts of 1968 (which the PCF did not support). The final break between *Tel quel* and the PCF, in 1971, occurred around the PCF's refusal to sell Maria-Antoinetta Macciocchi's book *De la Chine* (On China) at the annual fair of *L'Humanité*, a Communist Party journal. By that time, however, the political and aesthetic grounds for such a break had already been established.[12]

Tel quel's break with the PCF and its adoption of Maoism was officially announced in "Positions of the June 71 Movement," published in its fall 1971 issue. The issue opens with a quotation from Mao: "Between the new culture and reactionary cultures, a fight to the death is unleashed." The summer of 1971 had seen the *Tel quel* offices at Rue Jacob covered in *dazibao*—large posters expressing revolutionary slogans, typical of the Chinese Cultural Revolution. The political essays in the fall 1971 issue of

Tel quel (the rest of it was a tribute to Roland Barthes) maintain a revolutionary and combative tone: "We understand how, under such conditions, the Chinese cultural proletarian revolution, the greatest event of our time, undercuts the revisionist calculus, which will therefore do all it can to falsify the event. Well, we are going to do everything to clarify it, analyze it, and support it" ("Declaration," 134).[13]

The proclamation goes on to list various political mistakes made by *Tel quel* in its relationship with the PCF, the Soviet invasion of Czechoslovakia, and other issues, usually attributing them to a mistaken sense that "two become one," that is, that unity within the struggle against imperialism and the bourgeoisie justified compromise between a Maoist position and a PCF one. The "Positions" essay leads to a chronology of *Tel quel,* in which its errors and campaigns are clearly noted and explained in light of their new theoretical turn (for instance: "1968: . . . Incomprehension of the [correct] Chinese positions of the time. . . . Cover-up of contradictions. Those who continue to 'listen' to the Chinese cultural proletarian revolution constrain themselves in silence" ["Chronologie," 143]).

As a whole, the declaration and positions in this issue concern themselves far more with European politics than Chinese ones. Besides the various positive references to Mao Zedong's thought and the Cultural Revolution, no mention is made of conditions in China. But the ninth in a list of proposals made by the journal's editorial committee encouraged intellectuals both inside and outside *Tel quel* to "undertake the serious work of ideological and political reeducation," and suggested that *Tel quel* would eventually think through the political, economic, national and international implications of its political struggle (141).

The "work of ideological and political reeducation" became clearer in *Tel quel*'s spring 1972 double issue. Titled "Chinese Thought," it presented Parisian readers with a thorough and didactic examination of various aspects of Chinese culture. In contrast to the revolutionary tone of the "Positions" essay in the previous issue, the preface of "Chinese Thought" says the issue offers its readers the background necessary to understand the global political situation for which China has assumed a growing importance. More specifically, it asks readers to consider "the particularities of the language, literature, art, and philosophy of China, in order to better follow and understand the political, social, and cultural transformations that China today is producing and manifesting" (7). The claim, eminently reasonable in tone, is the emblematic expression of *Tel quel*'s pre-1974 interest in China. By focusing on specific aspects of Chinese culture *Tel quel* aimed to teach its readers the political meaning of contemporary China. The new China, in keeping with *Tel quel*'s theoretical perspective, was revolutionary both in culture and politics.

The 1972 issue on China reflected the two major lines of *Tel quel*'s inquiry: one more concerned with developing a theory of Maoism (and thus with contemporary China), and the other more interested in the radical possibilities of Chinese language and literature (and classical China). The force of each line depended on its relation to the other. Sollers would in 1981 refer to these as *Tel quel*'s belief in a simultaneous "revolution in action" and "revolution in language" ("Pourquoi," 13; trans. in Marx-Scouras, 174). In keeping with that idea, *Tel quel*'s Maoist politics maintained a vital link to textuality. In fact Philippe Forest refers to *Tel quel*'s Maoism as primarily textual: "Sollers' Maoism offers itself first as a textual Maoism which, from the outside, aims to make the poetics of an indecipherable language come alive and resonate in the henceforth deaf and overturned field of our own language" (379). Sollers's translations of Mao poems, for instance, fed into an existing squabble between René Etiemble and Michelle Loi, with Sollers's crowd holding that his translations were Maoist in method as well as content, thus putting all bourgeois translations in the shade.[14] Though Pound's translations had been connected to a "Chinese" method, the politics of his Chinese aesthetics—including his use of Confucian texts to bolster his support of Italian fascism—never broached contemporary China. This was *Tel quel*'s true innovation.

The role of articulating the Maoist and linguistic positions fell to Sollers and Kristeva respectively (though never exclusively). Sollers's major contribution here was his essay "On Contradiction," published in *Tel quel* 45 (1971), but he also wrote "The Philosophical Struggle in Revolutionary China" for the special issue on Chinese thought (1972). "Philosophical Struggle" focuses on ideological conflicts within China between those who wanted to follow the Soviet Union and those who wished to chart a separate course for Chinese Communism. The general tone is well captured by the essay's concluding sentences: "[The Chinese Cultural Revolution] is the battle of a long-repressed *thought,* of a mass revolutionary practice now consolidated in the light of day" (132). Sollers's emphasis on the movement of *thought* into the light of day recaptures *Tel quel*'s twofold vision of China as both intangible and real; like China itself, thought has left the dark corners of mind and stepped into the real, ready to revolt.

That long-repressed thought Sollers revealed to have been latent even in Chinese writing itself. In "On Contradiction" Sollers stressed the degree to which the dialectic is native to Chinese philosophy: "While in Greek philosophy [the idea of contradiction] does not appear explicitly until a century after philosophy's beginnings . . . in China it is born with philosophy itself" (*Sur*, 133). The major case in point was the word *contradiction* itself (*maodun* 矛 盾), which combines the characters for "spear" (矛 *mao*) and "shield" (盾 *dun*). This allowed Sollers to write that Chinese contains an inherent understanding of the dialectical principle, "Two comprise one that divides itself in two" (*Sur*, 132).[15] By the publication of *Tel quel*'s 1972 special issue "Chinese Thought," the journal's unsigned preface would be able to insist on the material nature of all Chinese thinking: "Chinese thought? Certainly not in the sense in which 'thought' exits for philosophy: sinology demonstrates that 'thought' in China is an indissoluble alliance of the 'sensory' and the 'intelligible,' of language and reality, of the subject and society" (6).[16] Sollers's praise for China depends on a critique of the West, whose thought (as the Western discipline of philosophy conceives it) has no native relation to reality.

Sollers's political interest in Maoism and his frequent turns toward language and philosophy form a counterpoint to Kristeva's work in *Tel quel*, which focuses largely on language and only occasionally turns to politics. In two book reviews in the special issue on "Chinese Thought," Kristeva explores the relation between China, its language, its poetry, and the West, insisting on the primacy of culture for revolution. She opens her essay on Michelle Loi's book on Chinese poets inspired by the West with the following rhetorical questions: "Isn't all sociopolitical turmoil in China unmistakably cultural? Doesn't the Chinese conception of revolution pass without detours through literature?" (66). For Kristeva the answer to both questions is "yes."

In her second review, Kristeva opens up the question of Western influences on Chinese poetry. She concludes:

> One thus gets the impression that occidentalism was mainly a current of
> democratization and antifeudalism at literature's ideological level, but that in
> what we call "form," it was never able to affect the secular particularities of
> Chinese poetry, which cross the codes of feudal regimes and correspond (1)
> to the specificity of the Chinese language; and (2) to the function of "litera-
> ture" in Chinese culture. Especially since these specificities indicate the uni-
> versal unconscious of symbolic function that Western literature itself is
> researching (with Pound for example), moving toward China even as China
> was looking West. (69–70)

Again here, the specific aspects of Chinese language and literature are
noted only to highlight their universal function, which contrasts favor-
ably with what the West has to offer. China's contribution to the West,
unlike the West's to China, concerns the "*universal* unconscious of symbolic function" rather than practical (and local) politics. While the West
offered a specific movement toward "antifeudalism," Chinese poetry
could all along "cross the codes of feudal regimes" and transcend the
local in favor of the universal questions of symbolic logic. Such an argument reflects *Tel quel*'s long-standing privileging of form over content;
here the Western contribution in ideology is clearly subordinated to the
literary form as such, which Kristeva insists is uniquely Chinese, both lin-
guistically and culturally. Like most Pound critics, Kristeva believes in a
correspondence between the aesthetic concerns of modernism and those
of Chinese poetry. Unlike them, however, this correspondence does not
produce for her an alarmed insistence on the dependence or indepen-
dence of one vis-à-vis the other. Because of the cultural specificities of its
language and culture, Chinese poetry for Kristeva appears to have
grasped well in advance of the West the fundamental problems of symbolic discourse.

Kristeva is concerned to show how much in Chinese literature anticipates the crucial problems in Western modernism, in many places echoing the theses of her then-unpublished *Revolution in Poetic Language*
(1974). In the first review, Kristeva offers the reader a reason to read Chinese poetry, which opens another horizon, "foreign to our literary norms,
but which seems more and more subjacent to our culture, and rejoins its
repressed, which pierces into the linguistic, ideological, and subjective
turbulences produced by modern texts" (59). More specifically, Chinese
poetry reflects a specifically modern experience of language and poetry,
exemplified in the West by Mallarmé and Joyce. Kristeva remarks that

despite any similarities among Chinese poets and modernist ones, differences in ideology and language mean their innovations have little in common besides "the objectification of the subject in a 'dream logic,' which probably translates the laws of the sublimation of negativity (of the death drive)" (59). What Chinese and modernist poetry share is their reflection of the universal condition of the Freudian unconscious. China's ability to seem "more and more subjacent to our culture" thus takes on a major importance: not only does Chinese literature articulate this unconscious, but it does so in such a way as to provide a didactic model for Western literature, which only through recent innovations in modernism has begun to do what Chinese literature has been doing for ages.

In 1971, a year before *Tel quel*'s special issue on Chinese thought, Hugh Kenner had wondered in *The Pound Era* if "the east, with centuries-long deliberation, were writing the macro-history of Western thought" (231). The idea—both there and in its Telquelian articulation—constitutes one of the most extravagant limits of the Chinese dream: the moment when (the) Chinese turns out to have been inside the West all along, and the dream-logic of Chinese thought appears for a moment to have produced the "Chinese dream" itself in some sort of astonishing and absolute *return*.

Both Sollers and Kristeva use the word *repressed* to discuss China: Sollers writes that the Cultural Revolution is "the battle of a long-repressed *thought*, of a mass revolutionary practice now consolidated in the light of day"; Kristeva claims that Chinese poetry "rejoins its repressed, which pierces into the linguistic, ideological, and subjective turbulences produced by modern texts." In Freudian psychology, the "repressed" is that which the conscious mind cannot bear to think; it lurks in the unconscious, manifesting itself in various deflected forms: puns, jokes, slips of the tongue, dreams. Used by Sollers and Kristeva with reference to China, "repressed" enfolds itself in a series of expanding metaphors, each, as Kristeva says, "more and more subjacent to our culture." In its most limited form, Kristeva understands Chinese poetry to express its own repressed. At another, broader level, Chinese poetry acts like modern poetry—and expresses aspects of the West's repressed. At a third, more global level—visible in the quotation from Sollers—Chinese Communist thought (and through it, most broadly, China itself) seems to be the resurgent repressed of global capitalism and imperialism.

Writing about the Maoist interest in China in the 1970s, Rey Chow remarks that "the mainland Chinese were, in spite of their 'backwardness,' a puritanical alternative to the West in human form—a dream come true" (*Writing*, 12).[17] Chow's calling China a "dream come true" seems a particularly apt way of talking about the properties of "China" for *Tel quel* in these years. It is precisely the way in which the Chinese dream becomes true—enters into the West's geopolitical field of vision—that grants it its political and emotional force. But it is the fact that China remained, in some sense, like a *dream*—a representation of the West's repressed ideologies and poetics—that grounded the Telquelian interest. What is at work here is something like *Tel quel*'s own "dream logic," in which China becomes the living, vivid manifestation of the West's unconscious. By freely, irrepressibly expressing that which the West is unable to know about itself—what Kristeva describes as "laws of the sublimation of negativity (of the death drive)"—China offered the Telquelians the uncanny feeling that the turn eastward involved not only seeing the other side of the world, but the other side of themselves.

GEOGRAPHY OF A DREAM

How do dreams come true? In *Drame* (1965) Sollers had mocked those who imagined they could find themselves by looking east: "The East? I'm asking you how to go towards the East? Why these vague, incomplete gestures? The east? E, A, S, T. How to go slowly towards the East? To the right of the image, more or less. . . . Couldn't we change places for a second? I'd like to see where I am, according to you" (32).[18] Sollers's aggressive questioning of the reader puns on the French words for "is" and "East" (both *est*), mocking the desire to move toward the East as a confused search for being itself. At the same time, Sollers seems to take the spatial metaphor seriously, imagining that the exchange of places might shed light on the self—though again here the sentence can be read two ways: the narrator might want to see *where* he is, or where he *is*—so that being and being in place dissolve into one another.

By 1971, however, Sollers would express astonishment at the idea that anyone could be missing out on China's potential effects on the world:

> It is stupefying to see the degree to which China has simply not existed for the great majority of Western intellectuals at the very moment when she was stepping over the threshold of history: except for Ezra Pound, who saw the

phenomenon "backward" and from a fascist perspective, and, of course, Brecht, who never ceased lucidly to approach this new reality. . . , one cannot find the slightest presentiment or reflection of the event among those who, nonetheless, shouldered the responsibility of an ideological avant-garde. (*Sur,* 126)

Sollers's presumption that China is ideal material for an ideological avant-garde suggests that whatever his notion of China was, it remained tied up in some sense of the radical possibilities of the East. In fact the demand that China's worth be recognized, though prompted in part by China's growing political and economic power, continues to depend on an "invented" or imaginary China, as the references to Pound and Brecht suggest. The major characteristic of China as *Tel quel* understood it had precisely to do with this movement between an exotic and ancient culture, disconnected from the political and economic geography of the modern world, and a powerful, exciting *actual* place able to participate and shape a geopolitical vision. During the years leading up to, and including, the trip to China, it is this China—the disjointed and yet intensely real object produced by these two visions—that drives *Tel quel*'s theorizing and its cultural politics, figured in the chimera of a truly *cultural* revolution.

The development of a China produced through this dual vision depended, I believe, on a general theoretical shift that occurred in Paris in those years. That is, the concept of *Tel quel*'s China would not have been possible without an underlying understanding of how such a vision could make sense. Presumably every understanding of China depends on such a vision. For Pound critics, for instance, one of the crucial questions turns on the nature of the China Pound perceived, whether whatever transformation he saw coming to him via Confucius and Li Po had anything to do with "real" China or was simply his own invention. For *Tel quel,* the question had a substantially different weight. There was, in the Paris of the late 1960s and early 1970s, an expression of what one might call a new theoretical geography, which in itself constituted another important context for the journal's relation to China. This theoretical geography stemmed from a new understanding of the relation between writing and the world: at some point a certain group of people began to write about the real world as though it were a text. In doing so, they undid the major premise of the question that haunts criticism of Pound's *Cathay*—Chi-

nese or English product?—by insisting on the inseparability of a culturally imagined version of "China" from a real one. By consciously challenging the separation between a real (political, economic) East and an
imaginary (literary, cultural, dreamed) one, these authors were able to
suggest that the imaginary China was, just like the real one, "in the true."

That last phrase belongs to French philosopher Michel Foucault, one
of the major architects of an understanding of social reality as "discourse," that is, an intertwined set of textualities that help create and
structure our daily experience of reality. Foucault published some material in *Tel quel* in the mid-1960s, but his association with the group ended
before *Tel quel*'s Maoist period. Nonetheless, Foucault's work was a vital
part of the intellectual milieu in Paris in those years, and so his ideas were
part of the air they breathed. Foucault's *Les mots et les choses* (1966; translated as *The Order of Things*) opens with a reflection on a Chinese ency-
clopedia whose distorted classification system structures a story by Jorge
Luis Borges:

> [T]he mythical homeland Borges assigns to that distortion of classification
> . . . is a precise region whose name alone constitutes for the West a vast
> reservoir of utopias. In our dreamworld, is not China precisely this privi-
> leged *site* of *space*? . . . There would appear to be, then, at the other extrem-
> ity of the earth we inhabit, a culture entirely devoted to the ordering of
> space, but one that does not distribute the multiplicity of existing things into
> any of the categories that make it possible for us to name, speak, and think.
> (xix)[19]

Throughout this paragraph Foucault moves subtly between the West's
simultaneously topographical and utopian sense of China. It is at the
same time a "precise region" and a "reservoir of utopias," a real place and
a nonplace (utopia). It is a *"site* of *space"* in a "dreamworld," a tangible
space in an intangible place. Foucault's most "realistic" formulation for
China—"at the other extremity of the earth we inhabit"—contains an
impossible metaphor, since the earth has no extremities along its East-
West axis. As China moves from a "dreamworld" to the earth's "other
extremity," its roles as utopia and literal topos fall into one; "China"
becomes the name of a place that exists both in the imagination and in the
world at the same time, like a dream from which one cannot be sure one
has woken up, or the reverse.[20]

The tense of "would appear to be" is crucial here. Foucault places the dreamworld at the earth's other extremity only by conjecture; in doing so he acknowledges that the projections of the dreamworld may not resemble reality. This "mythical homeland"—China—takes on, therefore, a largely literary function. It does so, crucially, without shame, without embarrassment; Foucault is simply stating the facts about the West's conception and ideology of China, not issuing a judgment on the dreamworld's relation to what things are really like. It is not, then, a question of distinguishing carefully between the dreamed and real versions of China (and then favoring one or the other). Rather Foucault acknowledges the real force of dreamed China, and the degree to which that China constructs the appearance ("there would *appear* to be") of Western reality. His "China" is, furthermore, multiple. Its "name alone constitutes for the West a vast reservoir of utopias." That is, China—the *name alone*—works not simply as a single vision of otherness, but as something like a Borgesian library, full of books with the same name but different texts.[21]

One of the more extensive and self-conscious elaborations of a theoretical geography like Foucault's comes from Roland Barthes's *L'Empire des signes* (*Empire of Signs,* trans. Richard Howard). Its approach to Japan is shaped by two major resistances: to an antiorientalist reading, and to a political one. The first few pages of *Empire* devote themselves to these refusals, and are layered with a typically theoretical self-awareness. Attempting to deflect an antiorientalist criticism *avant la lettre,* Barthes writes, "I am not lovingly gazing toward an Oriental essence—to me the Orient is a matter of indifference" (3). Indeed, the Orient's only relevance is that it allows the West to imagine itself, other-wise; taken, in sum, as a reservoir of features or ideas, the Orient can provide the West with the "possibility of a difference, of a mutation, of a revolution in the propriety of symbolic systems" (2–3). The very first paragraph of the book disabuses the reader of any notion that its subject is real Japan:

> If I want to imagine a fictive nation, I can give it an invented name, treat it declaratively as a novelistic object. . . . I can also—though in no way claiming to represent or to analyze reality itself (these being the major gestures of Western discourse)—isolate somewhere in the world *(faraway)* a certain number of features (a term employed in linguistics), and out of these features deliberately form a system. It is this system which I shall call: Japan. (3)

The crucial difference here is between the "fictive nation" that Barthes says he could write about and the "system" that he will call "Japan." "Fictive" is half of the real/imaginary opposition that structured the discussion of authenticity and Pound's China; the system Barthes will write about exists somewhere between those two fields, neither wholly fictive nor wholly real. Likewise, while Barthes will not claim to "represent or to analyze reality" itself, he takes his field of writing to be "somewhere in the world." It is this space, the in between of "real" and "fictive" Japan, that comes closest to *Tel quel*'s own conception of China.[22]

And yet Barthes's Japan is infinitely more literary than *Tel quel*'s China. While *Tel quel* made its China by combining a traditionally orientalist vision with a radical Maoist one, Barthes's Japan works more like a refusal of both positions. His Japan is structured like a language; it is a linguistic "system" built out of "features," not a country with particular customs or habits. What is at stake for Barthes is not so much Japan but a way of knowing it. While the production of information appropriate to the study of Japan is, Barthes recognizes, the legitimate task of certain members of Western culture, he himself will instead become the guardian of the Oriental myth. He writes: "Today there are doubtless a thousand things to learn about the Orient: an enormous labor of *knowledge* is and will be necessary. . . ; but it is also necessary that, leaving aside vast regions of darkness . . . a slender thread of light search out not other symbols but the very fissure of the symbolic" (4). Barthes's sense of the two obligations of Western observers stems from the major break in Western knowledge in the 1960s and 1970s, namely the difference between knowledge scientifically produced for the state and the antiscientific resistance to the discourse of "knowledge" as such, which takes the form of a critique of language's ability to represent reality. The image, however, is troubling, perhaps because Barthes's vision of a ray of piercing light had already been imagined, by Joseph Conrad, as an especially fraught metaphor for imperialism's drive toward the heart of darkness.

In any case, Barthes's use of a system called "Japan" to reveal that which the West might otherwise be unable to imagine is typical of the mood about the Orient among Parisian theorists of this time. What is worth pointing out once again is the way that the construction of a textual Orient—"Japan" as opposed to Japan—allows authors to create a kind of third space that attempts to shed the orientalism of a knowledge-based reading. Lisa Lowe writes, "The imagined Orient—as a critique of the Occident—becomes an emblem of his 'poetics of escape,' a desire to transcend semiology and the ideology of signifier and signified, to invent a place that exceeds binary structure itself" (154). Barthes had no doubt that scientific knowledge about the East would be produced; the necessities of global power and economics would dictate it. But the necessities of a conception of otherness that transcended signification—never popular as a government project—seemed to have no curator. Barthes's description in *Empire* of the Oriental myth depended less on its value as Oriental than on its value as myth.

While Barthes and Foucault differ in the particularities of their theoretical geographies, what they share is a way of writing about the world as a text—or perhaps better, a desire to talk about the world in textual terms. In approaching the world this way, both Foucault and Barthes independently reject the major principle behind much "so-and-so and China" criticism, namely that the crucial issue is whether a representation of China (or Japan, or anything) is accurate. Scientific accuracy, for both Barthes and Foucault, is only one perspective on "the true"; other, perhaps better, perhaps more useful perspectives are also available, and were, as Foucault argued, already part of the West's conception of China. The theoretical development in Barthes and Foucault of a certain way of talking about the East worked for *Tel quel* as a kind of unspoken justification for the group's China; it formed the epistemological ground upon which a new ontology of China—textual and real—made its stand.

As Rey Chow has noted, *Tel quel's* interest in China's Cultural Revolution is typical of a certain moment in Western intellectual history.

> The Orientalist has a special sibling whom I will, in order to highlight her significance as a kind of representational agency, call the Maoist. . . . Typically, the Maoist is a cultural critic who lives in a capitalist society but who is fed up with capitalism—a cultural critic, in other words, who wants a social order opposed to the one that is supporting her own undertaking. . . . What she wants is always located in the other, resulting in an identification with a valorization of that which she is not/does not have. (*Writing*, 10)

This seems a pretty fair description of *Tel quel's* motivations, especially during the group's (literally) Maoist period. At the same time, it does not capture the complexity of *Tel quel's* "China" as a theoretical object. The choice of "China" for *Tel quel* was not simply the choice of a "social order opposed to the one that is supporting [*Tel quel's*] undertaking"; if that were the case, any number of social orders would have done.

What mattered most to the members of *Tel quel* as they began to write and think about China was their sense, articulated in both political and literary terms, that China itself was speaking the West, and that the West had not been listening. It is at this level that *Tel quel* differs most from Pound or Brecht. In their cases, there was a general sense of the specificity of individual cultures and the difference between China and Europe that made the passage of ideas *as such* across those boundaries a difficult or even irrelevant proposition.[23] *Tel quel*'s interest in making contemporary China relevant to the West—part of the general field of vision of European aesthetics and politics—required the group to make quite different claims, particularly about the global nature of Marxism, Freudian psychology, and the problem of signification. The persistence of *Tel quel*'s globalizing vision—Maoism can rewrite Marxism; Chinese poetry speaks to the West's repressed ideologies and subjectivities— attests to a desire to allow China to be for and speak to the West. But the language in which China spoke was not natively Chinese in any sense. It belonged to Western philosophy and aesthetics—the dialectic, the symbol, and the unconscious—since that was the language through which the Telquelians understood the world. Especially for Kristeva, the presence of the problems of signification and the unconscious in China allowed her to prove their universal reach, since they surfaced in a culture that was, from France, "at the other extremity of the earth." In such a scenario, "China" could only ever be the double object that *Tel quel* theorized it to be: part word, part world, both a reservoir of utopias and a privileged site of space. As "China" moved from being merely a "reservoir of utopias" to playing the role of "dream come true" for *Tel quel,* it also came to embody the geo-theoretical effect that made it possible.

Consider these facts about "China" as it appeared to *Tel quel* in these years: (1) Its language uniquely combined signifier and referent; (2) its poetry articulated the universal and long-repressed (in the West) problem of symbolization; (3) its Maoism offered the hope of a truly cultural revolution. Each of these facts resembles the others, in that they all promise the disruption of vitally important and similar Western oppositions: text/reality, repression/consciousness, culture/politics. *Tel quel*'s China essentially works the same way. Its two faces—the ancient, unchanging, and mystical place that entranced Pound, and the modern, revolutionary, anti-imperialist nation—spectacularly meld the imaginary and the real. Part of what made that coming together possible was the theoretical ground laid by Foucault and Barthes, among others, in which traditional notions of representation and reality gave way to more complicated projections of linguistic systems and dreamworlds, blurring the line between actual and imaginary Chinas. For *Tel quel,* however, the very theory that supported such a sense of China seemed to be coming from China itself, as though China were justifying, once again in advance, the geo-theoretical conception that made itself possible. *Tel quel*'s "China" was therefore its own cause and its own effect.

To say all this is to say, psychoanalytically, that *Tel quel*'s China was in many ways a projection. In psychoanalytic terms, projection happens when something that comes from inside the self appears to be coming from the real world; the self projects its own ideas or thoughts or desires onto an outside object, which then appears to be the source of those ideas, thoughts, or desires. (In its psychotic form, projection results in hallucinations, so that thoughts take on a visual and/or auditory presence in the real.) When Sollers and Kristeva find, in China, the "repressed" that has eluded them in the West, or when they believe that China itself justifies their understanding of China (rather than the other way around), they are projecting their own ideas, thoughts, and desires onto China. Kristeva's sense, for instance, that Chinese poetry simply *coincidentally* reflects the fraught subjectivities and symbols of Mallarmé or Joyce, is typical of projective thinking. Classically, however, projection involves a dimension of denial, repression, or internal negativity, which is then "projected" outward onto an external object. The classic example is anti-Semitism. The "Jew" is the external projection of what we do not want to admit about ourselves. As I am using the term here with reference to *Tel quel* and China, however, the projected material is *positive* rather than negative—the external projection of what we *hope* is true about ourselves.

I make the observation that *Tel quel*'s China resembles a projection neither as a critique nor as a diagnosis. Such readings often operate under the assumption that naming the psychological malady at work explains the process in general. I note *Tel quel*'s projection here, instead, in order to remark the degree to which the group's psychoanalytic self-consciousness and the poststructuralist justification of its geo-theoretical China suggest that projection needs to be considered a vital part of *Tel quel*'s China rather than its external explication. What makes *Tel quel*'s China *unlike* a typical projection is the degree to which it was theorized as such. In the geo-theory of both Barthes and Foucault, or in Sollers's speculations about the "E, A, S, T," the sense that projection might be inevitable is met not with horror but with acceptance, and a sense of projection's possible utility.

Tel quel's use of China depended therefore on a highly articulated and self-conscious notion of China as Europe's other, and on the perceived ability of such an other to produce new knowledge about and understandings of the self. In thinking these problems, *Tel quel* produced via an aestheticizing reading a sense of "China" and "Chinese" that allowed the group not only to think the impossible but to *see* it, that is, to find in some version of the real world something that existed largely in the literary imagination. The story of this chapter is largely that story: the story of *Tel quel*'s China. What coalesced around the idea of China was a utopian vision that saw, however briefly, the ways "China"—as the name of the text in the world—might come to overturn the West.

1974: Chinese Theater

It is today perhaps obvious that people interested in the culture of a certain part of the world should go there. But that idea depends on a certain theorization of the relation between culture and geography, aesthetics and politics. By arguing for the reality-effect of China's politics and culture in the European world, the Telquelians were committing themselves to an understanding of "China" that had to take in China as a geopolitical entity. Such a necessity is clearest, perhaps, by comparison: Pound's understanding of China as fully located in its classical texts—and in marked contrast, in fact, with its political realities—allowed him to dismiss geopolitical China as irrelevant to what he wanted to do with his own China-idea.

And so, in April 1974, *Tel quel* went to China. Guided around the country by party minders, the Telquelians visited model factories, schools, archaeological sites, museums, farms, and hospitals, engaged in discussions with Chinese intellectuals, peasants, and factory workers (almost entirely via translation), and saw examples and performances of the new revolutionary art in theater and painting. The trip was, for the group, a political authentication of *Tel quel*'s political and cultural relevance in the place of genuine revolution; likewise, for the People's

Republic, it was an opportunity to bolster its image abroad and to present itself as international Communism's preeminent leader.

Upon the return to Paris, each of the Telquelians on the trip published an account and evaluation of the group's three weeks in China. These essays, articles and books, while ranging broadly across political positions, nonetheless had a few things in common. Consider these three excerpts from those responses:

> I wonder if it is really possible to draw any conclusion at all from the fictions we see. The characters are ultrastereotyped and papier-mâché. R. B. says they play their codes until the very end, and Ph. S. that these shows have nothing to do with what's playing today in China. Frankly, it's almost unbearable to watch a people, friendly, clearly artful and subtle, being represented by such mannequins. . . . What one has to point out here is the evacuation of any genuinely fictional dimension, of any subjective investment, of any suggestion of sexual identity. (Pleynet, *Voyage*, 81–82)

> In this country, site of a great historical experiment, heroism is not cumbersome. It could be said that it is confined, like an abscess, on the stage of the opera, the ballet, posters, where (is this an honor, or is it mischievousness?) it is always Woman who receives the task of making the body rear up on its political high horse, while in the streets, in the shops, in the schools, on country roads, a people (who in twenty-five years have already constructed a great nation) move, work, drink tea or do gymnastics without theatrics, without commotion, without striking poses, in a word, without hysteria. (Barthes, *Alors*, 119)

> [The theater] leaves no room for whatever in the psyche, the libido, the imagination, has not been channeled into political sublimation. As if the family, that harbor of the imagination, had consumed itself; and the desires of the community—represented by the desire of the girl—had vested themselves directly in politics, deeply and fully, but not without failure or drama. If this is not the reality, it is certainly the image that we are offered by ideology. (Kristeva, *About*, 155)

Despite their different arguments, what the three quotations share is a concern, either literal or figurative, with the Chinese theater. While, prior to the trip, the major Chinese aesthetic form in which the Telquelians interested themselves was poetry, in the group's reminiscences of the three weeks in China focus it is theater that most frequently articulates crucial moments of the group's experience. Whether used figuratively, to establish a metaphor for a whole social order ("a people . . . move, work, drink tea or do gymnastics without theatrics") or vis-à-vis an actual performance, the theater, and theatricality, together frame some important aspect of the Telquelian trip to China.

Any discussion of the relationship between *Tel quel* and Asian theater must begin where—not coincidentally—the last chapter ended: with Roland Barthes. And Barthes's relationship to Asian theater begins with *Empire of Signs* (1970), in which a Brechtian theatricality figures his understanding of all "Japanese" social relations. Comparing European and Japanese theater, Barthes writes:

> In our theatrical art, the actor pretends to act, but his actions are never anything but gestures: on stage, nothing but theater, yet a theater ashamed of itself. Whereas *Bunraku* (this is its definition) separates action from gesture, it shows the gesture, lets the action be seen, exhibits simultaneously the art and the labor, reserving for each its writing. . . . All this connects, of course, with the alienation effect Brecht recommends. That distance, regarded among us as impossible, useless, or absurd, and eagerly abandoned, though Brecht very specifically located it at the center of his revolutionary dramaturgy . . . that distance is made explicable by *Bunraku*. (*Empire*, 54)

The Western actor's attempt to act as though he were at one with his own speech reveals an embarrassing blindness common to all Western signification, namely the faith in a one-to-one correspondence between the production of meaning and the self. The actor in such a scheme is merely a special case of the general principle. For Barthes, we are all pretending, in one way or another, that we mean what we say, and that we are what we mean. As a social codification of that pretense, the actor effectively allows everyone else to imagine that they are not acting (since all the "acting" is happening on stage), thus providing a prophylactic against the following shame: subjectivity is not natural but performative. The most important fact for Barthes lies therefore in *Bunraku*'s acknowledgment of pretense, which allows for an open consideration—a "reading"—of social discourse without shame.

The major principle of Barthes's fictive Japan is that in its speech, culture, and daily life, signification never pretends—not because the "Japanese" are more honest, but because *they have nothing to betray*. All social acts of meaning thus take on the significance of Brechtian theater, exhibited with a self-conscious awareness whose value exists on the surface rather than in the unconscious. Throughout *Empire*, Barthes describes Japanese social discourse in terms that recall his descriptions of *Bunraku*, in which every element is gestural rather than natural. In cuisine, for instance, "*Sukiyaki* is a stew whose every element can be known and recognized, since it is made in front of you, on your table, without interruption while you are eating it" (19). Likewise on the street: "the spectacle of the Japanese street (or more generally of the public place), exciting as the product of an age-old aesthetic, from which all vulgarity has been decanted, never depends on a theatricality (a hysteria) of bodies, but, once more, on that writing *alla prima*" (80). And also in the bodies themselves: "The reason for this is that in Japan, the body exists, acts, shows itself, gives itself, *without hysteria*, without narcissism, but according to a pure— if subtly discontinuous—project" (10; emphasis added). In the last two of these situations, Barthes indicates the major corollary to the performative aspects of Japanese culture: the absence of hysteria (tied to theatricality or narcissism) in bodies and on the street confirm a sense that Japan, as Barthes imagines it, lacks an unconscious. (They also suggest that for Barthes, the unconscious is precisely that which appears when social codes require that we pretend not to see the fissure of signification.)

The Chinese situation is somewhat different, though once again theater is a major figure for Barthes's understanding of China's relation to the unconscious. Barthes's only reminiscence of the trip, "Alors, la Chine?" (Well, and China?), originally appeared in *Le Monde* only two weeks after the return from Beijing. It opens with a discussion of China's resistance to the Western search for knowledge, its deflection of the questions most pertinent to a scientifically minded European: "We shake the tree of learning so that the answers fall out and so that we can return with that which is our primary intellectual nourishment: a deciphered secret. But nothing falls. In one sense, we come back (outside the political response) with: *nothing*" ("Well," 116). For Barthes, this "nothing" is what is most radical about China. Constituted in response to questions about linguistics, sexuality, or morality, it offers nothing less than a refusal of the European *episteme,* a blankness that does not reverse or negate but defers. China offers no signifieds at all—or at least none recognizable as such—for the Western intellectual determined to "read" the culture's secrets.

"Alors" is a short essay—only five pages—and the first page and a half are devoted to an elaboration of this problem: Barthes says that in China "the ideological objects that our society constructs are silently declared *im-pertinent*" ("Well," 117), that is, not only irrelevant but (childishly) rude.[24] Barthes follows this with an exposition of what he calls China's "blandness" and its peacefulness, the pastel colors of its countryside, the uniformity of dress, the de-eroticization of its bodies. This blandness finds itself reflected everywhere, even in politics, which constructs itself repetitively and ploddingly through the combination of clichés. Aside from the political, Barthes says, only three aspects of Chinese culture offer themselves up for reading: cuisine, children, and calligraphy.

The rest of the social order is profoundly untheatrical. While in Japan, the theater itself seemed to mime the emptiness of all social signification (so that every gesture itself became "gestural"), in China, the melodramatic is confined to theater, and the social in turn presents a completely untheatrical, significative quiet. While tea drinking in *Empire*, for instance, was a ritual filled with empty signs, tea drinking in "Alors" has no real signs at all but simply constitutes itself as itself: "Tea is courteous, friendly, even; and also distant; it makes chuminess, effusion, all the *play-acting* side of social relations excessive" ("Well," 117; emphasis added). Likewise, Chinese bodies, bereft of fashion or makeup, function as bodies and nothing else: "the body no longer has to be understood; that here it stubbornly resists signifying, refusing to allow itself to be caught up in any reading, erotic or dramatic (except on the stage)" ("Well," 117).

When Barthes directly discusses the theater, it is because he finds in it the specifically theatrical gestures that are missing elsewhere in China. "Theatricality" here becomes the name of that which means more than it directly states; it refers to the connotative, performative, formal aspects of social meaning. Its importance is revealed in the final sentences of "Alors" as it was published in *Le Monde* in 1974:

> In this country, site of a great historical experiment, heroism is not cumbersome. It could be said that it is confined, like an abscess, on the stage of the opera, the ballet, posters, where (is this an honor, or is it mischievousness?) it is always Woman who receives the task of making the body rear up on its political high horse, while in the streets, in the shops, in the schools, on country roads, a people (who in twenty-five years have already constructed a great nation) move, work, drink tea or do gymnastics without theatrics, without commotion, without striking poses, in a word, without hysteria. (119)

When he refers to China's "great historical experiment" and the construction of "a great nation," Barthes seems to feel that what the Chinese are doing is actually heroic. He admires the idea that something would be heroic but that social activity would not take notice of it; when he says that the Chinese live "without theatrics" and "without striking poses" he praises their simple and modest relation to social meaning. As heroism disappears from daily life, the exclusive site of its performance and recognition becomes the theater. There, a gesture can be heroic because the space of theater effectively opens up a different realm of social meaning, in which heroism is marked *as* theatrical; in China, unlike the West, the theater remains in the theater (or in other theatrical social discourse, like propaganda posters) where it must be read as such.

Barthes's discomfort around the particular role of Woman in the Chinese theater—it is always "Woman who receives the task of making the body rear up on its political high horse"—does not interfere with the general argument. But this fact about Chinese theater will reappear in the work of other Telquelians, in each case as a nagging and potential "problem" with the experience of theater in China. The particular role played by women (in the character of Woman) in Chinese theater threatens to disrupt the notion of an undisrupted system, since in the West "Woman" names a highly visible and especially "psychological" kind of social being, one whose imbrication in the system of shame and signification cannot be in doubt. Barthes offers two possible interpretations in parentheses—honor or mischievousness—both of which deflect the question of Woman's "role" in Chinese society.

The problem of woman set aside, Barthes can conclude that in China, theatricality, poses—the whole hysterical apparatus of the theater—remains confined to the stage and outside social relations. "Hysteria" is the process in which the unconscious surfaces, becomes readable or visible. For Barthes, since theater (and nothing else) is hysterical in China, then theater is where the repressed surfaces: China once again takes on a special role in relation to repression. Where Kristeva and Sollers believed China to be expressing what the West repressed, Barthes finds simply that China has no repressed to express—except in the theater, where it is always marked as such. The China "without hysteria" in *Alors* is thus rather like the unhysterical "Japan" of *Empire of Signs;* the two fictive places have the same general *shape.* The presence of empty (and thus fully theatrical) signs in Japan mirrors the absence of full signs in China and gives the same result: they produce (and are produced by) a people and a culture effectively without a European unconscious, people whose culture gives the European intellectual nothing to read—and thus offers a radical rather than simple difference from Europe.[25] For Barthes, Chinese theater, by confining itself to the stage, seemed to offer a defense against the theatricality of everyday life.[26]

A fascination with Chinese theater, with China as theater, also motivates important parts of Kristeva's *Des Chinoises,* where its reading produces for her a statement of faith in China's profoundly radical social conception of gender. The book's next-to-last chapter ends with a lengthy treatment of Chinese theater. Kristeva opens the chapter by remarking on the same effect to which Barthes uncomfortably referred, namely the role of women in Chinese theater. At this point in *Des Chinoises,* Kristeva is trying to drive home her general point that China does not have gender in the way that the West does, and that what seem at first to be fairly standard Western representations of gender in the culture in fact prove that China has escaped merely reversing Western gender roles (by making women more powerful than men). Kristeva finds the evidence for this in her reading of the way women's bodies appear in public: "For the moment, at least, and despite the majestic Stanislavskian poses affected by women in posters or on stage, the trend does not seem to be toward an establishment of power with the help of women who, as former slaves, would become the new leaders of a new order" (*About,* 152). For Kristeva, this is good news; the trend of women taking up positions of power would indicate that the revolution was not challenging fundamental structures but simply reversing them. This good news takes place, for Kristeva, "despite" the women's Stanislavskian poses; the poses (because of their Stanislavskianism?) apparently suggest that women have actually taken up positions of power.

Stanislavsky's theater work opposes itself diametrically to Brecht's. Where Brecht was concerned to reveal the mechanisms through which actors performed their roles, Stanislavskian method acting urges the actor toward a complete identification with a role, so that actors to some extent "become" the characters they portray. While Brecht highlighted the artificiality of stagecraft in order to increase its didactic value, Stanislavsky aimed for the most "realistic" portrayal possible in order to urge the audience into an identification with the narrative and characters. While Kristeva describes the women's poses as "Stanislavskian," she also seems to have a sense of their "staged-ness." While "Stanislavskian" suggests genuine, realistic poses, the words "affected" and "majestic" (the latter seems to be used ironically) suggests that the women's poses provoke in Kristeva a sense of their artificiality and of their attempt to teach, to demonstrate (and are therefore unintentionally Brechtian). That is, she understands that the poses are supposed to have a Stanislavskian effect—to encourage women to take up a certain kind of power—and yet they have the opposite effect on Kristeva, since their affectedness reveals the intentional gesture behind them.

As Kristeva goes on to discuss other pieces of Chinese theater in an attempt to read the culture of the Cultural Revolution, she continues to experience its texts as "affected." When it comes to the revolutionary theater, cinema, and opera of 1974, she writes, heroines need frequent rescuing by the figure of "some representative of the Party . . . some *deus-ex-machina* who gives the performance a happy ending and validates the efforts of the heroine/pioneer. But (to our eyes at least) he is still a dramatic artifice, and nothing more" (*About,* 152). As with the women's poses, Kristeva finds the experience of the Party representative in some way excessive or superficial. She goes on to argue that the frequent appearance of the male representative does not constitute a significant cultural trend toward men in power, because he is a "dramatic artifice, and nothing more." "Nothing more" means that the male representative does not have a broader cultural meaning, that is, a meaning *outside* the theater.

In both these cases involving theater and the staging of the revolution, Kristeva identifies artificial moments in order to argue that they do not contribute significantly to a larger trend. In the same way that she discovers no trend toward women in power *despite* their affected poses, she finds in theater no significant trend toward men in power *despite* the male Party representative. Indeed, the very structure of Kristeva's reading indicates a certain distance from Chinese theater. Being able to call the poses Stanislavskian, or the Party representative a deus ex machina, requires recognizing them as a priori artificial, as theatrical "devices" named and known within a Western tradition of drama theory. At the point at which things *seem* Stanislavskian to Kristeva, they can only *be* Stanislavskian (that is, realistic) for someone else. When Kristeva identifies the poses as trying for realism, she also declares herself immune to their reality-effect. Such a view, as Kristeva herself suggests, depends in part on being a foreigner to Chinese culture; the Party representative is a dramatic artifice "to our eyes," where "our" refers to the Telquelians, but perhaps not to the eyes of the Chinese audience.

In search of a reading—foreign or Chinese—that will confirm China's dissolution of gender, Kristeva turns to revolutionary opera. There, she writes, the most repeated story is that of the young girl, whose precocious revolutionarism—guided, at the end of the play, by a Party representative—shows her family/village/classmates the way to a new society. What is striking for Kristeva is that this young girl is absolutely asexual—she carries with her none of the trappings of the Freudian family. Faced with this new archetype, Kristeva concludes that somewhere between the early twentieth century and the Cultural Revolution, the family has disappeared from Chinese theater, and politics has taken its place:

> [The theater] leaves no room for whatever in the psyche, the libido, the imagination, has not been channeled into political sublimation. As if the family, that harbor of the imagination, had consumed itself; and the desires of the community—represented by the desire of the girl—had vested themselves directly in politics, deeply and fully, but not without failure or drama. If this is not the reality, it is certainly the image that we are offered by ideology. (155)

Kristeva suggests that the spaces of the family, the erotic, the woman, have been closed down in favor of political concerns and a complete exteriorization of the psyche. The community itself becomes metonymized in the body of the young girl, who is never quite a heroine but who initiates and catalyzes revolutionary action (even though she ultimately must be rescued by the male Party representative). This process happens without sexuality, without libido, without any of the psychological trauma of the modern Western theater; "character" as the West conceives it has been flattened, as it were, onto a political screen. The "drama" of the Chinese theater revolves around this politicization rather than the vagaries of individual development.

Kristeva is not without resistance to this idea. She wants to find Woman, not bury her in the body politic; and yet the "ideology" of Chinese theater seems to have done the latter. It is at this moment that she turns to Brecht:

Brecht, the precocious "Chinese man" of socialism (cf. in his *Mei-ti,* for example) had realized that the failures of the Eastern regimes were not temporary mistakes or faults of such-and-such a personality; rather they were due to the fact that "something was missing." For me . . . what seems to be "missing" in the system is, indeed, the stubborn refusal to admit that anything is missing. More concretely, the refusal to admit that social entente, inasmuch as it is possible, is sustained by desire, by eroticism. (155)

Brecht's *Me-Ti, Buch der Wendungen,* a work of imitation Chinese philosophy that used "Chinese" names for European political figures (Kameh for Karl Marx, and so on), critiques the Communist regimes of Eastern Europe and the Soviet Union by placing them behind a Chinese screen; so imagined, their mistakes take on a certain epic quality that made them, for Brecht, easier to see. If Brecht is a "Chinese man" of socialism for Kristeva, it is because he saw that a Zhdanovian Communism had to suppress the element of mystery in the aesthetic, and deny that anything unspeakable or only obliquely representable existed underneath the social's skin. Kristeva's readings of Chinese theater put her on the edge of a Brechtian critique, one that would find in this particular Eastern regime yet another denial of the psyche, the erotic, desire—all the things that drive a psychoanalyst's sense of social ontology.

Even as she approaches this critique, however, Kristeva draws back. The search for that missing thing, she writes, echoing Barthes, is the natural reaction of a European scholar: "One's immediate reaction is, 'let's look for the archipelagos, they must be somewhere, well-camouflaged under Confucian civility and the elegance of the writings.' The big question, as they say, is precisely that" (156). The big question in question—and in many ways the question at the heart of *Tel quel*'s inquiry into China—is: what if, underneath the trappings of its Cultural Revolution, its Taoism and its poetry, China is just like the West's other East: Eastern Europe? Kristeva's "archipelagos" gestures toward Aleksandr Solzhenitsyn's *Gulag Archipelago* (1974), whose description of the Soviet Union's political prisons reshaped the intellectual landscape of European Communism. For Kristeva here, however, the search for "archipelagos"—the disruptions and imperfections of a seemingly seamless Communist system—is produced in part by habit, in part by fear.[27] The Western European Left's hopes in a Communist East in Eastern Europe and the Soviet

Union had, by 1974, been dashed to pieces; many in Western Europe were arguing, even as *Tel quel* went to China, that Chinese Communism was simply another failed iteration, Mao another Stalin. For Kristeva, who remained convinced that China would not simply replicate Eastern Europe, in culture or politics, the question was: how to explain the effective absence of desire on the Chinese stage?

This is the job of the chapter's final paragraph. Kristeva writes: "Unless, in the arrangement of the Chinese universe, this 'other scene' which in the West gives rise to 'the sacred,' 'the erotic' (or, when we ignore it, the 'totalitarian') is constantly present, as an undercurrent imperceptible to us, like Taoism—the subtle but permanent lining of all Chinese life" (*About*, 156). This speculative answer solves the problem of what is "missing." The apparent superficiality of Chinese theater does indeed conceal a missing side, but it conceals only because that negative side appears universally—it is hard to see because it is everywhere, and therefore is in some sense indistinguishable from the daily fabric of Chinese life and reality. Such a claim must remain unproven and theoretical for Kristeva, since the undercurrent in question *cannot be perceived* by Westerners ("imperceptible to us"). Kristeva knows its existence not because she has seen it but because it is theoretically necessary. The apparent lack of artificiality *for the Chinese spectator*—and thus the resistance of Chinese theater to analytic or literary critical interpretation—is thus revealed as a paradoxically *deep superficiality;* Chinese theater—and the affected poses of its women—is therefore "affected" and Stanislavskian all at once.[28] Ultimately, then, while appearing to read against the theatrical grain, Kristeva comes back to Brecht's position: one must see the Chinese theater as the Chinese do. Understanding the Chinese theater from the perspective of the "Chinese universe" allows her to find in the theater what she knew was there all along.

This reading of Chinese theater allows Kristeva to rediscover "woman" there—she whose life and psychology disappears in the plot returns in the permanent lining, not as a "woman" in the Western sense, but as an equal partner in the creation and use of power. In keeping with Kristeva's general argument about China, the space of the feminine is not, in China, a separate one, but is intimately tied up in and inseparable from the rest of the culture. This allows Kristeva to rearticulate her major critique of Western culture, namely that it opens up a psychically and socially separate realm for women as a way of controlling or hiding the psychic trauma of early childhood. While what seems to be "missing" in Chinese theater is in fact the space of woman ("No more arguments between women. . . . No more specifically female dilemma"), it is not in fact missing but integrated, part of the surface: "woman" cannot be seen in China because "woman" has not been separated out from the culture in general. Kristeva's chosen spectatorial relation to Chinese theater—indeed to the Cultural Revolution in general—allows her to perceive that.

In some way Kristeva's reading of China's theater allows her to develop to a powerful theory of realism, one marked by seeing things *as the Chinese do* (the point of view given by the "Chinese universe"). She begins with the premise that the West continually tries to conceal desire, even though it irrupts continually in the surface of the social body. China, on the other hand, does not hide desire, but recognizes its universal presence. It therefore has no "archipelagos"[29]—nothing sticks out—because desire is in such a system an "undercurrent" imperceptible on the social's glassy surface. Accordingly, what sticks out for the European witness is the fact that nothing sticks out—which gives rise to the sense that something is missing. Kristeva, however, transforms her sense that something is missing into a realization that what is being represented in the theater is in some sense that very fact. Therefore nothing is missing. In excising desire from its characters—in depsychologizing them—Chinese theater not only represents the universal presence of desire but *acts it out:* it is nowhere because it is everywhere. In Kristeva's theory of the imperceptible undercurrent (whose Western name is something like "woman") realism returns as a kind of hyperrealistic vision of its old self, in which Chinese theater is deemed to represent not only the full range of masculine power (visibly and universally) but also the full space of feminine power and matriarchy (invisibly and universally)—intertwined and (in)visible in China as they cannot be in the West. China is therefore more in tune with reality (as Kristeva understands it) than the West.

Kristeva's discovery of the missing in Chinese theater is remarkable for its imagination of an *other* system, one that might accept in the depths of its social structure the very conflicts that make Europe totalitarian with regards to desire, and through desire, to women. The excesses of such a reading, as Chow in particular has shown, lie in its sense that China is some sort of "absolute other" for Europe, or simply Europe's unconscious. This reading requires essentially conceiving of China as a kind of Europe upside down, complete with a neatly reversed metaphysics. In *Woman and Chinese Modernity,* Chow disagrees with three of Kristeva's major interpretations of China, arguing in each case that what appears to be a wholly other articulation of a concept (writing, the maternal order, Taoism) works in some ways like its Western counterpart, its difference a matter of articulation and presentation rather than kind. China is just another place, not the magical utopia Kristeva imagines it to be. Such a response corrects the Telquelian (or "Maoist" in the general sense) misperception of the East with the *facts,* insisting that the Telquelians have misnamed their dream-object.

And yet the factual correction cannot account, it seems, for the deliberate lack of innocence Kristeva exhibits in her readings of Chinese theater. Kristeva's willful disregard for the facts and her conclusion's twisted logic (1. Something is missing. 2. I cannot see the missing thing. 3. What is missing is "imperceptible") are gestures that deliberately ignore a "factual" or commonsense reading. Her writing in *Des Chinoises* is inflected neither by a reportorial mode nor by a reverent presentation of Chinese culture as the Chinese explain it to her. When Kristeva reads with a deliberate eye to China as she demands that it be, she deforms its theater into a theoretical object that works to her purpose: to provide an example of the way things *might* be, to offer the impression of a possibility outside the ken of Europe's knowledge-system. It is precisely at such moments that her readings fade into something like a Chinese dream, when the "unless" in this sentence—"Unless, in the arrangement of the Chinese universe, this 'other scene' which in the West gives rise to 'the sacred,' 'the erotic' (or, when we ignore it, the 'totalitarian') is constantly present, as an undercurrent imperceptible to us, like Taoism"—opens up through its unjustifiable logic this utopian impossibility: that a society might accept desire, not suppress it.

Both Barthes and Kristeva used their theatrical turns to find in China a European other, a system in which the theater, standing in for a whole system of social signification, could indicate a positively valued superficiality—China is the place where the repressed (figured by "woman") does not interrupt the surface of the social, where gestures like tea drinking have no secret depths (no "playacting"). Such a view is in marked contrast with that of Marcelin Pleynet, who wrote as though the theater itself were leaking uncontrollably into his quotidian experience. Pleynet's *Le voyage en Chine* (The trip to China), published in 1980, consists largely of his diary entries of late April and early May 1974. Though written at the height of *Tel quel*'s Maoist period, the diary entries show little interest in the political aspects of the trip. Rather the text manifests a continual and suspicious concern with both the staging of *Tel quel*'s trip and the aesthetics of Chinese theater, and in doing so offers a vision of China quite different from Barthes's, even though mediated through the same cultural metaphor.

It all begins with a trip to see a historical re-creation: "When we got to the house/museum where the first CCP congress took place, in front of the red table with a teapot and several teacups on it, R. B. tells us that he had at first thought that the table was set for us, and that we had to sit on the stools (for a moment I had had the same idea). It was explained in time that we were facing a reconstruction of the room (table, cups, and teapot included) in which the first CCP congress took place" (41). The staged nature of the table and teapots here only becomes clear as Pleynet and Barthes understand it as a restaging, an intentional re-creation of an original scene. But it is the scene's striking resemblance to their daily experience of China that causes confusion; both Barthes and Pleynet refer to the series of reception rooms and cups of tea that form the background of their conversations with the Chinese. As the trip wears on, it is precisely the dailiness of the staging that will begin to annoy Pleynet, as though this first scene were merely an extreme version of all their social interaction.

The museum-quality of the tea scene finds itself repeated particularly in a visit to recently uncovered archaeological sites. In the book's preface, Pleynet thanks French sinologist Marcel Granet, whose histories of China introduced generations of French students to the subject. Faced with the Communist Party tour guides' sanitized version of Chinese history, Pleynet feels frustrated. In one instance, a planned trip to two ancient temples is canceled because, Pleynet suggests, of the Party's antireligious stance. "They tell us they're closed, but it's quite obviously the same Marxist childishness which reduces 6,000 years of history to a few vulgar sociological sites, which keeps us away from anything that might give that history a dimension worthy of it. In short, everything that doesn't bring into focus the most stereotyped of fictions (of culture or history) is either hidden or forbidden" (85). It was in fact the "stereotyped" setting of the tea party that caused Barthes's and Pleynet's confusion; the scene, just like so many other scenes, offers itself first to its most banal interpretation. What is missing at the archaeological sites is any sense of the *depth* or *magnitude* of Chinese history, of China itself, in the face of the superficial and the stereotyped representation put forth by the CCP (whose superficiality denies history the "dimension" that might be "worthy" of its depth). Furthermore, the tour guides' version of history is couched in completely unconvincing terms: "The research, if it isn't completely untrue, stumbles over primary truths whose heartbreaking childishness in the face of the centuries that they imagine they explain is more depressing than anything else" (84–85).

It is not, then, that Pleynet acutely pierces the veil of Maoist truths, but rather that the Maoism is so deeply unconvincing as to be absurd, like a child's lie. Out of these pages comes not the critic's triumph but rather the reader's immense disappointment, not with China itself, but with the Communist Party's guided tour and its general cultural aesthetic, whose preferred narrative mode is the most obvious melodrama. Nowhere is this clearer than in Pleynet's discussions of the theater, which form a counterpoint to his anger about the Party's staging of Chinese history. He remarks on a performance of Chinese opera,

> I wonder if it is really possible to draw any conclusion at all from the fictions we see. The characters are ultrastereotyped and papier-mâché. R. B. says they play their codes until the very end, and Ph. S. that these shows have nothing to do with what's playing today in China. Frankly, it's almost unbearable to watch a people, friendly, clearly artful and subtle, being represented by such mannequins. . . . What one has to point out here is the evacuation of any genuinely fictional dimension, of any subjective investment, of any suggestion of sexual identity. (81–82)

As with his commentary on Chinese history, here Pleynet defends a perceived reality against its representation by the CCP. Whereas earlier the depth of history itself was covered over by the Party's "childish" representation of it, here the subjective depth of the people is erased by the mannequin-like performances on stage. In both his first sentence and the remark he quotes from Sollers, Pleynet indicates his belief that these representations have only the most tenuous link to actual China—a sense that

China (and Chinese people) are somehow *more* than what they seem to be in the museums or on stage.

The critique does not merely revolve around some sense of "the people," however; it extends to a general disagreement with the chosen cultural aesthetic of the Communist Party, which Pleynet feels repeats the worst of socialist realism. Remarking on an exhibition of paintings in the village of Huxian, Pleynet says: "No matter what the arguments about the works' political didacticism are, everything happens as if there is no painting, as if the work had no reality other than its propaganda function" (91). And later, commenting on the final scene of a ballet: "Finally a red sun rises over the mountain, and the performers turn toward it as if toward holy communion. All this is obviously pretty hard to accept as such" (97).

The refusal to "believe in" or enjoy the representations by the Communist Party point to the limits of Pleynet's political commitment. He remains, in front of Chinese theater, a demanding reader of culture. At the same time, however, it is important to recognize that Pleynet's demands depend on a preconceived and quite traditionally orientalist view of China, its history, and its people, namely a sense of their profound *historicity* and *artfulness* ("clearly artful and subtle"). When Pleynet denounces the Party's new theater, he denounces it in part in the name of that history and that artfulness, speaking for China in a moment when he cannot agree with its official self-description. Rey Chow has described such a position as typical of many Western sinologists who identify with China's classical culture: "In the case of the sinologist's relation with his beloved object, 'China,' melancholia is complicated by the presence of a third party—the living members of the Chinese culture, who provide the sinologist with a means of *externalizing* his loss and directing his blame" (*Writing*, 4).

Pleynet's anger directs itself, however, at the Party rather than the People. His readings of Communist-supported theater essentially mirror his sense of the whole trip as politically staged (and childishly so at that). China's masses and its culture, in contrast to the Party, benefit from some of *Voyage*'s most lyrical and literary descriptions: "The stereotypes of Xi'an's guides and interpreters cannot keep one from seeing the masses of the villages and countryside which move attentively, with curiosity and calm, into another way of life" (93). Pleynet here sounds like both Barthes and Kristeva: as we have seen, the word "attentively" is at the center of Barthes's appreciation of China, while the "calm" villagers might stand in for those in Kristeva's Huxian (she describes them, however, as "not even curious"). Similarly, the land itself cannot be blamed for China's political mischief but instead points the way toward a more classical (and orientalizing) reading, one that clearly shares something with Fenollosa: "Whether it's the Great Wall, or the landscape's rice fields, the sign, the trace that the Chinese leaves always has two measures, that of man and that of the space he lives in: the fixation of one in the other—the vast, ideogrammatic writing of space" (122).

The approach to China in the pages of *Voyage*—especially in contrast to Pleynet's earlier Maoism—confirms his *literary* commitment to China, which not only survives Maoism's political failure but is, in *Voyage*, allowed to return and issue judgment upon it. When it does so, Pleynet repeats the classic tropes of an avant-garde literary orientalism (as modeled by, say, Pound). In the interstices of a certain Taoism, a sense of the Chinese as attentive or calm, and the visceral presence of Chinese writing, appears a China that seems able to contain all the necessary possibilities for a genuinely new literary vision. Given Pleynet's sense that the good things about China and its people are drowned out by Communist propaganda, it comes as no surprise that the one performance he enjoys in China is markedly more popular than the rest:

> At seven o'clock our guides come get us to take us to the theater. The auditorium is full. The whole group seems to think that this is a more "popular" audience. The stage is Chinese, the orchestra is on the stage behind a screen. The game, the song, the music, the actors' makeup seem a good deal less Westernized than what we saw the night before. It's a familial show, and in the audience one sees several women with very young children in their laps. The public cheerfully interrupts the action to applaud the actor in the main role or some particularly brilliant acrobatics, or the victory of good over evil. Last night there wasn't a single round of applause during the whole show. When it's over, like every other time, we're invited to leave before the crowd; tonight the whole auditorium rises and applauds us. (101)

What seemed earlier to be a frustration with an overly obvious and melodramatic stagecraft (not just in theater but everywhere) not yet named "Western" here receives that appellation. The appreciation of "less Westernized" stagecraft, the sense that the audience is more popular ("un public plus populaire"), the spontaneous applause, all combine to create a sense that at last, the Telquelians are witnessing something that is in some way *naturally* Chinese, getting an unscreened glimpse of the true subject of their interest.

If theater matters to Pleynet's experience in China, then, it does so only to reveal the other side of its Janus face: artifice. In contrast to Kristeva, who drives through this initial impression (as she did with the Stanislavskian gestures) toward a positive reading, Pleynet feels, both in theater and the historical or archaeological presentations he attends, that everything is *staged* with an eye toward maximum political effect. His genuine pleasure at more popular theater has to do with the fact that it feels natural, spontaneous—even the audience's reaction to the foreigners feels unforced. Pleynet's Chinese experiences, as managed by the Communist Party, gave him the sense that he was never really seeing genuine China—in either its classical or folkloric versions—but instead a trumped-up and aesthetically vacuous melodrama. The cultural side of the Cultural Revolution, at least, had nothing revolutionary or even interesting about it.

When theater opens up a place of comparison for the whole "playacting" side of social relations (Barthes), an experience of revolution in gender roles (Kristeva), or an experience that figures the more general staged fakery of the CCP's tour of China (Pleynet), it reveals itself as a powerful, malleable trope for the Telquelians' Chinese experience. More than that, it also opens up a space for Brecht—Kristeva's "Chinese man" of socialism—at the zenith of *Tel quel*'s relationship to China. As the circular history of Barthes's phrase "without hysteria"—appearing first in the *Empire of Signs* (1970), then in the review of Brecht's *Mother Courage* (1971), and finally in "Well, and China?" (1974)—suggests, Brecht seems to be both borrowing from the East and, uncannily, explaining it in advance. Such a reading of Brecht confirms Shu-hsi Kao's sense that Brecht is, despite his disavowals, undeniably "Chinese." At the same time, it suggests that Barthes's experience of East Asia happens *through* Brecht to an important degree—that a Brechtian theory not only of theater but of social activity prepares Barthes for a particular experience of the East by giving him a framework within which to read it. Likewise, for Kristeva, Brecht—socialism's "Chinese man"—both "is" Chinese and explains it. His political analysis of Eastern regimes—the idea that "something is missing"—allows Kristeva finally to unlock the aesthetic secret of Chinese theater: that there is no secret at all.

It thus seems clear enough that for *Tel quel*, Brecht was "Chinese." But it is also possible that its "China" was Brechtian. Brecht's presence adds yet another layer of complication to the shape of *Tel quel*'s China. To recap: Brecht sees Mei Lanfang in 1935; he imagines, in the A-effects essay, that what he sees in that performance resembles what the Chinese audience sees. Renata Berg-Pan argues that in fact what Brecht sees is Brechtian, not Chinese, by pointing out that Chinese audiences find the gestures Brecht found so alluring (the biting of the hair) formal and even dull. Brecht, in the second half of "Alienation Effects," dismisses the effect's Chinese origins and argues for its "profitable" German use. This produces the mystery of Brecht's China, which rejects its own Chinese-ness, but is nonetheless received as "Chinese" and as part of a broader European idea of what "China" means (Kao). In 1970, Barthes, in Japan, finds elements of the Brechtian theater (which he believes Brecht has learned from the East) in Japanese social discourse. Returning to Paris, he sees *Mother Courage* and describes it using a phrase, "without hysteria," that he used in *Empire of Signs*. Three years later, he uses the same phrase in "Alors, la Chine?" In a parallel development, Kristeva, reading China in terms defined by the history of European theater (cf. the Stanislavskian poses), uses her sense of Brecht's political analysis (first published in the fake voice of a Chinese philosopher) to discover the secret of "Chinese" theater, a secret that turns all Chinese discourse into a Brechtian play whose every gesture is to be read superficially. Extricating from all this a discrete chronology of origins is probably not possible. Even if one could figure out whether or not Brecht's A-effect was or was not truly Chinese—whether China influenced Brecht or Brecht influenced the way the Telquelians saw China—it is too late in the game to do anything about it. By the time *Tel quel* travels to China, Brecht's A-effect has knotted itself into a larger discourse on "China" that has as much force in the perception of reality as actual China itself.

What is there to learn from this coincidence between Brecht, theater, and *Tel quel*'s China? Within two years of the group's return, the Telquelians would have turned their backs on almost everything they wrote about China in and around 1974. As an intellectual habit, then, thinking China through theater has a relatively short shelf life; no one claims for it any serious influence on the group's later ideas, or on the development of postmodern thought and theory. *Tel quel*'s repudiation of this moment in 1974 certainly suggests that in hindsight the group—much like its critics—found its trip more than a little embarrassing.

At the same time, as the apotheosis of a certain moment in postmodern aesthetics and politics—the last moment (in Europe) of pure faith in a simultaneously cultural and political revolution—1974 still has something to teach. It marks, first of all, the high-water mark of a European intellectual relationship to China that can be said to begin as early as Leibniz, and carries on through Hegel,[30] and past Hegel to Fenollosa, Pound, and Brecht. It is also a particularly important moment in the history of *Tel quel,* as the return from Paris would bring about the group's apolitical turn and the retreat to the aesthetic. From that vantage point, one sees articulated around 1974—some for the first time, some simply in repetition—many of the most important ideas that the Telquelians were bringing to the intellectual table. Some of these would be picked up and, stripped of reference to political China, would ground the intellectual work that "theory" brought into the American academy (particularly in Kristeva, whose *Strangers to Ourselves,* though it never mentions China, repeats ideas Kristeva first articulates with respect to Huxian). Inasmuch, then, as the ideas developed around the trip are important, the habitual reference to the theater marks it as the aesthetic form that most eloquently expresses its experience, for good or ill—as against, as I have suggested, poetry, which had been the emblematic form of *Tel quel*'s earlier interest in China.

As an expression of the China experience, "theater" lends itself to a variety of suggestive figures: one could argue that the theater of revolution that was China 1974 did create, ultimately, the audience it deserved: an audience for whom, once out of the building, all the spectacular pleasures of the play melted into nothingness, an audience whose major effect was, after 1974, disappointment. If nothing else, the frequent reference to theater in Barthes, Kristeva, and Pleynet indicates that they found it to be a useful or intriguing manner in which to read China—though this does not mean necessarily that China was "theatrical." It does suggest, however, that the Telquelians may have come to China with the theater—and Brecht—in mind, and that the actual performances they saw served, accordingly, as metaphors for a much larger sense of what China could or should mean for them. Despite whatever differences one may perceive between "China" as seen by Brecht and *Tel quel,* there is little doubt that for the Telquelians Brecht—who, as Sollers wrote, "never ceased lucidly to approach this new [Chinese] reality" (*Sur,* 126)—and through Brecht, Asian theater, were not only ways of thinking *about* China, but ways of thinking *through* it.

Chinese (Re)turns: 1974–1990

WITH AND WITHOUT UTOPIA: 1974–76

Back from China, the trip's promise evanesced like so much stage smoke. For some members of *Tel quel,* disavowal took longer than others, but all of them—except, perhaps, Barthes—would eventually repudiate some or all aspects of their Chinese interest. Among the first to do so was *Tel quel*'s editor at Seuil, François Wahl. In June 1974, a month after the return from China, Wahl published a series of articles in *Le Monde* under the title "La Chine sans utopie" (China without utopia). The articles compose a cautionary tale for would-be reverse ethnocentrists: part pragmatic warning, part theoretical resistance to the project the Telquelians (Kristeva, Pleynet, and Sollers) were, in his view, doomed to articulate upon their return to Paris. The article's four parts, published over four days, each tackle a different aspect of the Cultural Revolution, and work together to expose what Wahl sees as the ongoing and pernicious influence of the Soviet Union and Stalinism in China—the very threat of China as Eastern Europe Kristeva would resist in *Des Chinoises.* For Wahl, China's refusal to disavow Stalin's political crimes, its ongoing emphasis on a Soviet-style industrialization, and its socialist realist model of cultural production, all contribute to a sense that China is fully imbricated in an economic and political model that the West already *knows.*

The structure of Wahl's general argument allows us to see not only what he is for but what he is against. For Wahl, a China without utopia is one that does not create a radically new space but simply reflects and repeats a familiar one. If Europeans can see China as (potentially) another Soviet Union, they cannot also take it as a utopia; rather, China is too much in the world to be anything but another instance of government in terms the world already understands. Such an attack responds directly to the kind of cultural Maoism *Tel quel* espoused leading up to the trip and immediately after it, which depended on a sense of China as radically "other" and thus as a possible utopia. Wahl's production of political, cultural, and historical knowledge about China is intended to deflate such expectations.

Alongside this argument comes, however, a sense of disappointment, a sense that China, in not being Chinese enough, has in some way let Wahl down. When he describes his experience in China, the things he finds most strange and surprising turn not on cultural differences but on cultural similarities. Describing, for instance, the Beijing cityscape, he writes: "As soon as one gets to Beijing, one has the strange and worrying sense of finding oneself in Eastern Europe . . . you might think you were in East Berlin. Where is China?" (June 16–17, 4:3). The meaning of "China" in this last question effectively captures Wahl's disappointment. The question is not, "Where is the geopolitical space recognized as China?"—Wahl knows full well where he is. It is something more like, "Where is the Chineseness of China? Where is that which I think of as culturally Chinese?"

Wahl's sense that the positive difference of China has been subsumed by a Soviet model (of thinking, of living, of Marxism, of culture) appears over and over in "La Chine sans utopie." Take for instance this complaint about Beijing's Soviet-style architecture: "The imposition of a construction style cannot be secondary, inasmuch as what manifests itself there is the European-style project of industrial urbanization in its Soviet iteration, not even retouched, not even 'sinified'" (June 16–17, 4:4). The Soviet structures—whose appearance in architecture merely reflects their appearance in thought—are most offensive because they have not *even* been retouched or made Chinese. China appears to be offering not something like "Soviet Communism with Chinese characteristics," but a Soviet Communism *tout court*, a full-scale repetition without a difference. Wahl's frustration comes out most clearly in the June 18 article on Stalin, where he asks the following rhetorical question: "Does the China of the Cultural Revolution intend—as it has been affirmed in the West—to propose a 'different' model of knowledge?" (6:6). The answer—"One can only say that the Chinese themselves give us no reason to think so"— expresses well Wahl's sense of the Cultural Revolution as an enterprise doomed to repeat the past rather than able to create the future. And the absence of a Chinese "difference" is the symptom par excellence of the problem.

Wahl states his major thesis most explicitly in the title of the fourth article, "Cultural Revolution or Westernization?" which deals with the realm of culture. This article, which is far more critical and sure of its criticisms than the previous three, accuses China of having Stalinized its literary culture and thus of playing into the hands of the West. Early on, Wahl lays out the unpleasant facts: "As for 'literary' books, that is, symbolic practice as such, one must—if one wants to understand China—come to grips with the fact that there *aren't* any" (June 19, 8:2). The absence of symbolic practice extends outward, Wahl writes, so that all cultural productions, including theater, propaganda posters, puppet shows, the cinema, are governed by the triumphalist cliché.

Tel quel met Wahl's articles with a scathing critique. The journal's first post-trip issue argues in an unsigned editorial that Wahl's point of view has been influenced by his refusal to see what he cannot accept: namely that China could produce a difference that would be meaningful in the West. All of Wahl's complaints about Sovietization, *Tel quel* argues, stem from his desire to keep China in the past, as an object for his own ethnocentric fantasies rather than a force in the contemporary world: "Without [westernization] China would remain forever 'eternal,' that is, a semi-colony under a feudal regime" ("En Chine," 8). *Tel quel* reserves its most serious criticisms for Wahl's claim that China has abandoned its Chinese past in favor of westernization. Wahl had argued that China, in attempting to follow the Soviet model, had forgotten all its culture, and that doing so would result in its inevitably following the Soviet line: "A China without a cultural past is, one finally sees, a China bound hand and foot to the language of the West" (June 19, 8:6). *Tel quel* responds: "Was China free relative to the West during the Opium War, colonial occupation, or Soviet 'management'?" (9). *Tel quel*'s articulation of China's progress in terms of its battle against imperialism underscores its anti-European political commitment; for Wahl, on the other hand, the Chinese past that matters lies well before Western colonization, in its Buddhism, Taoism, and Confucian philosophy, which might serve as a bulwark against westernization.

Tel quel's reply to Wahl's notion that China cannot be the West's utopia is, in short: of course it can't. "When one is in China, one senses very clearly the moment in which the Chinese *can no longer* answer *our* questions. Indeed: they are our questions. And we do not know how to answer them ourselves, whence the temptation to make the Chinese responsible for them, instead of taking account of a new reality: theirs" (7). Echoes here of Barthes's wariness about carrying Western hermeneutics east; but for *Tel quel* the question is not about new knowledge but a new "reality"—a fully other hermeneutic face-to-face with the West. China is not a utopia; it is a place in the world, and that is the reality with which the West must account.

In *Tel quel*'s remarking of Wahl's sinophobia, and Wahl's of the journal's sinophilia, one feels the presence of antiorientalism, the not-yet-declared theory that would rise to judge all Western comers to the Chinese scene. As far as the facts were concerned, history gives the victory to Wahl. But his value here has little to do with that judgment; rather he serves most importantly as an instance of a rhetorical *style* about China whose differences from the Telquelian model correspond to a substantial difference in political commitment. Wahl's reasonable, unhysterical presentation of the facts—the series opens with a lengthy explanation of the role of Confucius in ancient China—is emblematic of a certain type of criticism leveled against *Tel quel* during these years, which confronted the group's baroque, elaborate theoretical and stylistic expressions with a rational and journalistic history lesson and good clean common sense (and sometimes a more mainstream orientalism). The disagreement between Wahl and *Tel quel* thus depends not only on a different understanding of what was happening in China, but also a different understanding of *how* to understand. Compared with the Telquelians, Wahl seemed to many observers to be pursuing a useful explication of the conditions in China, rather than a self-centered reverie built on a strident political position. Wahl's articles on China exhibit not simply a different opinion than *Tel quel*'s, but a different sensibility.

Such a sensibility could not have been any more opposed to Barthes's. Wahl's arguments exemplify what Barthes had called, in *Empire of Signs*, a Western, "scientific" approach to the Orient. That approach's relation to "China" as an object of knowledge was journalistic, historical—and therefore profoundly opposed to the kind of textual reading that supported Barthes's "Japan," or *Tel quel*'s China for that matter. Wahl's interest in a "China without utopia" articulates precisely his opposition to an imaginative, "unrealistic" relation to China; his political realism was at the same time a rejection of the literary mode. That this sensibility breaks down along lines of science versus literature, or rational realpolitik versus utopian dreaming, repeats once again the debate over translation in Brecht and Pound (philology vs. song), with its attendant mapping onto West versus East.

When Barthes's "Alors, la Chine?" was republished by Christian Bourgeois as a pamphlet in 1975, Barthes added an afterword that appears directly to respond to Wahl's explicitly "scientific" take and reaffirms his faith in a nonjudgmental response to China. Conceiving of his essay as a kind of "negative hallucination" fully outside the traditional political mode, Barthes stakes a claim to a new kind of political engagement: "This negative hallucination is not gratuitous [*gratuite*]: it is an attempt to respond to the way many Westerners have of hallucinating the People's Republic of China—in a dogmatic mode, violently affirmative/negative or falsely liberal. Is it not after all a wretched notion of politics to think it can occur in language only in the form of a *directly* political discourse?" ("Well," 120).

Rather than a wholesale rejection of politics, Barthes here offers a redefinition of the term, suggesting that attacks on *Alors*'s political naïveté depended on an impoverished notion of politics itself. If Barthes's negative hallucination is not "gratuitous," that is because it has a political value of its own, as a political response to the necessary politicization of China (itself, as Barthes notes, a kind of hallucination). This defense also provides—in advance, as it were—a response to a certain antiorientalist critique and its relentless pursuit and demystification of Western hallucination. A reading of China that remains sensitive to and unashamed of internal experience, as does Barthes's, might resist its critics best as a work of literature rather than as a work of politics. Such a practice would confirm Barthes's general "refusal" of China, a refusal that he saw as both a negation of the demand to discuss China politically and as a way of reflecting what he saw as China's own refusal to be a screen for Western projections.

That mode of refusal is in keeping with Barthes's direct experience of China. He writes almost nothing about what he saw or did there. Kristeva and Pleynet report, however, that he sometimes did not get out of the bus at tour stops, preferring to stay inside and take pictures through the window. Perhaps this is why *Alors* itself has the hazy quality of a dream. Barthes's "negative hallucination" never describes anything specific about China; instead he gives an endless series of collective nouns and lowercase people, producing a sense of China as seen through the distance of a telephoto lens or a bus window: quiet, spacious, passive, with nothing in close-up. The essay's opening scene—and it is a scene—reads like stage directions from a kind of play where all the characters are archetypes:

> In the calm, soft light of the reception rooms, our hosts (workers, professors, peasants) are patient, conscientious (everyone is taking notes: there is no feeling of boredom, but rather a peaceful feeling of team work). Above all, they are attentive, unusually attentive, not to our identity but to our attention *(non à notre identité mais à notre écoute)*. It is as though, in the presence of a few unknown intellectuals, it is still important for this immense nation to be recognized and understood, it is as though what is requested of foreign visitors is not the response of a militant agreement, but one of assent. ("Well," 116)

The scene as it is played does its best to be profoundly untheatrical; for Barthes, the expectation of "assent" rather than criticism seems to put China wholly outside the economy of the Western audience, and himself, as audience to that audience, outside such a role as well, without hysteria. And yet, in its description of this quiet space, the text is not without its own emotions: a sense of astonishment, of gratitude, perhaps, at the quality of attention given. Face to face with the "immense nation" of China, Barthes describes himself as an "unknown intellectual," but the felt disparity in importance does not return in the social relation, where Barthes is the one attended to, listened to.

Taken as a prescription, the moment, like the rest of *Alors,* is not without its problems, most notably its adherence to what Spivak identified in Kristeva as the Western intellectual's self-centeredness in the face of the other. Certainly *Alors* and *Empire* can be understood as typical of a Western confusion between one's cultural other and one's absolute other (that is: the Chinese equal what I am not). The degree to which the places Barthes describes obtain their signifying value from their being not-the-West can only result from his own peculiar *lack* of attention to the actual situations there. At the same time, one finds in Barthes an attentiveness to something that may never have been in any China except the one he saw. More so than any other text in this chapter—even Pleynet's diary—Barthes's text asks of the reader an attentiveness not to China itself but to Barthes's own experience and to the space within which he moves. That space may have nothing to do with China per se, but it has very much to do with a certain hallucination of China and a certain understanding of the conditions of social speech. If Barthes traveled, as it were, through a penumbra of zero-degree social discourse where all the meaning made was his, it was because of his insistent inattention to Maoist politics: the negativity of his hallucination was political. Rather than imbuing China with something—for instance, all the utopian possibilities of the revolution—Barthes gave it nothing. For him, more so than for anyone else on the trip, China was not really in the world; it was, like his Japan, a purely personal space.

Barthes's China is, as much as Wahl's—though in the other direction—outside the Telquelian mainstream of this period. The fall 1974 issue, titled "In China," offered *Tel quel*'s first responses to the trip. The issue opens with five articles, two unsigned, three signed by Sollers, that articulate a sense of China's continuing relevance and importance to the desired revolution. Beginning with an unsigned editorial whose final line asks, "ARE YOU GOING TO REVOLT? YES OR NO?" *Tel quel* stresses the Maoist obligation: "The study of Mao is in this case the number one imperative" (3). This political imperative remained part of *Tel quel*'s global vision through sometime around 1976.

Of the group, Sollers in this period most forcefully stresses the historical weight of *actual* China and its effects on the general practice of beliefs. Armed with a sense that fear and repression motivated Europe's lack of interest in China, Sollers again and again offers China as the only alternative—ideological, political, sexual, poetic—to Western thought and civilization. At one point, he suggests that "until the Chinese revolution, *it wasn't certain*, historically, that Christianity would not remain the universal return of the repressed. Well, there it is, it's decided. The east wind wins out over the west wind" (11). And later, in an essay titled "La Chine sans Confucius" (China without Confucius), Sollers writes: "From my point of view, I would say that the religious and idealistic worldview that has always been that of *all* exploiters currently has only one serious enemy: China" (14).

Sollers fleshes out these political concerns with an interest in Chinese women. In "Quelques thèses" (A few theses), Sollers writes that the first question of the petit-bourgeois is always, "'what about sexual life in China?' Which one can understand this way: above all, tell me that obsessive neurosis remains central in all societies. Above all, tell me that there is no *woman* (which is to say: confirm that the phallic market—woman as object of exchange among men—isn't put into question) etc." (10). As in all other aspects of life, women in China represent an *other* system, have an other relation to sexuality and culture than that of Western women (Kristeva's two articles later in the same issue confirm this reading). For Sollers, Chinese women, like the rest of China, work best as a challenge to Western thinking. At the same time, however—like Barthes, like Kristeva—Sollers does remark on the role of women in Chinese theater: "is it a coincidence that the main characters in the operas are women, that it's women who are most often charged with taking care of the culture's memory?" ("Mao," 18). As in Barthes, the nagging feeling that something might be wrong here comes in the form of a question, a hesitant step that avoids a more directly critical reading.

In comparing the Sollers of this time to Barthes, one remarks the persistently political and dogmatic form of Sollers's discourse on China. Unlike Barthes's "negative hallucination," which attempted to invent a "China" that could work as an epistemological object with no clear ontological referent, Sollers's China remains profoundly and forcefully material, part of Sollers's interest in aggressively *worlding* a closed Europe. Sollers's ongoing interest in Maoism—articulated most fully in 1974's *On Materialism,* which reprinted several essays on Maoism (including "On Contradiction") as well as his translations of Mao's poetry—depended on and grounded an experience of China as in the world. In his essays in the fall 1974 issue of *Tel quel,* several anecdotes about his visit to China, quotations from Chinese people he met while there, and a brief discussion of Deng Xiaoping's recent statement to the United Nations all attest to that belief.

In keeping with Sollers's political narrative, Marcelin Pleynet in the same issue confirmed that *Tel quel*'s vision of China as a paradoxically real utopia remained alive and well. In "Pourquoi la Chine populaire?" (Why popular China?) Pleynet lays out the justification of *Tel quel*'s Chinese interest. In doing so, he attacks Wahl's "China without Utopia" and another essay, published in the journal *Esprit,* called "China without Lyricism."[31] Both essays attempted to present a China without the utopian or lyrical extravagances of the French Maoists, presenting instead a more "realistic" picture of China. Pleynet responds that any "realistic" approach to China must first face this undeniable fact: "China is a socialist, Marxist-Leninist, revolutionary country. All debates on the objectivity of the story or account of a trip to this country, can in no way abstract this fact" (32). And yet this fact can, in Europe, only be studied in an abstract fashion, by reading the work of Mao Zedong. Hence the need for a trip to China:

> It required the sensory experience of a three-week trip for the concepts [of Maoism], now become concrete reality, to find their true dimensions. Who speaks of utopia, of lyricism? . . . Three weeks in China taught me to understand the effectively political dimension of this utopia (this non-topia), this lyricism: that of language, of a thought, capable of displacing itself in a dialectical leap from its own "utopia" to its topic; shouldn't the first thing one does be to give oneself the means to make progress? (33)

Yes, Maoism is both lyrical and utopian, Pleynet argues. But in China, that utopianism and lyricism are given a real dimension through the political activity of the Chinese people; they become *facts.* Under Mao's direction, the Chinese can move from "utopia" to a "topic," a reality. The real "progress" of the Chinese people is thus linked to the "means" Mao provides; the relationship between these two things is not direct but dialectical. So anyone who wants to talk about China without lyricism or utopia—especially when they do so in the name of the historical facts—misunderstands the basic historical fact of Maoism, which is lyrical, utopian, and real all at once. Wahl's argument is patently incompatible with the fact of Chinese Communism as it exists both in Mao's writing and in actual China.

Unlike Sollers's more directly political discourse, Pleynet's language here emphasizes the way that the literary (lyrical) and the political are, in China, irrevocably and equally entangled. Such a model effectively mirrors the group's own relation to China, in which their own utopian and lyrical thoughts work dialectically with Chinese reality. For Pleynet, the visit to China was necessary because it allowed thought to be hammered into shape in the forge of phenomenological experience, producing the combination of "revolution in action" and "revolution in language" that the group was trying to theorize. The trip was therefore intimately linked to avant-garde writing:

> This trip stemmed for me from the basis of an experience and a practice of modern poetic language, and from the consequences that such a practice must produce. I consider this trip to be logically (biographically) a consequence of a certain kind of practice of avant-garde writing, of which I must say that it has never been stopped but on the contrary has been taken up in the massive deployment of the battles through which the Chinese people, in the name of their independence and liberty, assault the sky. (39)

With this final image, Pleynet enacts the simultaneously literary and political nature of his interest in China. The phrase "assault the sky" is both lyrical and utopian, and adds to the real activity of the Chinese people the metaphorical dimension Pleynet felt it had.

The fall 1974 "In China" issue was to prove the high-water mark of *Tel quel*'s interest in China and Maoism and the acme of its dual conception of China. In the years following the return from Beijing, *Tel quel*'s China—once solid enough to support a revolutionary politics and aesthetics—melted away under the pressures of global history (including the revelation of the atrocities of the Cultural Revolution) and changes in the group's theoretical and aesthetic interests. As time passed, political China faded from *Tel quel*'s table of contents. A 1975 editorial still asked, "Who is refusing the living questions about China, and especially the questions asked here about China?" (5). But *Tel quel* itself was no longer posing those questions. Sollers published two more translations from Mao in *Tel quel*'s issue 66, but in October 1976, Sollers wrote in *Le Monde*, "On the subject of the situation in China today, one mustn't, in my opinion, speak of 'doubts' or 'worries,' but of genuine drama" (qtd. in Forest, 483–84).[32] In the winter 1976 issue of *Tel Quel*, the following note appeared on the journal's last page, under the heading "About 'Maoism'":

> Information continues to appear, here and there, on *Tel quel*'s "Maoism." Let's make it clear that if *Tel quel* did, for a time, attempt to affect opinions about China, largely in order to oppose itself to the PCF's systematic deformations, it cannot but continue to do the same today. For a while, in fact, our journal has been the object of attacks by "real Maoists." We cheerfully grant them the title. The events currently in progress in Beijing can only open even the most hesitant eyes to what one must call the "Marxist struc-

ture," whose sordid manipulations of power and information can now be verified. . . . Myths must be finished with; *all* myths. (104)

The final two sentences here call up Wahl and Barthes, respectively. *Tel quel* now seems willing to posit the existence of a "Marxist structure" that governs both the Soviet Union and Communist China, which is what Wahl had argued all along. At the same time, the demand that myths be finished refers not only to political myths but orientalist ones; Barthes's "negative" valuation of China would in such a rubric be one possible response.

After its rejection of Maoism, the group never regained the political engagement that had driven it in the late 1960s and early 1970s. Instead the journal returned to the more primarily aesthetic concerns of its earliest issues—concerns it had never abandoned—and ceased to articulate itself as part of a recognizably political movement. On this subject Philippe Forest provides the most eloquent narrative:

> It is possible that, in the Chinese estrangement, something secret and decisive on which the future of *Tel quel* depended played itself out. Julia Kristeva gives it voice: "A group holds through mania, one calls it enthusiasm. Bizarrely, it's the febrile, and, in short, factitious enthusiasm of the Chinese that dislocates the mania of their pilgrimage. [*Tel quel*] would perhaps survive the return from China, but its spirit certainly would not. Mania was diverging into skepticism; the group was exploding" [*Samouraïs*, 251]. The voyage of April 1974, as we would see, would not announce the writing of any *Mea Culpa;* there would be no thundering revelation of a "return" from China. But, more subtly, the Telquelians abandoned somewhere between Beijing and Xi'an that which gave their political passion its sense. (478)

Forest is not alone in construing *Tel quel*'s post-1974 period as one of "abandonment"; Marx-Scouras writes that after 1974, *Tel quel* "relinquishes" the dream of revolution and "abandons" its Marxism (180). Ffrench, for his part, attributes the rejection of Marxism in part to *Tel quel*'s new theory of "exceptions," in which no collectivity is possible. He writes that the "dissolution of *Tel quel*'s Marxism is determined as much by the internal logic of the thought and practice of the review as by the general disillusionment with the Left in France at this time" (207).

Whither China? The disappearance of the geopolitical reference coincides with the dissolution of *Tel quel*'s Marxist politics. Those politics gone, the group itself dissolves into its constituent parts, becoming a set of individuals only loosely joined by an undefinable aesthetic project. Or, perhaps, this is the way it always was. The end of *Tel quel*'s interest in actual China—which came so quickly on the heels of the group's having been there—also marks the end of the dual conception of China that had sustained and driven that interest. The fall 1974 issue's vibrant defense of the utopian, lyrical possibilities of the Chinese revolution would turn out to be the last gasp of *Tel quel*'s China.

POSTMORTEMS: 1979–90

Pleynet's 1980 *Le voyage en Chine* offered the first wholesale revision of *Tel quel*'s Chinese experience. The book contains Pleynet's diary entries from the 1974 trip and a preface, dated 1979, that offers the reader advice on how to read the diary. *Voyage* thus comes out of two times simultaneously: while the journal entries are written in the present tense of 1974, the book's preface treats them as part of the historical past. This dissociation does not remain unexplained, but the text bears the mark of time uncomfortably. If he has not published these journal entries until now, Pleynet writes, it is because he had for a long time not been able to read them: "I was reading them, in fact, from the perspective of what I had wanted to believe, at all costs, about the destiny of modern China. That is, from a perspective to which they only barely testify" (14). In other words, the journal, written in 1974, nonetheless represents opinions about China that Pleynet can only publicly articulate in 1979. The preface thus asks the reader to read the journals *out of time,* that is, into the same time as the preface—a time after the dissolution of Pleynet's Maoism and the abandonment of political China.

In closing down the historical distance between 1974 and 1979, the preface argues for the integrity and value of the journal entries *in the present*—not as relics of an earlier and dated relation to China but as evidence of a still-valuable and important literary thought. The preface does this largely by distinguishing between a political or Maoist relation to China and a literary one, effectively splitting *Tel quel*'s China in two. The political relation, whose mode is reportorial or investigative, will, Pleynet writes, inevitably succumb to Communist Party propaganda, either by repeating it or by refuting it. Neither case can produce anything but the most clichéd travel narrative: "Considering the conditions under which the trips took place, and the state of affairs in China today, is it possible to do otherwise? Everything also doubtless depends on what one goes looking for, and I have to say that I myself was taken in by the conventional protocol of such trips. Two articles published in *Tel quel* after my return carry its unmistakable trace" (13).

In one of those 1974 articles, Pleynet had praised the direct and productive dialogue between the French visitors and their Chinese hosts by quoting from Barthes: "It seemed to me that, as R. Barthes wrote in *Le Monde,* our Chinese hosts were especially attentive, 'unusually attentive, not to our identity but to our attention,' and that every encounter or visit we had was determined first of all by the quality of that attentiveness" ("Pourquoi la Chine populaire?" 34). In the *Voyage* preface, the dialogic table has turned:

> If it weren't for, I must say, the peculiar manner in which a writer, or better yet a poet, has of apprehending the spectacle of the world, if it weren't to some degree for the defenses of that eccentricity, I wouldn't have brought back anything else from China. But this eccentricity created a situation where, in a certain way, I was never completely the person to whom the Chinese politicians and unionists were speaking. I could hear, obviously, the grounds and logic of their speeches, which even convinced me sometimes. But, as frequent, repetitive, and hammering as the speeches were, my living relationship to the reality they represented remained somewhere else, completely other. (14)

Pleynet reveals the Chinese as essentially incapable of "attending" to him, since they never actually speak to him, but only to some political version of him. The shift from a political (and blind) relation to China—exemplified in Pleynet's stridently Maoist and Leninist 1974 essays—to a literary one allows Pleynet to *see through* the Chinese political performance, or even to see it as performance in the first place. Pleynet's view of the "spectacle of the world" works in part because it allows him to stand, *as an audience member,* in front of those who do not even know they're part of the spectacle. It is not simply that the Chinese misrecognize Pleynet and he recognizes them, but also that he recognizes them in their misrecognition.

The experience of China offered in the preface, and designed to condition the reading of the journal entries, is therefore an experience of profound otherness—not that of the Chinese, but of Pleynet himself, adrift in a world where the vast majority of signification means nothing to him. Such an experience is deeply incompatible with the engagement of a political Maoism and the desire for revolution right here right now. Pleynet's preface invites the reader to effectively separate political China from Pleynet's experience. As Ffrench remarks, it is only once the political intensity faded that the "singular experience of the writer had become a point of interest in the Chinese context" (205).

Pleynet begins by describing his discomfort with what he had originally felt as the political purpose of the trip. He says he felt totally bewildered and out of place in China: "I very quickly found myself too far out of my element to reconcile whatever was familiar (Western) about the Marxist arguments put forth by our Chinese interlocutors with my own presence in this faraway country, much less an even more faraway culture and a past" (*Voyage*, 14). In his 1974 articles on Chinese Maoism, Pleynet had written from a position of mastery about the meaning of China and its revolution. Here, his approach is more classically orientalist. Western Marxism seems absurd or ineffectual next to China's history, its culture, and its unbridgeable *distance* (Pleynet is "too far" from his element). China thus regains (or had perhaps never lost) all the attributes of its classic otherness—its endless history, its artful culture, and its difference from Europe—that had been erased in the approximations of Pleynet's Maoism.[33]

This clear separation between a political China and a literary/cultural one would have been impossible to publish in *Tel quel* in 1974. It was, however, Pleynet's experience—or his memory of that experience—and it cannot be described in the language of the political essay. It is in this mood that Pleynet turns toward literature: "I have, therefore, in seeking to transcribe the strongest emotional moments of the trip into a poetic language, borrowed as though naturally a poetic form I would call translated from the Chinese" (*Voyage*, 15). China itself—not political China, but literary/cultural China—gives Pleynet the voice he needs to express his experience. The poems that result are interspersed throughout *Le voyage en Chine*, and testify to Pleynet's investment in a China whose particulars resemble the 1915 Ezra Pound far more than the 1974 *Tel quel*.

The value of the poetic form, taken from classical Chinese literature, leads Pleynet to a wholesale dismissal of contemporary, Maoist China: "Though Marxist rationality might explain history, it will never grant it either reality or weight, and man, lost in the forest of characters and symbols belonging to an ancient world, seized by truth, will never fail to project himself, to implicate himself in the description and reinvention of the thousand fables that bear, we all know, the traces of his life and his culture" (15). With his dismissal of Marxism, Pleynet effects a return to the traveler's individual experience, and recognizes that his understanding of China comes of necessity through his own needs and histories. This marks, in its literary commitments, a turn toward the position Barthes held all along, in which the meaning of the Chinese experience does not flow through the great events of geopolitical history but rather according to the demands of an individual psyche essentially inimical to politics.

Before coming to a reading that tries to read Pleynet where he is, it is worth noting that what we can see—and what he presumably could not see—is the way in which his narrative picks up so many of the traditional tropes of orientalism, or orientalism-as-Maoism, in Chow's sense. In particular Pleynet's description of man as lost in a "forest of characters and symbols belonging to an ancient world" seems typical of a return to a well-nigh Poundian vision of classical China.[34] So while *Le voyage en Chine* demands to be read as an individual and literary experience of China, one can also see it as a common one, repeated any number of times by any number of travelers or writers who demand that the Chinese represent for them the good that they cannot find in the West. In such a reading, we understand Pleynet's experience not through the lens of individuality but that of history, and rightly explain it by pointing to the general history of orientalism, which leads us to the history of colonialism, and colonial desire, and through that to the general encounter between China and the West.

To see the experience as an individual, literary one requires, then, a sort of refraction, in which we try to bend our current historical vision to the demands of Pleynet's own text. In that text, the return to France is also a turn to a new historical awareness, one produced by the felt immensity of the Chinese landscape. Pleynet writes: "Upon returning to Dreux I see the spire of the cathedral at Chartres, which I want to see again today to understand, or not to understand—that which, above and beyond the news (the presidential elections), mingles in and out of the great human adventures in the kind of giant documents (caught up in the passage of centuries) that we carry, that we live, most often maybe, at ground level" (122). In this moment, the Chartres cathedral becomes something like the Chinese countryside or the Great Wall, an object that testifies to the passage of geologic time across the human time of each individual life. The Chinese experience—regardless of what it may say about China, really—grants Pleynet a new vision, a defamiliarizing vision, in which daily life suddenly takes on the tint of its own macrohistory, even as that macrohistory's permutations work themselves out in the dailiness of living. Is China—real China—necessary to such a vision? For Pleynet, even as he moved toward an abandonment of his "Chinese" politics, the answer appears to be "yes."

In 1981, Sollers published his interview with Shu-hsi Kao, "Pourquoi j'ai été chinois" (Why I was Chinese), in what would prove to be one of *Tel quel*'s last issues.[35] The interview is preceded by a 1974 photograph of Sollers in China, standing among three larger-than-life Buddhist statues, whose presence testifies to China's legacy as more than simply the "indefensible engagement" of *Tel quel*'s Maoism (Forest, 484). In the interview, Sollers takes up a historical position that places the trip, his early novels, and *Tel quel*'s Maoism firmly in the past. He does not do so to disavow all of *Tel quel*'s commentary on China, but rather to place its varying aspects within a nonutopian historical narrative. He is able in the interview to separate a series of mistakes made around China from what he continues to argue were good ideas coming out of *Tel quel*'s Chinese interest. This allows him to retain most of the essential features of *Tel quel*'s fascination with China at the level of culture and literature.

Any reading of "Why I Was Chinese" must take account of its title. In French *chinois* has two meanings; while in its most common usage it means "of or from China," it can also mean "complicated, bizarre, excessively subtle" (something like what "Greek" means in "It's all Greek to me"). More specifically, *Chinois* with a capital *C* is a noun that means "male Chinese person," while *chinois* (lowercase *c*) as a noun refers to the Chinese language, and as an adjective means both "of China" and "complicated." In Sollers's title it is used as a lowercase adjective, but it is not clear in which sense.

All this is troubled further by what Sollers says about Chinese. Writing of the "emptiness" of certain aspects of Chinese thinking, Sollers remarks on the apparently "other logic . . . in what is called Chinese thought [*la pensée chinoise*], thought that seems to be of an other order or an other nature. For me, it seems to come from inside me, spontaneously, even though I don't look Chinese [*bien que je n'aie pas l'air d'être chinois*]. So it's strange for a Westerner to not find among the coordinates of his own culture something that he finds instead completely clearly in an oriental one" (24). Sollers here contrasts two states: first, that of knowing "Chinese thought" from the inside by virtue of being natively Chinese, and second, that of knowing "Chinese thought" from the inside as a Westerner. Sollers argues that the second condition is his, that he "spontaneously" knows something that resembles "Chinese thought" in that it offers an "other logic" or an "other order." Although to say "resembles" is not quite right; it is unclear whether Sollers believes that what he comes to know is the *same* as Chinese thought, or simply *like* it. In any case, for most people, being culturally Chinese grants access to the other logic. For Sollers it comes counterculturally.

Crucial to either interpretation is that there exists something called "Chinese thought," which demonstrates a nature or logic fully "other" to a traditionally Western one. How Chinese—in the sense of being from China—is this thought? Later Sollers says of his practice of writing: "The stakes of this kind of writing would only be completely comprehensible one day by starting with Chinese. It's not that people will understand the book [*Nombres*] just because they learn Chinese. But if a Chinese person managed to detach himself completely from the language . . ." (28).[36] Here being Chinese seems to get in the way of understanding the "other" logic of Chinese thought expressed in the Chinese character (and transitively in *Nombres*). And learning Chinese (presumably as a Westerner) does not guarantee an understanding of it—it is a necessary condition, not a sufficient one. Rather the "other" logic of Chinese writing (which Sollers takes throughout the interview to be identical with Chinese thought) is accessible via a certain "detachment," a detachment that depends nonetheless on knowing Chinese. It is about, it seems, a certain estrangement, so that one has to come to Chinese as a stranger (whether as non-Chinese, like Sollers, or as a "detached" Chinese person) in order to grasp the particular logic of this thought.[37] In such a scenario, the "Chineseness" Sollers approaches may have little to do with real China, but real China is no longer really in play here, except as a geographical marker for an idea. One might remark here on the difference between Sollers and Brecht. The latter, experiencing alienation in front of the Chinese theater, imagined a "Chinese" audience that experienced the same thing—for Brecht the "Chinese" audience was actually, legally, ethnically Chinese. For Sollers, a Chinese mode of thought has little to do, in 1981 at least, with actual China—in fact the less it has to do with real China the better.

Given Sollers's claims to have access to this Chineseness, why does he say he *was* Chinese, past tense? His continuing sense of Chinese writing as offering a site of logical (natural, ordered) otherness is remarkably consonant with the classically reversed ethnocentrism of his earliest positions on Chinese writing. What has changed, however, is his political detachment, which shapes the interview's role as a commentary on, and repudiation of, *Tel quel*'s Maoist politics. The Chinese person who knows Chinese but cannot "detach" himself from language might be understood as prototypically Chinese—that is, as having a fixed national and cultural identity. Sollers, in this interview, offers himself as a detached (and estranged) subject not once but twice: first in his claim that, though he grew up in the West, his thought has always had an "other" logic (so he is detached from the West), and second in his disavowal of Maoism (so he is detached from China). In both cases Sollers is concerned to separate something that might be called "Chinese thought" from China itself, and through this to retain the specificities of his thought while shedding the historical burden of China. Such a position contrasts dramatically with the writing that appeared in the *Tel quel* of the early to middle 1970s, in which China and its politics (sometimes even its geography, its mountains and rivers) were taken as the natural and original source of Chinese philosophy. It is for this reason that the tone of the interview—as well as the attitude in critical appraisals of it, which seem to take it more or less at face value—presents "*Tel quel* and China" as part of a historical past that has been refuted by the present. This is true not only at the level of Maoism (the revelation of the Cultural Revolution's atrocities) but also for *Tel quel* as a collective enterprise (whose unity has now been dispersed).

"Why I Was Chinese," even as it suggests the end of an era, also offers indications that China—as a notion rather than a nation—was alive and well for Sollers in 1981. But the notion of China Sollers appears to hold in "Why I Was Chinese" is not the same one he had in 1974. While things that are Chinese (in nationality) continue to exist, "China" is no longer the exclusive name of his "Chineseness" (in the figurative sense). That is, the figure of "China" no longer denotes a major theoretical approach to geography or an understanding of the relation between aesthetics and politics, the word and the world. Instead, "China" in 1981 seems to mean something like what most people mean by "China"—an actual geographic space identified with a particular cultural history. This is not to say that Sollers had abandoned the literary principles that had driven his avant-garde writing in the 1960s and 1970s (on the contrary, his novel *Paradis,* published serially in *Tel quel* until 1981, is the most extravagantly literary of his works to that point). But those principles did not of necessity have a geographic location, and did not therefore come under the name of China, even though they resembled a "Chinese" logic. Thought had escaped geography.

Perhaps the clearest symptom of Sollers's shift is his take on Chinese politics, where he finally raises the question of woman. In a discussion of the aftermath of the Cultural Revolution, Sollers remarks on the trial of Jiang Qing, Mao's widow and one of the Gang of Four accused of being behind the revolution's disasters. His concern, muted in 1974, that "it's women who are most often charged with taking care of the culture's memory" ("Mao," 18), here returns with a vengeance. Sollers remarks that Jiang Qing is being made the scapegoat for China's desire to repress the Cultural Revolution: "there's the fact that it's the widow of the Great Man, and that, consequently, there is something there that is probably intolerable for Chinese society, sexually" ("Pourquoi," 23). The revolutionary possibility of Chinese women has disappeared or been obscured; the 1974 suggestion that Chinese women were somehow outside the Western phallic economy is no longer in effect. Sollers's claim that Jiang Qing's being female is "intolerable" sexually marks China with the same Freudian structures familiar to him in the West. Sollers: "What seems completely symptomatic, recently, is that in the end Chinese history becomes a history of women. The symptom has become feminine" (23).[38]

The split between political China and aesthetic "Chineseness," first figured in Pleynet and given full voice in Sollers, finds itself carried to its apotheosis in Kristeva's later writings about *Tel quel*'s Chinese period. It requires, as with Pleynet, a rewriting of the trip's motivations and purpose designed to erase its Maoism. On the subject of Mao in particular, Kristeva writes in a 1984 essay that "Joseph Needham . . . had no trouble convincing me that Mao, poet and writer, was the most faithful modern version of ancestral Taoism" ("Memory's Hyperbole," 275). Mao is not identified with his political role at all; instead Kristeva names him a poet and writer, and associates him with the philosophical religion of Taoism. It is Mao's role as a "modern version" of an ancient Chinese thought that makes him appealing; this principle in general is taken to have guided the 1974 trip: "it was classical China, dressed in the worker's blue suit of socialism, that we had gone to find, more interested in Ming tombs or Buddhist steles than in the stories . . . of the friendly Chinese activist comrades" (275). The emphasis on Chinese *history* as opposed to the *stories* told by the friendly comrades reveals, in the difference between the singularity of the former and the plurality of the latter, something of the reverence for China's past accompanied by a "realpolitikal contempt" Spivak describes in her "French Feminism" essay.

Kristeva confirms Sollers's discussion of *Tel quel*'s political dissolution, writing that "for most of the Paris-Peking-Paris travelers . . . this arduous journey, one that from the outset was more cultural than political, definitively inaugurated a return to the only continent we had never left: internal experience" (275). As with Sollers and Pleynet, Kristeva here rejects the political part of the China trip but retains its value at the cultural and individual levels, as the opportunity to experience individually a quasi-didactic strangeness whose effects she continues to feel. That moment lives on: "I loved—I still love—to lose myself, as in a dream, in the characters of Chinese texts that my professor at Jussieu had rudimentarily taught me" (275). Here the dream is named at last: it is where you lose yourself, a space produced not, it would seem, by any actual relation to China, but rather by the relation between Kristeva and China, between her sense of self and her sense of strangeness.

In the 1984 essay, Kristeva also seemed to promise a fuller accounting of her trip to China. Writing that she was only presenting "visible surface effects," she remarked, "Only a diary, a novel, could perhaps one day restore the wild indecency of it" (275). Kristeva's *Les Samouraïs*, which includes a fantasy-sequence in which the Roland Barthes character is arrested and tried in China for propositioning a young man, partakes fully of both the personal and the wildly indecent.[39] The autobiographical novel, published in 1990, is less an explanation than an embrace of Kristeva's relation to China. The 1984 essay "My Memory's Hyperbole" had read like a history; *Les Samouraïs* has an unrestrained, baroque feel. Stylistically, it resembles at times 1974's *Des Chinoises,* but is frequently more personal, offering impressions of China concerned less with the female protagonist Olga's role as a representative of Western feminism and more with her individual experience. In *Les Samouraïs* "China" names a relation to the self rather than a political response to the world.

Such a conception is already visible in the title of the section dealing with the trip: "Chinese." On the section's second page, Kristeva explicitly recalls the word's figurative meaning in French:

> Besides, what could be more "Chinese"—bizarre, aberrant, lunatic—than China? To tear one's self away from oneself through the Chinese. To break the mask of conformity. To dive, not just to the roots . . . but beyond them, into total unrootedness. To discover a counteridentity. To rejoin one's own absolute foreignness under the form of a giant as civilized as it is behind the times: the atomic bomb of demography, the genetic Hiroshima of the twenty-first century. (196)[40]

The meaning of "Chinese" in quotes is given by Kristeva—bizarre, aberrant, lunatic—before she comes to China. The figurative and the literal are thus reversed, so that the trip to China becomes not a search for the political realities there but a hunt for lunacy, aberrance, an experience fully outside the self, any self, and into the foreign confines of one's own mind. "Chineseness" thus becomes the primary rather than the secondary meaning of "China."

At the same time, Kristeva's differentiation between China and Chineseness distinguishes precisely a constructed European notion of "China" (in scare quotes) from real China. In acknowledging the double meaning of *chinois* in between dashes, she also recognizes that its figurative meaning figures importantly in the construction of the Western conception of China, so that for the West, China is always already "Chinese." Such a formulation recalls Eliot's differentiation between the as such and the as we know it, and Said's distinction between the "brute reality" of the Orient and the West's "representation." Unlike Eliot and Said, Kristeva makes that distinction explicit by refusing a sense of China as the true and original model for invented "China," the original from which the copy came. The value of the "China"/China pair thus lies not with actual China (and its demographics, its modernity) but with an understanding of actual China that uses literary tropes to make it an oneiric object. Kristeva does not say "China has many people," but "China is a demographic atomic bomb." A sense of China as "Chinese" (in the sense of bizarre, extravagant) flows from the second version only, and imbues actual China with all the qualities of its mythic, dreamed version.

In keeping with her interest in Chineseness as a property not of China but of the West, Kristeva in *Les Samouraïs* extends and relishes a personal identification with Chineseness. The novel's female protagonist is Olga, a Bulgarian intellectual who has moved to Paris and become involved with the avant-garde literary journal *Maintenant* (Now). The novel is narrated largely by an omniscient third person, but includes as well journal entries from another woman who attends *Maintenant* meetings and reports watching Olga listening to her lover, editor Hervé Sinteuil, talk about Mao: "I watch her face while Hervé tells us about Mao's poetry. Her Asiatic features are impenetrable; she really does look Chinese" (189). Later, visiting Buddhist caves in Longmen, a Chinese woman asks Olga a question in Chinese; Olga begins to reply and her accent gives her away: the woman runs away shouting "Foreigner! Foreigner!" Olga is delighted: "She thought I was Chinese!" (250). In both these instances the outside observer (one French, one Chinese) find in Olga's features something genetically Chinese. In the first, the observer remarks not that Olga looks like a Chinese person *(une Chinoise)*, but rather that she looks "Chinese" *(chinoise)*, with its attendant dual meanings. In the second, the Chinese woman takes in Olga's "Asiatic features" and mistakes her for one of her own. Kristeva indicates Olga's pleasure in the misidentification; unlike the others on the trip, Olga is eager to identify with China and Chinese people. This is so in part because Olga has a strong sense of the Chineseness inside her. As it gets articulated in the real, a trip to China gives Olga an opportunity to ask questions about her own identity: "Not 'who am I,' but, in a more meditative, more intellectual way: what are the extreme faces, the *chinoiseries* that I feel in myself and cannot formulate?" (197). In other words, going to China (or being mistaken for Chinese) offers Olga a vision of the places where her self does not hold together but remains foreign, strange, impenetrable.

In the quotation above, Kristeva makes *chinoiseries* a synonym of "extreme faces" by putting them next to one another, calling up the series of references to her looking Chinese. Even in *Des Chinoises* Kristeva had remarked that she "owe[d] her cheekbones to some Asian ancestor" (12). In *Les Samouraïs*, looking Chinese continues to have very much to do with access to the logic of estrangement in which Kristeva interests herself. There is no question, then, that Kristeva's facial resemblance, even genetic heritage, relative to ethnic Chinese, constitutes a central image and metaphor in her articulation of her own right to and interest in strangeness. Compare this construction of interest in the "other logic" of "Chinese thought" with Sollers's remark that he has access to Chinese thought even though he does not "look Chinese." Sollers's argument is that understanding the other logic of Chinese writing requires a detachment from culture and ethnicity rather than a connection to it. (Recall here Pound's statement, "Serious approach to Chinese doctrines must start with wiping off any idea that they are merely Chinese" [*Selected Prose,* 83].) Kristeva—both in *Des Chinoises* and *Les Samouraïs*—offers a completely different relation to China, one in which she literally *projects* (throws) herself into the scene of otherness.

Olga's thinking in this way is repeatedly presented in *Les Samouraïs* as an intellectual choice rather than a matter of temperament. In one sequence, in the village of Huxian—the same place whose description opens *Des Chinoises*—Olga is overwhelmed by the paintings of a Chinese woman who, with no formal training, produces work whose aesthetic is a long way from the propagandist socialist realism elsewhere in China. Olga asks her how she does it; the woman responds: "I don't paint what I see, but after I've slept. When I come home from the fields, I'm tired, I dream a lot, always in color; when I wake up, I paint what I've seen in my dreams. Well, not completely: I can't remake the dream exactly; the painting represents rather something that doesn't exist and which is between my dream and my life at work" (235). Olga is amazed; this woman, with no formal schooling, appears to be articulating exactly her own theoretical training, giving voice to the grounding principles of Olga's aesthetic vision. The character Sylvain (like Marcelin Pleynet a critic of painting) is amused: "Let's not exaggerate, Sylvain said in the same playful tone, are you seduced by this lady or by your own vision?" (236).

Sylvain here articulates the classic criticism of *Tel quel*'s trip to China, namely that in looking East, it simply found a way of exteriorizing the ideas that belonged to its own particular vision. The "discovery" of a Chinese peasant who speaks precisely the understanding of the space in between dreams and life necessary for the group's theoretical conception of China strikes Sylvain, as it has many critics in the real world, as too much of a happy coincidence, a simple projection onto the other of one's own wishes. Against this, however, Kristeva presents Olga's thought as the product of a decision taken with open eyes rather than an exoticizing blindness.[41] As Sylvain explains at length why these peasant painters cannot produce anything like a Cézanne or a Mondrian, Olga withdraws from the conversation: "Sylvain, always so demanding. . . . And in the end, he wasn't wrong. But what good did it do, if it kept him from appreciating that which arises without doing violence to custom, but still lets itself go to the laws of dreams?" (238).

The distinction between truth and utility is crucial to Kristeva's understanding of the China trip for the characters of *Les Samouraïs*. The three young men on the trip—Sylvain, Hervé, and Stanislas Weil (Wahl)—continually exhibit a suspicion, at times derisive, regarding especially China's self-presentation with regards to modernity, industry, culture, and politics. For them, the Chinese dream disappears in the very moment of coming to its place; while Hervé, for instance, frequently expresses amazement and interest in China and its culture, he and Sylvain together frequently make fun of the group's interpreters, or remark that the historical presentations describing China's ancient matriarchy are "too harmonious to be true" (247).[42] Olga at one point complains that Hervé turns everything into a pretext for joking around. But the novel, through Olga, does not criticize the truth of the men's sentiments, or the arguments that ground them. *Les Samouraïs* appears to argue for an alternative based not on realism but on dreaming, attentive not to historical knowledge or political development but to the incommensurable foreignness of being.

Such a position, in keeping with the extravagant style of *Les Samouraïs,* explodes through and beyond the simple treatment given it in "My Memory's Hyperbole":

> China came in to take the place of an anti-origin, the deepest, the most ancestral, the race of ancestors with slanted eyes, but also the most unreal, therefore the most painless, impersonal, without childish colors, just a puzzle of mirages. A kind of theater of identities where one takes up masks to evoke the essential, while the masks just disorganize everything supposed fundamental. (197)

The memory returns us, hyperbolically, to the site of the theater, which seems able, in various moments, to stand in for the general trajectory of *Tel quel* and China. For Kristeva, the "theater of identities" produced by the experience of China seems to reflect the whole world of social relations, in which unreality itself is a condition both of the essential and its disorganization. Here as elsewhere, the reference to theater indicates not merely a sense of China as theatrical, but more importantly, of self as audienced, as given meaning by and through the experience of being China's living spectator. The identity disrupted by the taking up of masks is Kristeva's; the fundamental disrupted is that "supposed" by European, not Chinese, culture.

It is precisely such an experience—the sense of China itself as alive, and of the self as interpellated by that aliveness—that differentiates Kristeva's *Les Samouraïs* from "My Memory's Hyperbole." In "My Memory's Hyperbole," the experience of China itself is deemed only marginal to the intellectual insights of its Taoism or its writing system. *Les Samouraïs*, whose recollection one might truly call hyperbolic, approaches in its style and its emotional weight the earlier writing about China, including *Des Chinoises,* that experienced the trip as an earthquake measured on some Richter scale of the Western mind.

Nowhere is this clearer than in *Les Samouraïs'* final evaluation of the experience of Huxian. In the novel, the scene appears much as it does in *Des Chinoises:* the foreigners arrive to face a crowd whose gaze indicates an absolute disconnection from common humanity. Hervé remarks that the Chinese "exclude us from their visual field, while we try to include them in our thoughts. Are these as different as they seem? Or is it just two ways of dismissing the Unknown?" (232). Olga is left with the same experience of total otherness that surges from the pages of Kristeva's *Des Chinoises.* But *Les Samouraïs* does not find the experience quite as revolutionary as did *Des Chinoises*—there remains little of the sense of wonderment at the bursting of China into the real world. Instead it is a reminder of what Olga already knows. As Olga ponders what to do in the face of an experience of total otherness, the novel gives two possibilities. They appear not at the end of the "Chinese" section, but in the beginning of the next one, in some sense already outside the frame of reference given by 1974:

> Either you fold yourself into a disabused and solitary contemplation of the world in which you yourself are a hanger-on, because capable of whipping your own bitterness to the point of sympathetic irony, thanks to champagne, a martini, or any other comparable help.

Or you continue your voyage toward other Huxians, to show all the extraterrestrials who surround you the thing you knew all along, but of which they seem unaware: just like Huxian, the world is made up of incommensurable isolations.

Olga chose the second solution. (284)

"Huxian" here becomes the universal name of the thing "China" stood in for: the place where, when you go there, you feel you are not at home. The Chinese experience, so dramatic and breathtaking in its 1974 version, has turned to a simpler, less spectacular knowledge. In its awareness of the world's incommensurable isolations, the text abandons the Chinese dream by relegating its utopianism fully to the past; neither possibility can hold open the most intense wish of *Des Chinoises:* that this otherness might step across the divide that separates cultures and peoples and upend what the West thinks it knows. While in its "Chinese" section *Les Samouraïs* had at times recaptured the Chinese dream as it appeared in 1974, here that dream seems fully foreclosed, understood not as a missed opportunity but as an opportunity that never was. The memory of Huxian—"indestructible," Olga calls it—suggests that the trip to China occurred largely so that it could reveal, at the far end of history, its own ontological impossibility.

Conclusion

What seems naive about it all, ultimately, is the goal of the Chinese dream itself. At the century's twilight most of us were sophisticated enough to scoff at utopian pursuits, in China and elsewhere; today we favor smaller, more local interventions. I have tried in the last chapter to imagine, however, what it might have been like to have faith in a utopian vision, and to feel it coming alive, as it were, in the blood and roots of China. It is differently alive, I think, in different moments in the Telquelian trajectory, and is at its least interesting in that period when the group's political interest trumped its literary one—except in the case of Barthes, who maintained all along a disdain for the political stereotype. But when the dream does happen, it engages a hermeneutic that makes some unusual and interesting demands on our conception of the symbolic order. *Tel quel*'s "fact-finding" mission to China found, it would seem, few of the facts about the Cultural Revolution and Chinese politics; it did, however, produce a certain set of knowledge-objects that cannot be called "facts" in the traditional sense of the term.

All this is shaped, as it never was with Pound or Brecht, by the lived experience of geopolitical China. At various moments in the previous chapter I suggested that the relationship to classical China lasted longer than the Maoist one—a tendency visible most clearly in the abandonment of Communist China after 1976 or so, which did not substantially affect what I called in Pleynet's case a more "literary" relation (directed specifically toward classical China). This suggests that there may have been a fundamental incompatibility between a contemporary vision and an idealized notion of classical China (which is timeless, enduring, artful and subtle in its aesthetic, and so on), since *happenings* in contemporary China were able to disrupt or disturb the very timelessness of the classical China in question—especially, it would seem, when seen from up close. In the Telquelians' writing after 1976, the "choice" of China is inevitably described as stemming from an earlier interest in classical China or Taoism.[1]

Why this difference? It may have something to do with the referential stability of classical China, which unlike Communist China could not offer its practice as a counterexample to theory. The trip to China undid whatever fantasy the Telquelians had about contemporary China, but could not touch their sense of the deeply rooted radical potential of classical China. In the throes of their political relation, the Telquelians occasionally discovered the roots of the Cultural Revolution in the ancient and timeless Chinese past (in its unchanging writing system, in its mountains and rivers, or its prehistorical matriarchy). In so doing, they made the new revolution not especially revolutionary, but rather the natural outgrowth of China's ancient and inherent radical possibilities. The pastness of the past allowed for a less rigid relation between *Tel quel*'s "theory" and Chinese "practice."

Classical China was important for Pound and Brecht, too, though differently in each case. With a single exception, Pound never followed his derisive 1936 take on contemporary China with any commentary on its post-1949, Communist version, though he lived until 1972.[2] It is almost as though contemporary China simply did not exist for him, even as he continued to translate and retranslate the classic Confucian texts into English. As for Brecht, he seemed committed up to his death in 1956 to the possibilities of Chinese Communism, and declared Mao Zedong's *On Contradiction* to be 1954's "book of the year." At the same time he maintained an interest in classical Chinese philosophy and poetry, though his aesthetic or intellectual commitment to China never rose to the dizzying intensities of either Pound's or *Tel quel*'s. But even Brecht conceived of Chinese modernity as European—his careful planning of the setting for *The Good Person of Szechwan* testifies to his sense of European modernity as somehow disruptive of a classical China (with Peking Opera gods) already in place.[3] Later in life, perhaps the clearest instance of Brecht's fascination with China's "classical" modernity came when he translated Mao's poem "Snow," written in a classical style and translated by Brecht with the same strategies he had taken from Waley. Originally translated into German by Fritz Jensen as "Chinesische Ode" (Chinese ode), "Snow," a highly charged political poem in which Mao declares himself superior to China's early emperors, became in Brecht's hands "Gedanken bei einem Flug

über die Große Mauer" (Thoughts during a flight over the Great Wall").
Brecht's title highlights the coincidence of modernity (with "flight") and
ancient China (the Great Wall), implicitly comparing the long glance back
into Chinese history with the perspective afforded by an airplane flight
over its surface.[4]

In each case—Pound, Brecht, *Tel quel*—what appears to be at work is
the old story about classical China and its unchanging, mystical truths.
To the extent that each Westerner comes to China with its mythical
unchanging version already in place, such similarities are not surprising.
Even the assertion that China "enters without complexes into the modern
world" (Kristeva) posits a China already *there* doing the entering, a thing
totally outside both the world and its modernity, waiting to be seen, to be
acknowledged, to be made available. Perhaps, then, one could differentiate the three subjects of this book by remarking how each one conceives
differently of the force responsible for China's entrance into modernity:
for Pound, himself; for Brecht, the West; and for the Telquelians, the
Chinese themselves.

The "China" at work in these texts is stabilized by association with
classical China. Such stability is gained partially by a freedom from Western influence. For observers of China—both Chinese and Western—
since the mid-nineteenth century the process of modernization/Western-
ization essentially undoes China's ontological untouchability by
(allegedly) introducing economic, cultural, and technological *change* to a
previously immovable society. In comparison to its classical version, contemporary China (the only China the West has ever really known, in this
century or any other) is contaminated, shifting, and impure. The irony of
all this is that classical China's mythical stability makes it an incredibly
reproducible object. Classical China exists always as an object of knowledge rather than an object of experience. It is thus *available for thought*—
transportable to new contexts—in a way that is not as readily present for
notions of contemporary China, which can always be countered with the
"facts."

Indeed, the question of the geopolitical or economic *facts* returns
importantly here. Their status is intimately linked to the kind of "scientific" knowledge about the non-West that Roland Barthes believed best
located outside the field of a genuinely critical vision. Today an important and common critique of the West's Chinese dreams turns precisely

on such a distinction, arguing that the aesthetic, nonfactual side of a dreamed China is precisely what is wrong with it. Such a critique has been most elegantly made, to my mind, by Kojin Karatani. Karatani argues that a literary orientalism, even in its most respectful mode, fails to see other human beings as people. "Aesthetes," he writes, "think that kneeling before the beauty of the other is the same as respecting the other from an equal position" (152). The problem, Karatani argues, is that by granting some other culture the aura of aesthetic otherness requires "bracketing" other concerns, including those that might see individuals as more than objects of analysis or beauty. To Karatani's immense credit, his essay does not argue that all aestheticizing relations are morally wrong, just that they should sometimes stop to "unbracket" that which they have put aside in order to pursue their aesthetic or theoretical interests. It seems to me that such an attitude is a good model for thinking about Western writing on China, since it offers an opportunity to both understand and read the texts in the spirit in which they were written and to remember—occasionally or often—that what those writings gain (the ability to see a new "China," for instance) depends in large part on what they do not, or do not want to, see.

Karatani goes on to say that part of what the kind of aesthetic appreciation "kneeling before the beauty of the other" produces is something he calls, after Walter Benjamin, an "aura." In his essay on the work of art in the age of mechanical reproduction, Benjamin says that the art work's aura disappeared as a result of the technological possibility of reproducing it. Karatani responds: "But the truth is the opposite: It was mechanical reproduction that prompted an aura to emanate from artworks of the past. And this can be amplified further: It is the mechanization of production that endows handmade products with auras and changes them into art. . . . The point is that an aura does not exist in the object" (152). One can profitably think of "classical China" as something like the handmade work of art, since it develops an aura precisely at the moment when technological (and other) changes appear to make it irreproducible—so that "classical China" becomes the name of something that is irretrievably in the past, something that had to be lost for people to realize they ever had it.

The auratic appeal of classical China is one answer, I suppose, to the question that dogged the preface: why do Westerners interest themselves in China? But it is clearly also such a *general* answer that it brings up more questions than it resolves: Is everyone's classical China the same? If not, how do particular social circumstances in realpolitikal China affect particular instances of classical China? What about circumstances in Europe, or in the lives of individual authors? As soon as one names "classical China" part of the structure of Chinese dreams, all the most obvious questions immediately go to work, fragmenting whatever sense of generality might have been gained. (And in any case it is clear that the aura of classical China counts only as one factor among many.)

In the preface I suggested that such general answers to the "Why China?" question tend to produce, mistakenly in my view, some either ontological or quasi-ontological version of either the West or China in order to explain why natives of the former get interested in the latter. Such explanations attribute either to the West (via a generally supposed curiosity, or an imperialist drive to knowledge) or to China (via an enchanting mysteriousness, or an ancientness worthy of attention) the qualities necessary to provoke the West's interest in China.[5] Thus the answer to "Why China?" becomes something like, "Because it's so ancient and fascinating" on the one hand or, "Because the West's political and economic power made it possible or desirable to be so interested" on the other.

Both answers offer a certain kind of reading in advance of the text. The first, which years of critique have taught us to recognize as absurd, depends on some unprovable sense of what China "really" is. As an answer, it is the one also given in the texts, though rarely directly, of Pound and the Telquelians, as they turn to classical rather than contemporary China as the mark of Chinese Chineseness. It is easily readable into those texts in part because the texts themselves appear to believe in it. The second answer—the orientalism-critique one—essentially debunks the first by pointing out that any ontological construction of China necessarily stems from Western desire rather than from anything in China. For those who answer "Why China?" this way, "China" in Western texts is always something that the West makes up itself, something whose causes lie largely with the demands of Western aesthetics, thought, or political economy. At its most simplistic such an answer attributes the West's interest in China to a general ontological principle of the West itself—curiosity, a drive to knowledge, an imperialist vision— which layers itself on top of the particular social circumstances that produce the Western interest. A book attentive to the particular circumstances of Western interests in China in France and Britain might finally answer the question of why by naming all such interests "orientalist," while differentiating carefully between various kinds of orientalism. The fragmenting, specifying questions—Are all orientalisms alike? How different does one have to be from another before it becomes something other than orientalism?—reveal the limitations of such an approach.

It seems, even after this limited consideration, that any general answer to the "Why China?" question will be frustrating, because any answer that pays attention to specificity will have a hard time constructing a general theory that remains specific enough to be useful. Is "Why China?" a bad question? I have discussed the ways in which the question conceals a naturalized ideology of interests and expectations about Western interests in China, one I do not especially agree with. Beyond that, I have argued that two major types of general answers to the question essentially solve the problem by attributing to either China or the West an ontological stability that I do not believe they have. Part of my goal has been to suggest that there are other, better questions out there. Indeed this book might be thought of as an extended meditation on the kinds of questions one ought to ask about the representation of otherness when the side that does the representing is *(a)* part of a cultural or geopolitical dominant, and *(b)* identified positively with the otherness it represents. Inasmuch as there is a general theory of Chinese dreams at work here, it tries simply to cover some of the ground laid out by those criteria.

Each chapter leaves us with one or two crucial, almost-impossible questions whose possible answers shape the most essential directions of reading and criticism. For Pound, that question is about translation, and goes to the heart of what counts as "China": Who owns the Chineseness of China? The way one answers that determines how one takes Pound's *Cathay* (English product or Chinese one?). And that same question is, I think, behind Eliot's distinction between China "as such" and "as we know it," that is, between a China produced by European knowledge and one that exists in a reality belonging to the Chinese themselves. Reading through Pound's high-wire translations of Li Po in *Cathay* as well as the "sinified" style of his *Cantos,* one comes up against this question again and again, as the Poundian reading, though mistaken, takes its plunge into the heart of European thought *in the name of* Confucius and classical

China. In such a circumstance, what one confronts are the ethics of representation, which rewrite the same question in a slightly different form: How should people go about representing cultures to which they do not belong, across the divides of global power and oppression—especially when not representing is not a real possibility?

In the Brecht chapter, on the other hand, beyond the well-nigh blinding influence of Pound, the most interesting question raised lies precisely with otherness, or rather with the difference between *Befremdung* (strangeness) and *Verfremdung* (alienation)[6] as it applies to others in general and China in particular. Is it possible to look past the strangeness of otherness? Brecht's insouciance on the question of the Chinese everywhere *except* the A-effects essay offers him a way to stage what was a remarkably intense relation to China and Chinese thought as not much of a cross-cultural big deal. Indeed, the way Brecht managed to separate Chineseness from his own work probably accounts for his flying under the radar, as it were, of contemporary scholars on East-West comparative literature. But as I discussed in the chapter, Brecht's forceful, innovative theater—particularly *Der gute Mensch von Sezuan*—brings up precisely the sorts of questions about the value of Chineseness *as* strangeness that Brecht generally did not address in his own work. *Der gute Mensch* itself, then, both as Brecht worried about it before his own performances (as in the discussion of rice versus bread), and as it has been performed (as with the National Theatre production) continues to make relevant the question of how China looks on Western stages of all types.

For *Tel quel,* finally, the real question revolves around the appearance and use of dreams, of the relation between something like Barthes's mythical Japan and an actual 1974 car ride from Xi'an to Huxian. Is fantasy responsible to reality, and if so, how? The entire trajectory of *Tel quel's* China, from its most intense political iterations in the late 1960s and early 1970s ("Long live Mao Tse-tung's thought!") to the slow romance of memory in Kristeva's 1990 *Samouraïs* or the nostalgic revenge of Pleynet's diaries, revolves around the promise of a dream come true. China's betrayal—both its betrayal of the Telquelians and their betrayal of China—offers an astonishing instantiation of the stakes of imagination, hope, disappointment, and memory as the group experienced and articulated them over the course of several decades. In every instance, the shadow of realpolitikal China, with its undeniable historical facts (the most unpleasant of which *Tel quel* had plenty of opportunity to hear well before the 1974 trip), casts itself long over any judgment of the Telquelian theorization and use of "China" for their own political and aesthetic purposes in Paris. How one judges their fantasy against that reality drives any reading of those texts.[7]

More so than Brecht's or Pound's, the Telquelian interest in China resonates with the "Chinese dreams" of the title, perhaps because in their repudiation of China the Telquelians give the appearance of a certain "waking up" (even though Pleynet's continued commitment to classical China and Kristeva's hyperbolic haze of memory suggest the ongoing pull of a certain dreamlike interest). But Brecht and Pound are dreaming as well, as long as one understands that dreams are something one can have while awake, in the form of those hopes, desires, and expectations that give life to thought.

It should be clear by now that "China" is the name of a particular epistemological formation, a way of knowing the world. Or rather "China" does not name the epistemology, but is a particular example of a more general type. We do not yet have a word for the type, though we have words for the kinds of things such a type *does*. As Said points out in *Orientalism*, European ideas like "China" have a way of reshaping realities elsewhere, both in small, individual ways—the experience of a Western tourist in China who has read *Des Chinoises* or *Cathay* differs, presumably, from the experience of one who has not—and in larger, more geopolitical ones (the World Trade Organization, human rights, military intervention). Such changes come, in some sense, *after* the idea has already been conceived, and so the degree to which a particular "China" has anything to do with actual China (leaving aside the question of who gets to decide what actual China is, or is like) shifts over time. If the name for this shift—for the degree to which ideas come to affect realities—is "orientalism," then it seems to me we are still missing a name for the idea *before* it enters into the orientalist process . . . though admittedly speaking of a "before" and "after" in this process is not easy.

Let me try to make some general statements about the shape of the kind of epistemological formation of which "China" is an example. It is defined first of all by a reference to an actual place, a place to which it has ultimately no clear referential relation. As Haun Saussy remarks, the ideas voiced around "China" are "not about China, or not exactly, *though they have to seem to be so in order to do the critical work they do*" ("Outside," 853; emphasis added). That is, the knowledge produced by the Chinese reference depends in some way on a recognized geographic reality for the force and attractiveness of its vision—think here of Barthes's fictional "Japan." And at the same time, it has nothing to do, or nothing exactly to do—it is difficult to be precise here—with that place. Rather it gives the name of that place to something defined generally by its being directly opposed to the source of the idea: "China here appears as the symmetrical opposite to what the reader already knows in the West" (Saussy, 853). What we have, then, is an idea that depends for its force on the existence of a place with a particular name, but has no real intellectual relation to that place—rather the idea is produced almost entirely in reference to the self, to what the self is *not* (as Spivak says of Kristeva). More specifically, the Chinas produced in Pound, Brecht, Kristeva, and the others oppose themselves directly to some of the West's major philosophical and cultural markers: science (including the entire process of rationality, philology in translation, usefulness), the alphabet (and its debased and fractured signification, primacy of speech over writing, loss of direct reference), and the unconscious (not simply Freud's version, but a more general sense of a split between desire and its articulation, the tendency to split mind and body, leading into the family, sexuality, and so on). Against these, "China" is *not* the West; it is mystical, ideographic, and completely unhysterical.

So used, "China" gives voice to the mysterious or magical discovery of "other" systems of reading or writing, acting or even living, that have reshaped or tried to reshape the way the West thinks about language, culture, or politics. Seen in Pound, Brecht, and *Tel quel,* "China" does not simply add a superficially exoticizing dimension to an otherwise interesting project. Rather, something in the felt Chineseness of "China" authorizes or produces the aesthetics or politics at hand. Such an authorizing presence is clearest, perhaps, in the two translations of *Cathay*'s "unusual" language, from Chinese into English and from romanticism into modernism. But it is also there in the "Chineseness" of Brecht's alienation-effect, and through that effect, the gestural theater of the *Berliner Ensemble* (as Barthes noticed in 1971). And one sees it as well at the nucleus of *Tel quel*'s poststructural innovations; as Saussy has remarked, the entire enterprise of poststructuralism and deconstruction has "been thinking from the outset about China and the cultures influenced by China" ("Outside," 849).[8] To say all this is to say that "China" is a way of knowing that is central to the development of some of the major aesthetic and philosophical trends of the twentieth century.

A book on the history of "China" in the West, rather than the history of China in the West, would be doing "sinography" rather than sinology, reading "China" as it is written into the fabric of Western life and thought. With the neologism *sinography,* I make a deliberate gesture toward Marie-Rose Logan's introduction to a 1974 *Yale French Studies* special issue on "Graphesis," in which she defines *graphesis* "as an operatory process through which 'writing' actualizes itself in a (written) text," and says that it "de-scribes the action of writing as it actualizes itself within the text independently of the notion of intentionality" (12).[9] That is, I take sino-graphy, literally the "writing" of "China," to be the study not simply of how China is written *about,* but of the ways in which that writing constitutes itself simultaneously as a *form* of writing and as a *form* of Chineseness, in a gesture whose style and content are always already turned back on themselves in an (un)concealment of their own origin. This double movement, in which any particular writing of China both establishes a particular Chinese difference (from the West, from itself) and simultaneously posits China as the origin and source of the difference that makes its difference visible, as it were, in the object of study I hope to name with the term *sinography.* Taken in this way, sinography relates to sinology as historiography does to history: as "a textual examination of the bases of judgment" (Saussy, 886). To read sinographically would be to abandon the attempt to force every reference to "China" into truth or falsehood, without at the same time abandoning the question of reference altogether—rather, the question of reference would have to be folded into the broader discussion of writing "China," a discussion, to paraphrase Logan, of the action of writing China as it actualizes itself within the world-text independently of the notion of authenticity. In a sinographic reading, for instance, "*Cathay:* English or Chinese?" is interesting *as a question,* not merely as a prelude to an answer that would declare the book of poems authentic in one way or another. Indeed the question of authenticity, of reference to genuine Chinese poems (Qian: "*Cathay* is first and foremost a beautiful translation of excellent Chinese poems"

[*Orientalism,* 65]) would be understood as precisely that which was at stake in the asking of it. Such a reading would attend above all to the writing process as a process, and to the ways in which that process (style, trope, plot, figure, vocabulary, pidgin, example)[10] does not simply think *about* China, but actively thinks it into "being."

In the Freudian model of the dream as a wish fulfillment, the dream is divided into its manifest (surface) content and its latent content. Writing to me about "Why China?" Christopher Bush asks:

> What is the wish fulfilled by a Chinese dream? What lack does "China" seem to address? To what extent is China merely manifest content that needs to be gotten beyond in order to discover the motivating latent symptom or complex underneath it all? To what extent does the manifest content, the letter of the dream, "China," matter? If pushed too far, the latent/manifest distinction is frustratingly empty: turns out the asparagus is a penis, so it could have been a sausage or a train or a shark, so don't spend any more time than necessary on the asparagus.

This is where one ends up once one gives up on the actual Chineseness of the dream. After someone like Spivak has pointed out that Kristeva is reading the West, not China, then really there is no point in talking about China at all, since to do so is simply to keep mentioning the asparagus, and so "Why China?" is just a bad question. And yet, Bush continues: "Material and historical conditions do, after all, matter; just as an egg seldom functions as a phallic symbol, it is hard to imagine *Tel quel* having found a model culture in, say, medieval Scotland." This puts us right back where we started, with some obligation to think about what in actual China might have made it the figure for these particular dreams. We can look at the asparagus and say, well, it resembles a penis, which is why it is a good figure for latent content about penises. What is it about the shape of China that has made it a likely candidate for Western dreams about science, translation, writing, politics? It seems to me that sinography must attempt to answer this question if it is to be honest about the "material and historical conditions" of the West's "China." *Chinese Dreams* has been a book about the movement between the manifest and latent content of the Chinese dream, a book that has read as closely as possible the interaction between those two forms of content as they play themselves out in Western intellectual history. I am defining "China" as an idea produced precisely by the interaction between these two forms of content, an idea whose most luminescent possibilities stem from the fact that the latent and manifest content might be the *same thing*. In this "China" differs a great deal from the asparagus—as only a psychotic would confuse the latter, outside the dream, with a real penis. "China" thus resembles a living psychosis—which is simply to say once again that it is shaped like a *dream*.

Inasmuch as "China" seems to be a defining trait of certain subcultures important to the development of modernism and poststructuralism (London 1915, Moscow 1935, Paris 1974), it can function, sinographically, as a yardstick of their epistemological convictions—ultimately the Chinese dream is a way of knowing the world. If to us, today, the excesses and projections of these "Chinese" dreams seem dated, even absurd, that may also be the measure of a change in the kinds of thought the West has come to value in the intervening decades; in some sense simply naming the thought a "dream" creates a distance from the moment when it seemed quite real to the person thinking it. That most folks do not now dream in the same way says something about the kinds of knowledges we have come to believe in. And yet: "If what we once loved seems now to stand on shaky ground, it would be absurd, sacrilegious, to believe that it never made sense, that we were mystified" (Picon 377).

In the wide world, of course, the contributions of Pound, Brecht, and the Telquelians are not particularly well known. In fact, history's best-known "Chinese" dream is not a Western one at all. It belongs to the Chinese Taoist philosopher Zhuang Zhou, who famously dreamed he was a butterfly, and upon waking up, could not be sure if he was Zhuang Zhou having dreamed the butterfly, or the butterfly dreaming it was Zhuang Zhou. In the English translation by Burton Watson, the brief episode reads:

> Once Zhuang Zhou dreamt he was a butterfly, a butterfly flitting and fluttering around, happy with himself and doing as he pleased. He didn't know he was Zhuang Zhou. Suddenly he woke up and there he was, solid and unmistakable Zhuang Zhou. But he didn't know if he was Zhuang Zhou who had dreamt he was a butterfly, or a butterfly dreaming he was Zhuang Zhou. Between Zhuang Zhou and a butterfly there must be *some* distinction! This is called the Transformation of Things. (Chuang Tzu, 49)[11]

As scholars of Taoism read the passage, it is either about the difficulty of properly perceiving reality, or about the fluid and transformative nature of that reality and its experience. Consciousness is located neither in

187

Zhuang Zhou nor in the butterfly, but in some dream-space between them; in some interpretations the critic says that Zhuang Zhou realizes that the sense of self, too, is nothing but a practical illusion.

There are any number of ways this story and its interpretations might be made to stand in for the West's Chinese dreams.[12] This is one of them: in every chapter of this book I have at some point referred to this sentence of Hugh Kenner's: "If so, then Fenollosa's sinological mistakes, rectifying 17th-century sinological mistakes, owed their right intuitions (brought with him from Massachusetts) originally after all to China: as though the east, with centuries-long deliberation, were writing the macro-history of western thought" (231). This idea, which offers up Western knowledge in the form of an incredible Chinese return, has its resonances vis-à-vis both Brecht (think of his struggle with the difference between the A-effect in China and in Europe) and *Tel quel* (where the revolutionary potential of this Chinese writing is at its clearest). One might say that Kenner—or Pound, Brecht, or the Telquelians—momentarily wake up from a dream of Chineseness only to wonder if it couldn't be, maybe, that the Chineseness is dreaming them. Following this through the conventional understandings of the Zhuang Zhou story, one could go on to wonder if the Western self were not, also, a practical illusion. Whatever distinction exists between the West and "China"—and there must be some distinction!—nonetheless reveals itself, in this fanciful analogy, to be caught up in the fateful ephemerality of self-recognition.

Notes

PREFACE

1. And more recently: reading the *New York Times* this morning, I came across a review of a new book by William C. Hannas, in which he apparently "blames the writing systems of China, Japan and Korea for what he says is East Asia's failure to make significant scientific and technological breakthroughs compared to Western nations" (Eakin).

2. Going the other way, from China to the West, has also been a burgeoning topic. The field of "Chinese comparative literature," which usually engages Chinese literature and Western theory, has its intellectual home in the Association of Chinese Comparative Literature, founded in 1987. For a brief history of that field, see Yingjin Zhang.

3. The phrase "Chinese dreams" is, as far as I know, my own; it echoes, however, the title of *Rêver l'Asie,* a collection of essays published in 1994. In the introduction to the collection, editor Denys Lombard imagines the mode of exotic literature as an "exorbitant" expression of a particularly Western habit (11).

4. One corollary of this is that in French, *l'est,* unlike *l'orient,* has referred not so much to East Asia as to Eastern Europe. This is discussed more fully in the *Tel quel* chapter. For a concise treatment of the historical meanings of *Western,* see Williams, 333–34.

5. Or, as Rey Chow puts it, "The theorization of Chineseness . . . would be incomplete without a concurrent problematization of *whiteness* within the broad frameworks of China and Asia studies" ("On Chineseness," 8–9). Likewise, much work has been done and remains to be done on China's own "Chinese dreams."

6. In the context of Rimbaud's "A Season in Hell" this line is about the impossible desire to escape Western modernity for something prior to or outside of it—as against a "use" of the Orient as a site for pilgrimages or (military, economic) pillaging, in which it is already captured inside the West's field of political and economic interest.

CHAPTER ONE

1. Qian shows that *Cathay* underwent several revisions, from an original sequence of eleven poems to the final version Pound submitted to Elkin Matthews (60–61).

2. The character *qing* 青 can mean both blue and green in different contexts. Fenollosa's notes are reprinted here from Wai-Lim Yip's *Ezra Pound's "Cathay."* The words in brackets below Fenollosa's transcriptions are Yip's corrections to those notes.

3. For a good introduction to the discipline of translation studies, in which questions such as this one are answered in a variety of possible ways, see Bassnett.

4. For more on Pound's repetitions, see Kenner, *Era,* 193–94.

5. Despite these criticisms, Waley would later tell John Gould Fletcher that his own translations owed a debt to Pound's *Cathay* (see Yip, 163–64). Yip also insists that Waley in many cases "took over Pound's diction and sentence structure" (164).

6. Kenner argues in *The Pound Era* and elsewhere that Pound's "errors" are in fact produced by a consistent aesthetic rather than wild guessing. Pound's other, earlier translations from Anglo-Saxon and Latin came in for expert criticism of much the same order as did *Cathay.* Writing in 1953 about Pound's translation of the Anglo-Saxon *The Seafarer* (published in *Cathay*), for instance, Kenneth Sisam argued that the problems in the translation were produced by either "careless ignorance or misunderstanding" (Carpenter, 154).

7. Ming Xie writes that "Waley recognized that Giles belonged to the older order, making Chinese lyrics sound like W. S. Gilbert, and that Pound was actively experimenting with advanced techniques which were hammering nails into the coffin of traditional rhyming forms" (174).

8. In *Transpacific Displacement,* Yunte Huang writes, "the desired immediacy of ethnographic truth cannot be achieved by means of the Imagistic 'direct treatment of the "thing"'; instead, it is contingent upon the intertextual relations in the world of intertexts (92). Though I have not used the word *intertext* here, it captures well the movement back and forth between *Cathay*'s ethnographic Chineseness and the poetic newness that would come to difine its modernism.

9. "Fan-Piece" was included in the first Imagist anthology, *Des imagistes,* which first appeared in 1914 as a number of *The Glebe.* According to Donald Gallup, Pound sent the manuscript for the anthology to *Glebe* editor Alfred Kreymborg in the summer of 1913 (137). But Zhaoming Qian dates the poem's composition to November 1913, by which time Pound would already have been in contact with Mary Fenollosa and thus fully embroiled in a general turn toward Chinese material (*Orientalism,* 54).

10. That "Fan-Piece" first appeared in *Des imagistes* indicates once again the slippage between Pound's orientalism and his modernism.

11. Huang shows that Upward had not just made the sequence up "out of his head," but in fact used a book of Giles's translations as a source and inspiration (68). "Reminiscence" here therefore tropes a more literal "re-membering," in which Giles's versions are taken apart and put back together again.

12. While referring to Qu Yuan as an Imagist is clearly at some level a joke, it also reflects Pound's sense that he and Qu Yuan were doing the same thing, an idea that depends on believing that he had unmediated access to Qu Yuan's mind and was not

simply understanding Qu Yuan within the mediated frame of his own personal experience of poetry.

13. For a lengthy discussion of the appearance of the phrase that inspired Pound's recollection in the Fenollosa notebooks, including a brilliant demonstration of the way Pound retranslated Fenollosa's notes to make his Chinese references adhere more closely to his own sense of what Chinese ought to be, see Huang, 43–50 and 70–73.

14. For instance, the character *qing* 青 , meaning "green," "blue," or "youth," appears in *qing* 清 , meaning "clean" or "pure," *qing* 情 , meaning "feelings" or "affection," and *qing* 請 , meaning "request" or "ask." It also appears in *jing* 睛 , meaning "eyeball," and *jing* 精 , a character whose meanings include "meticulous," "sperm," and "goblin" depending on context. In each case the radical (the strokes to the left of the original *qing* 青) hint at the character's meaning—the heart radical on the left of *qing* 情 , or the speech radical on the left of *qing* 請 . Fenollosa might claim that the "youthful" (青) "heart" (心) denotes purity, and that the original relation was visual not phonetic.

At the same time, it is worth noting that most native readers of Chinese do not think of *dong* 東 (east) as a combination of sun and tree. When I mentioned this idea of Fenollosa's at a presentation at the American Comparative Literature Association, a Chinese woman sitting next to me gasped in amazement and proceeded to show her neighbor why this was true. Though Fenollosa's sense has been articulated by some scholars in China, current scholarship on the issue suggests that the character 東 stems originally from a pictograph of a drawstring bag.

15. Songping Jin writes that while scholars agree that Chinese contains phonetic elements, Fenollosa also takes part in an interpretive school Jin calls "etymorhetorical" (known as the *xiao xue* tradition in China), in which associations made for the purpose of rhetoric supplant "actual" etymological evidence. (In French, for instance, one might associate *pouvoir* [power] and *savoir* [knowledge] with *voir* [to see], even though etymologically there is no relation.) Jin's generous interpretation of Fenollosa seems to elide, however, the seriousness with which Fenollosa takes the actual, not rhetorical, visual nature of the Chinese character.

16. A sense of the Chinese past as essentially *available* to Western scholars is part of what Said defines as one of the major principles of orientalism. As Said puts it, "The scientist, the scholar, the missionary, the trader, or the soldier was in, or thought about, the Orient because he *could be there*, or could think about it, with very little resistance on the Orient's part" (7). In other words, orientalism is not simply a set of "facts" about the East, but a general way of thinking about those "facts" as material for a certain kind of consumption.

When it came to China in particular, there existed in the West around 1915 a persistent tendency to see contemporary China as the degraded and hapless remnant of a once-great civilization, a country whose culture needed to be rescued from its politics. This point of view was succinctly laid out by Fenollosa in his essay on the Chinese written character: "Several centuries ago China lost much of her creative self, and of her insight into the causes of her own life; but her original spirit still lives, grows, interprets, transferred to Japan in all its original freshness" (56). Not surprisingly, such a view mirrored the relative national positions of Japan and China in the early 1900s. Japan's successful modernization had made it an Asian superpower and an equal of the European nations, while China still struggled to join the industrial age. Possibly the clearest instance of the difference between China and Japan relative to Europe occurred on May 4, 1919, when the Treaty of Versailles allowed Japan to keep Germany's Chinese colonial possessions, which it had taken over during the war, effectively giving it the same status in China as any of the European powers.

17. The classic sinological critique of Pound's *Cathay* was made by George Kennedy, who argues that Pound's fanciful translations of the *Cathay* poems and the Confucian classics demonstrates at times "a totally irresponsible attitude toward the Chinese language" (462). Kennedy concludes that "Pound is to be saluted as a poet, but not as a translator" (462).

18. Kenner's position on *Cathay*'s style agrees with his reading of its meaning: its primary function, he declares, was as an anti–World War I volume, rather than as any representation of Chinese poetry or an exemplification of Imagism.

19. For more on Kenner's sense of a Poundian "era," see Perloff.

20. Kenner's claim that Pound was not seduced by ideograms is in line with a long-standing Western fear that close contact with a cultural other would cause the writer to "go native" and lose a sense of Western objectivity. The implicit sexuality of "seduction" is typical of a Western treatment of the East as sexually dangerous.

21. Jang does not give Eliot's full sentence: "Pound is the inventor of Chinese poetry *for our time.*" "For our time" is a crucial part of Eliot's emphasis on the culturally constructed value of *Cathay*'s "illusion." Eliot never claims that Pound has actually invented Chinese poetry. Jang here participates in the larger trend of quoting Eliot as though he were only praising Pound.

22. The words "west leave" in the original mean to leave the west, not to go west. "Ko-kaku-ro" is in fact the Japanese sounds for Chinese characters referring not to a specific place but to a particular type of building. "Ko-jin" is not a person's name but instead means "old friend." (See Jang, 358, and Kenner, *Era,* 204).

23. Hearing Pound's rhythms now, attuned as our ears have been by years of poetry under his influence, is likely to be considerably different than having heard *Cathay* as part of the fabric of early modernism. "Ko-kaku-ro" may in fact sound slightly inauthentic.

24. Kenner's position was common for Pound critics who had little Chinese in the 1960s and 1970s. For a treatment of *Cathay* largely in its relation to Europe and English poetry, see Davie.

25. Even though he is explicitly disagreeing with Kenner, Qian is not immune to Kenner's influence. At one point Qian writes that "after two and half years of sniffling and squabbling, [Pound] managed to have Fenollosa's essay on 'The Chinese Written Character' published" (*Orientalism,* 64), a sentence that picks up on Kenner's "half-century of sniffling and squabbling" in *The Pound Era.*

26. Another stance is taken by Xiaomei Chen in *Occidentalism.* In the book's

third chapter, "'Misunderstanding' Western Modernism: The *Menglong* Movement," Chen traces the history of a movement in recent Chinese poetry that claimed to be influenced by Pound. She thus subjects "Pound and China" to an interesting reversal, in which Pound's "misunderstood" poetics return to the site of their origins only to be in turn "misunderstood"; her subject is not so much "Pound and China" but "China and Pound." And the Chinese "misunderstanding" of Pound, Chen writes, "is as profound as its better-known Western Orientalist counterpart" (69). Chen goes on to explain that the Chinese "misunderstanding" of Pound appeared relative to an official "understanding" of his work as decadent and capitalist; she consequently views the "misunderstanding" as a rebellion against an official totalitarian discourse.

In reversing the polarity of cross-cultural influence, Chen unmasks the particular ethnocentrism of Pound and China criticism, which invariably treats the East as the object of the West's intellect, failing always to consider that the reverse might also be true. This tendency is as present in Pound as it is in the majority of his criticism, for which the question is always: What did Pound learn from (the) Chinese? Kern, for instance, quite explicitly makes this point, writing that "my concern in this book, however, is less with Chinese language and literature per se than with their construction and representation in the West, mostly in the work of Anglophone writers whose own knowledge of Chinese is often quite limited" (xi).

27. For more on the use of the figure of "the solitary boat" in Chinese poetry, see Eoyang.

28. Pound does, as usual, make several changes (errors?) to his translation, which Sanehide Kodama catalogs in "The Eight Scenes of Sho-Sho." In a revelation typical of much *Cathay* scholarship, Kodama discloses at one point that Pound's choices in translation have mirrored the traditional Japanese aesthetic concept of *yugen,* though there "is no evidence that Pound was familiar with the term" (141). Thus the "native" interpreter verifies and vouches for the unconscious authenticity of Pound's translation. Building on and extending Kodama's work, Qian considers Canto 49 in the context of Chinese ekphrastic tradition, ultimately arguing for a reading of the Canto as an "ekphrasis of an ekphrastic tradition in the Far East" (*Modernist,* 124).

29. As Cookson explains, Geryon is "the monster and symbol of Fraud in Dante's *Inferno,* where he is associated with usurers" (50).

30. Such a claim should be made tentatively, if at all. Confucian scholars could be bought out by ruthless despots just as professors can today. As far as imperialism goes, most of China today is an imperial expansion that cooled down several hundred years ago. Incidentally, Pound's translation of the Confucian *Zhong Yong,* rendered in English as *The Unwobbling Pivot,* became in Italian *L'Asse che non vacilla* (The axis that does not vacillate), with the attendant wartime pun on *Axis.*

31. For a reading of Pound's Confucianism, see Dasenbrock. For a critique of Pound's translations of the Confucian Odes, see Dembo. Both Dasenbrock and Dembo discuss the texts, however, as though Pound were simply making a scholar's mistakes.

32. By contrast, Qian's latest book, *The Modernist Response to Chinese Art* (2003), devotes a full chapter to the appearance of Chinese characters in the later *Cantos*; I discuss it further below.

33. In 1938, Mao Zedong's Communists and Chiang Kai-shek's Nationalist forces were fighting each other and Japanese invaders.

34. In particular Pound's interest in government via an enlightened dictator—a ruler easily modeled along Confucian principles for guiding Chinese emperors— turns the Confucian principles into international ones in *The Cantos* and finds its luminary exemplars in John Adams and Benito Mussolini, among others.

35. Though *xin* is the first Chinese character in *The Cantos,* it was not added by Pound until the 1956 edition.

36. Except in one instance, where Dorothy Pound accidentally added a punctuation mark.

37. For an essay that treats the characters in relation to Derrida on writing and speech, see Ira Nadel's "Visualizing History," which thinks the Chinese characters as a type of visual sign, akin to a poster or a graphic.

38. In his "philological" readings of Chinese, Pound has any number of mistakes or poetic "misreadings." But the question here is not one of accuracy but of method.

39. Kern's use of "primitive" reproduces certain stereotypes without necessarily being useful to describe Chinese. In the history of Western modernism, "primitive" modes of speech, like the "primitive" African art that inspired so many modernist painters and sculptors, were deemed closer to the truth of things than their Western counterparts, a view that surely enacts a certain orientalism even though it may be true.

CHAPTER TWO

1. A peasant's coat made of straw (Waley's note).

2. An umbrella under which a cheap-jack sells his wares (Waley's note).

3. [Waleys Gedicht ist ein ungewöhnlich anschauliches Beispiel für die Schwächen einer allzu wörtlichen Entsprechung, da er das Problem dadurch zu umgehen versucht, daß er zwei Wörter einfach unübersetzt übernimmt. Das beeinträchtigt seine Version ganz erheblich. Er erinnert den Leser an die Schwierigkeit seiner Aufgabe, auch daran, daß es ein chinesisches Gedicht ist, das hier übersetzt wird. Die Wörter im Chinesischen zu belassen, bedeutet eigentlich das Eingeständnis einer Niederlage. Es irritiert den Leser, der ja nun selbst das Geschäft des Übersetzers besorgen soll. . . . An ihrer Stelle führt er [Brecht] etwas ganze Neues ein, das jedoch die essentielle Bedeutung des Originals bewahrt: den unterschiedlichen Rang der zwei Freunde. Der Wasserverkäufer bewahrt das chinesische Milieu und wird sofort verstanden. (37)] All translations not otherwise attributed are my own.

4. "Vorstädte" means suburbs, and refers to European urban development, in which the rich live often in the city center and the poor live in the outlying areas. I have used "slums" here to avoid ambiguity for American readers.

5. One could also make the case that the colloquial language of Brecht's translation is appropriate to the general tone of the original Chinese poem. Given that

Brecht rightly understood Bo Juyi as a didactic poet, and thought of himself as one, this affinity is not surprising. Whether "didactic" meant the same thing to both poets is, of course, the next question.

6. Or simply take the change as insignificant. Lane Jennings writes that "Brecht adds two closing lines to his version in order to make three complete quatrains out of Waley's ten-line fragment. There is no attempt here to extract political meaning from the lines" (125–26). This response shows how one might take the poem if one does not know about the original; once that knowledge is obtained, however, it not only enables but provokes the kind of reading given by Tatlow.

7. A good instance of this appears in Brecht's "Das letzte Wort," in which he says that the best Chinese poets—including Bo Juyi—were often sent into exile by princes, and that this demonstrates that their poetry was not simply "art for art's sake" ("noch war diese Kunst lediglich eine Kunst, zu gefallen") (qtd. in Jennings, 92). Brecht goes on to compare the Chinese poets to German writers in his time, who fled Germany and the National Socialists.

8. One alternative reading of sympathetic understanding is given by Shu-hsi Kao: "le fonctionnement ici de la re-connaissance se fonde sur une pré-connaissance historiquement circonscriptible et culturellement intournable. Profondément enrac-inée dans l'imaginaire européen, la fameuse 'connaissance de l'Est' . . . est un fait de langage, une formation discursive/conceptuelle ayant pur [*sic*] nom la 'Chine'" [The function here of *re*-cognition founds itself on an historically circumscribable and culturally unbridgeable *pre*-cognition. The famous "wisdom of the East," which is profoundly rooted in the European imaginary, is a fact of language, a discursive/conceptual formation whose name is "China"] (93). Kao argues that what Europe recognizes as "China" is in fact not China (or Chinese) at all, but rather a "fact of language," a European concept of what counts as "Chinese." In other words, what seems to be a new "sympathetic understanding" is actually *preconceived* and *historical*, stemming from a long-standing European tradition of imagining "China." The shock of recognition, the question of resemblance, the problem of influence: all these are in some way configured ahead of time (*pre*-cognized) by the sense of what counts as "Chinese." I will have more to say about this later on in the chapter.

9. For an extensive discussion of the similarities between Brecht and Waley, see Kloepfer, 137–39.

10. I would be willing to accede to a third factor. Inside this book, "Brecht and China" as it comes out of the poetic translations cannot be raised outside of the more general theory of Eastern influence on modernism raised in the previous chapter. While at times I will want to argue that the similarities say therefore as much about certain tendencies in literary criticism and biography as they do about the true reasons for each writer's translations of Chinese poetry, any claim on my part that this is the case labors under the weight of the reading I produced in chapter 1. Simply put, it is hard for me not to think Brecht through Pound. Much of this chapter might be read as an attempt to get out from under the weight of that thought.

11. Brecht published "Der Tschingtausoldat" in a local Augsburg newspaper in

1915. The poem is a more or less patriotic treatment of the last moments of a German soldier defending colonial possessions in the Chinese city of Qingdao against the invading Japanese. The German soldiers all perished.

12. Lane Jennings's dissertation, "Chinese Literature and Thought in the Poetry and Prose of Bertolt Brecht" was approved in 1970, but has not been published. The first text to raise the more general question of an intercultural Brecht was Reinhold Grimm's *Brecht und die Weltliteratur* (1961). More recent work in German has been done by Han-Soon Yim (1984), Weigui Fang (1991), Weijian Liu (1991), Albrecht Kloepfer (1997), and D. Stephan Bock (1998). Tatlow's latest book on Brecht and East Asia, *Shakespeare, Brecht, and the Intercultural Sign,* appeared in 2001.

13. Tatlow is not alone in making the comparison; Weigui Fang's *Brecht und Lu Xun* (1991) connects Brecht to the Chinese author at least partly via a metonymic movement through Pound's phrase "MAKE IT NEW" and the title of Lu Xun's short story collection, *Old Tales Retold* (Gu shi xin bian) (30).

14. As for a more direct influence, no one has shown that Brecht ever read more than one of Pound's poems (Tatlow, *Mask,* 113). Brecht's poem "E.P. Auswahl seines Grabsteins" refers to Pound's long poem *Hugh Selwyn Mauberley.* For the English translation see *Poems,* 384.

15. Bridgewater, like Tatlow, uncertainly dates Brecht's encounter with Waley's poems from 1938. I can only imagine his delight in discovering that current scholarship says that Brecht saw the poems first in 1929, which would allow Bridgewater to sweep all of Brecht's work from 1929 to 1938 into his theory.

16. The original "pidgin" English first developed in nineteenth-century Canton, where it was used as a means of "business" ("pidginess") communication among Portuguese, English, and Cantonese speakers. See Spence, *God's,* 8.

17. I do not mention Renata Berg-Pan here because her chapter on the question of style, "Affinities between Chinese Poetry and Brecht's Verse," repeats practically word-for-word Lane Jennings's dissertation chapter on the same subject. Berg-Pan's acknowledgment of her debt to Jennings "for several ideas presented in this particular chapter" (347) seriously understates the case. For instance, compare Berg-Pan's unattributed "If written out in two lines instead of four this poem could even stand as a translation of a Chinese couplet with five characters per line. Literally rendered into English, such a couplet would read: 'Leader says this way fame: Subject says this way grave'" (261) to Jennings's quotation above.

18. Tatlow, who resists most successfully the tendency to work backward from Brecht's work to a China that would ground it, concludes at one point that Brecht, too, "makes it new" when it comes to Chinese poetry (140). This echo of Pound's famous injunction to "make it new" indicates how heavily Pound bears on the sense of what it means to translate from Chinese.

19. Willett's translation of *Verfremdung* as "alienation" has been lamented by many Brecht scholars, in no small part because "alienation" already names a well-known Marxist concept (*Entfremdung* in German). Willett gives the source of Brecht's *Verfremdung* as the Russian formalist Viktor Shklovsky's phrase "Priem

Ostrannenjia," or "device for making strange" (Brecht, *Theatre,* 99). As Fredric Jameson and others suggest, "estrangement" is a better translation (85n).

20. But in his 1934 production of *Die Horatier und die Kuratier,* Brecht "used individual actors to represent entire armies by attaching flags to their costumes. Each flag represents a unit of soldiers, and as the battle progresses, flags are removed to indicate the losses suffered by each side. . . . Brecht's source for this particular adaptation of Chinese technique is not known" (Jennings, 86). In Peking Opera, the flags do not represent specific soldiers or units of soldiers; Jennings speculates Brecht got the idea from an illustration.

21. In the original: "All dies is seit langem bekannt und kaum übertragbar." *Übertragen* is given in my bilingual dictionary as "transferable."

22. [Wohl auf Grund schlimmer Erfahrungen bei westlichen Gastspielen oder vor westlichen Zuschauern in China, fand es der große chinesische Schauspieler nötig, von seinem Interpreten wiederholt versichern zu lassen, er stelle zwar Frauengestalten auf der Bühne dar, sei aber kein Frauenimitator. Die Presse wurde informiert, der Doktor Mei Lan-fang sei ein durchaus männlicher Mann, guter Familiervater, ja sogar Bankier. Wir wissen, daß es in gewissen primitiven Gegenden nötig ist, zur Vermeidung von Insultationen dem Publikum mitzuteilen, der Darsteller des Schurken sei selber kein Schurke. Diese Notwendigkeit ergibt sich natürlich nicht nur aus der Primitivität der Zuschauer, sondern auch aus der Primitivität der weslichen Schauspielkunst.]

23. Such an epistemological test, as I suggested in the section on Brecht's translations, is essentially rational, and dominates most understandings of what it means to represent artistically. This book constructs itself to some extent around figures—artists and their critics—who resist that epistemology in reading China.

24. A corollary response is Tatlow's: "What appeared to him [Brecht] as magic were signs in a language he did not fully understand" (*Mask,* 312). For more on Peking Opera's development, see MacKerras, *Chinese Theater,* especially Scott, "The Performance of Classical Theater."

25. Earlier, Brecht had argued that if the Western actor gave away his tricks, all that would be left would be "a quickly-mixed product for selling in the dark to hurried customers" (*Theatre,* 94). His claim that Chinese actors profit from their secrets neatly completes their reversal.

26. [dépend évidemment de la mesure dans laquelle on veut bien retenir et souligner l' "étrangeté" du fait chinois dans l'oeuvre et la pensée de celui à qui l'on doit le concept de *Verfremdungseffekt.*]

27. [Bref, la référence chinoise offre à Brecht un double bénéfice: d'une part, l'occasion de puiser dans le fonds communautaire de l'imaginaire européen pour y trouver la figure déjà "familière" et re-connue de l'Autre chinois, et d'autre part, la possibilité d'exploiter l'infinie altérité de cette figure pour en fair la clef de voûte de son édifice conceptuel du *Verfremdungseffekt.*]

28. [Brecht a pu trouver dans divers courants philosophiques chinois, dans les formes traditionnelles de la poésie chinoise, et surtout dans la pratique théâtrale chi-

noise, des éléments qu'il a par la suite assimilés au point de les faire siens, et qu'il a su maintenir dans leur "étrangeté" inaugurale. C'est là, pourrait-on dire, une forme de contradiction permanente.]

29. Scholarship on this issue is unclear. John Fuegi and Paula Hanssen suggest that Hauptmann translated all of Waley's poems into German. But Lane Jennings quotes Hauptmann herself as saying she first translated four of the six translations that Brecht published in 1938, and that he did the others himself (91). This is strange because Brecht's English was by all accounts quite weak.

30. *Brecht and Company* (published as *The Life and Lies of Bertolt Brecht* in its British edition) is the focus of some 150 pages of critique by established Brecht scholars (including John Willett) in *Brecht Yearbook* 20 (1995). The authors fault Fuegi for making some very basic errors about Brecht's work, and for drawing hasty conclusions from what evidence he does have. Nonetheless, the claim that Hauptmann played a vital role in the Chinese translations (acknowledged by other scholars before Fuegi) appears to be true.

31. [Das Studium dieser Bücher warf mich tatsächlich um. Da waren Sachen, die sehr Brecht ähnlich waren . . . Dann fanden sich (chinesischen Studenten), die mit mir über Waleys Übersetzungen chinesischer Gedichte sprachen. Ich bearbeitete bzw. übersetzte übers Englische etwa 10. Die zeigte ich Brecht.]

32. Tatlow appears not to have known of Hauptmann's vital role in producing the Brecht translations, since he does not mention her importance in either *The Mask of Evil* or *Brechts chinesische Gedichte* (Brecht's Chinese poems). Paula Hanssen states that though Tatlow was in contact with Hauptmann while writing *Brechts chinesische Gedichte*, she did not tell him about her contributions (88). Tatlow writes that Brecht translated the Waley poems in 1938, shortly before their publication (*Mask*, 140).

33. Hauptmann clearly believed that what resembled Brecht in Waley was not Waley's work, but something about the original Chinese, since she went on to discuss them with Chinese students and even at some point tried to study the Chinese language (Hanssen, 83).

34. Brecht's play *Der gute Mensch von Sezuan* is known in English as both *The Good Woman of Setzuan* (trans. Eric Bentley) and *The Good Person of Szechwan* (trans. Ralph Manheim, in *Collected Plays*). "Person" is a better translation of *Mensch*. The National Theatre production, following *pinyin* romanization, used *Sichuan;* elsewhere in the chapter I will follow the Manheim translation. In *Coining Poetry,* Stephan Bock, punning on the homophony between the German *Sezuan* and *Setzung,* place or location, argues that any "translation" of *Sezuan* into "Sichuan" or "Szechwan" misses the point. He goes on to say that "Sezuan" (or rather the Chinese words *si chuan,* which mean "four streams") should be understood as a "hemispheric doubling" of biblical Mesopotamia—known in German as "Zweistromland," the land of two streams (244).

35. [Sezuan ist die Welt der modernen, gespaltenen, pluralistischen Gesellschaft. "Sezuan" ist ebenso ein Modellfall wie—einige Jahre vorher— "Mahagonny." Brecht hätte genau so gut den Titel Der gute Mensch von

Mahagonny wählen können. Es handelt sich nicht um eine Chinoiserie, sondern um das Modell einer modernen zerrissenen Gesellschaft.]

36. Kloepfer makes this argument in relation to East Asian influences on Brecht's poetry, writing that Asia did not provide local "color" but rather stood in for difference in general, and that it simply affected Brecht's modernism by offering him an example of unrhymed, unmetered poetry (28–29).

37. Tatlow continues: "Indeed, if we assume instead the opposite hypothesis—that Brecht really knew nothing about Mencius—the parallel is all the more intriguing" (471). I touched on this sort of idea when discussing the "independent" development of a certain strategy of Chinese translation in both Brecht and Pound, but it bears remarking again here, because it raises this question: Is it possible for two people ever to think the same thought? How similar do they have to be before we recognize the similarity as such, or at least as uncanny? That is, could it really be that Brecht and Mencius came to similar general theories about the individual's relationship to society? Tatlow is not alone to be tempted by such an idea; think here of Hugh Kenner's phrase, said about Fenollosa, that it was "as though the east, with centuries-long deliberation, were writing the macro-history of western thought" (*Era*, 231). The "as though" allows Kenner to push this idea a long way; Tatlow's take on the difference between an *apparent* ("as though") similarity between Brecht and Mencius and a genuine one is less clear.

38. Kenner's angry defense of Pound's mistranslations—"Let us be quite clear that they are deflections taken with open eyes" (*Era*, 213)—suggests that such a structure, and the ideology of authorship that accompanies it—is not the exclusive concern of Brecht critics.

39. This is perhaps why it seemed natural for the National Theatre production to include pictures of London's homeless in its program, so that the audience could see the relevance of the Chinese parable "at home." As though to further stress the necessarily comparative reading, the pictures appeared alongside photos of the Tiananmen massacre. While the homeless photos clearly ask the audience to consider the plight of the poor, their juxtaposition with the Tiananmen photos bizarrely invites the reader to figure the value of London's poor and China's dead in a relative calculus of oppression.

40. This is true even though narratively the play has nothing to say about Western imperialism in China, and so on.

41. One more such instance: a photograph of Karl von Appen's design of the Berliner Ensemble's 1957 production features in the background this blown-up newspaper headline: "Kolonien bleiben Kolonien" [Colonies remain colonies] (Thomson and Sacks, 120).

42. Bock writes of *Der gute Mensch* that the difficulty of tying it to specific meanings is so severe as to demonstrate the power of poetics as a mode of *resistance* to interpretation ("Der gute Mensch von Sezuan ist . . . einziges Zeugnis der Kraft des Poetischen wie zugleich Schreckbild jedweder Rezeption" [514]). Bock's book *Coining Poetry* is a real tour de force of postmodern Brechtianism; its allusive, tempestuous desity makes it difficult to do justice to on any terms but its own.

CHAPTER THREE

1. In the United States, *The Kristeva Reader* was published in 1986, *The Irigaray Reader* in 1991, and *The Cixous Reader* in 1994.

2. A fourth study, by Niilo Kauppi, instead reads the journal through an "adapted structural constructivism" largely inspired by the work of Pierre Bourdieu. *Tel quel,* Kauppi writes, functioned for consumers of the avant-garde like "the symbolic goods department of a large department store like Bloomingdale's: there, side by side, they could find all the radical products at a relatively low price" (359).

3. This is not to suggest that Europe was not aware of China before 1966. China's involvement in the Korean and especially Vietnamese civil wars were part, as Philippe Forest notes, of the general geopolitical background for French avant-gardists in the 1960s.

4. [arrivée du dialogue entre Occident et Orient, question du passage d'une écriture aliénée à une écriture traçante, à travers la guerre, le sexe, le travail muet et caché des transformations.]

5. [A l'ouest, la foule; à l'est, le peuple. A l'ouest, l'image; à l'est, la scène. A l'ouest, les signes sans racines et accumulant les signes sans prise sur l'axe profond du dehors. . . . A l'est, la force invisible des mutations complètes et sans reste, l'écriture carrée qui ébranle le sol le plus assuré, l'inscription commune à la boue et au sang.]

6. [repartant avec elle dans la violence échappant aux lois, dans la convulsion et l'emmêlement du meurtre remontant par ses jambes, ses doigts, recevant aussi "à travers la perception"—voir, entendre— 見 —et passant ainsi par la portée complète provoquée par le jeu des mains.]

7. The link between Sollers's *Nombres* and Pound is clearer in Sollers's use at one point of the character *zheng* 正 , which formed part of the Confucian expression *zhengming* 正 名, or proper naming, that had fascinated Pound (*Nombres,* 80).

8. As I said earlier with regards to Pound, the vast majority of speakers of Chinese would never think of this as they said the word *jian,* even though everyone knows about the word's etymology. Whether it affects a general cultural understanding of seeing as such is another question.

9. I owe this formulation to Jane Gallop's essay "The Translation of Deconstruction."

10. [D'un côté, la guerre du Viêt-nam est perçue comme une ignominie, une sauvage boucherie; de l'autre, la situation chinoise semble annoncer la possibilité d'une révolution à l'intérieur même de la révolution. Sur cet arrière-fond—réel et mythique—se déroule au loin l'histoire intellectuelle française.]

11. [L'Asie mythique qu'inventèrent Pound et Artaud s'inscrit à nouveau dans l'histoire des peuples.]

12. Among others, these included, importantly, the Sino-Soviet split of 1960, which reverberated through European Communist parties and made side-choosing requisite.

13. [On comprend donc comment, dans ces conditions, la révolution culturelle

prolétarienne chinoise, plus grand événement de notre époque, dérange le calcul révisionniste et qu'il fera tout pour la falsifier. Eh bien, nous, nous ferons tout pour l'éclairer, l'analyser et la soutenir.]

14. For more on this see Etiemble.

15. In a note to me about this chapter, Haun Saussy remarks that Mao's slogan in the Chinese context refers to his exploitation of his prestige to split the Party or the people again and again, his personal prestige ensuring that his side would always emerge on top: a formula for continual radicalization underwritten by personality cult. He adds: "A non-admirer of Sollers could apply the parallel to him, too."

16. Note here than instead of Sollers's principle of "one that divides itself in two," we have two (the sensory and the intelligible) becoming one.

17. I would argue that it was not "in spite of" but because of their "backwardness" that the Chinese were such an attractive model for *Tel quel.* The "backwardness" at the level of technology and economy offered the possibility that a new system might be constructed, rather than the challenge (of the West) of having to take apart a culture before rebuilding it. In fact, the Chinese were "backward" in just the right way—modern enough to enter the modern world, backward enough not to have been corrupted by capital.

18. [Mais l'est? Je vous demande comment aller vers l'est? Pourquoi ces gestes vagues? Incomplets? L'est? E, S, T. Comment aller lentement vers l'est? A droite de l'image, en somme. . . . Ne pourrions-nous échanger nos places une seconde? J'aimerais bien voir où je suis, d'après vous.]

19. Evidence for this claim, Foucault suggests, lies partially in the Chinese writing system, which "erects the motionless and still-recognizable images of things themselves in vertical columns" (xix). Foucault's interest in verticality is repeated in Sollers's *Sur le materialisme,* where Sollers writes not only of the characters in columns but of the verticality of the wrist that paints them. Sollers's quote is reprinted in Barthes's *L'Empire des signes.* For a reading of this moment in Foucault, see Zhang Longxi, *Mighty Opposites.*

20. For another reading of this passage in Foucault, see Zhang Longxi, *Mighty Opposites,* 19–22.

21. One other marker of the odd coincidence between Borges's work and the more general theoretical geography that I am elaborating comes in Guy Debord's *La societé du spectacle* (1967): "The spectacle is a map of this new world—a map drawn to the scale of the territory itself" (*Society of the Spectacle,* 23). This sentence repeats the plot of Borges's brief "On Exactitude in Science" (1960), which tells the tale of an empire in which "the Art of Cartography attained such perfection" that "the Cartographers Guilds struck a Map of the Empire whose size was that of the Empire, and which coincided point for point with it" (325). This same Borges story later reappears as a central metaphor in Jean Baudrillard's *Simulacres et simulations* (1981).

22. Fredric Jameson's claim that Brecht's China is neither kitsch nor historical depends on precisely such a Barthesian sense of the real. In fact, it is probably only in light of Barthes's Brecht-inspired work that one can look back from 1998, as Jame-

son does, and see more clearly than most the ontological paradoxes of Brecht's China.

23. For Pound, it is slightly more complicated: he could use Chinese ideas because as ideas, they belonged best to those who used them. But for him true "Chineseness" was located entirely in classical China, and in those who were willing to learn from it.

24. In French, the oppositions between features of a pair of phonemes are described as *pertinent*. So Barthes is also saying that the entire Western meaning-making structure is washed out by the gray of China.

25. Such a notion is complicated, however, when Barthes discusses Chinese politics—the only text, he writes, that China offers up for reading (10). This acknowledgment is not allowed to affect his general argument.

26. For a more detailed reading of Barthes's "unhysterical" take on East Asia in relation to orientalism-critique, see Ha, 110–21.

27. This opens up the always interesting question of how much the Telquelians could have and should have known about China's political repression. One cannot argue that they did not know at all about Maoism's ugly side, since the word was coming from all sides of the political spectrum—even as some rightists denounced Mao, others supported him, and many on the left (including *Tel quel* editorial manager François Wahl) were criticizing him as well. The point then is not that we now have better information about Chinese politics than Sollers et al had in 1974, but rather that their reading of the information they were getting was happening within a too-fixed, too-binary frame of reference that reduced all criticism of Mao to simple sinophobia. For a contemporary, pro-Chinese, anti-Mao take that is scathing about *Tel quel*'s exoticism, see Leys, *Les Habits neufs du president Mao* (1971) and *Ombres chinoises* (1974).

28. Not content with posing the possibility of such an undercurrent's existence, however, Kristeva's next question simply takes it as a given: "Will this 'permanent lining' of Chinese socio-political life preserve China from the totalitarian blindness typical of our Western rationalism, until, with the help of economic development, a new discursive, familial, feminine and masculine realization of 'what's missing' may be achieved?" (156). What begins the paragraph as speculation ends it as certainty. The move from tentative proposition to a rhetorical question that assumes what had been speculative a short time earlier occurs several times in *About Chinese Women*. It is remarked by Spivak: "In ten pages this speculative assumption has taken on a psychological causality" ("French Feminism," 137).

29. "Archipelagos" are, like islands, pieces of land that stick out of water. Kristeva is using the term here also as a metaphor to represent things that disrupt the smooth surface of the social.

30. For more on this, see Saussy, *Problem*.

31. I have been unable to identify the essay's author.

32. Part of what provoked this turnabout was, for Sollers, the Chinese leadership's decision to mummify Mao's dead body.

33. Barthes had used the word "faraway," in English, to describe "Japan" in the opening pages of *Empire*. Here it translates Pleynet's *lointain*.

34. The phrase "forest of characters and symbols" [la forêt des caractères et des symboles] plays on Baudelaire's poem "Correspondances" as well as on a traditional Chinese title for dictionaries or reference works (as "forests" or "seas" of information).

35. In summer 1982 *Tel quel* switched publishers from Seuil to Denoël, and later to Gallimard. The journal changed its name to *L'Infini* and continues publication.

36. [L'enjeu de ce type d'écriture ne serait compréhensible un jour complètement qu'à partir du chinois. Ce n'est pas parce que les gens vont apprendre le chinois qu'ils vont comprendre le livre. Mais si un Chinois arrivait à se détacher complètement du chinois . . .]

37. The logic of Sollers's thinking here may be a particular case of a more general Western relation to otherness: in his book on American Westerns, Armando Prats writes of the white hero who "goes native": "He may enjoy his clear epiphanies about the Indian, but these tend to emerge from an uncorrupted moral center that the Indian can only mirror and confirm. . . . for all his complete and thoroughgoing Indianness, the white hero *never loses his individuality to tribal identity*. Indianness remains ever the token of his distinction *as a white man,* so that he wears his Indianness as a stamp of high privilege, of a moral aristocracy of one, not only among mere whites but among all the other Indians, who neither chose to be Indian or ever seem to know fully the blessings they enjoy" (131).

38. As many critics have noted, the coincidence in much French theorizing of this period between the otherness of a certain thing (the East, language, etc.) and the otherness of woman is worth thinking about. See Chow's *Woman and Chinese Modernity*.

39. The novel's title echoes that of Simone de Beauvoir's *Les Mandarins* (*The Mandarins,* 1953), which describes the life of Parisian intellectuals in the 1940s. The difference between Beauvoir's title, which refers to China's quasi-nobility of intellectuals charged with directing the course of the state, and Kristeva's, referring to the members of a Japanese warrior class, speaks to a different sense of the role of the public intellectual in society.

40. [D'ailleurs, quoi de plus "chinois"—bizarre, aberrant, lunatique—que la Chine? S'arracher à soi-même à travers les Chinois. Casser le masque de la conformité. Plonger non pas jusqu'aux racines . . . mais au-delà, dans le déracinement total. Se découvrir une contre-identité. Rejoindre son étrangeté absolue sous la forme d'un géant aussi civilisé qu'attardé: la bombe atomique de la démographie, le Hiroshima génétique du XXIe siècle.]

41. Recall here Kenner's claim that Pound's "errors" in translation were not errors, but "deflections taken with open eyes" (*Era,* 213).

42. The character of Armand Bréhal, a stand-in for Barthes, is a special case. *Les Samouraïs* presents him as a doddering old queen whose naive misunderstandings of psychoanalysis and culture lead him to (mis)take all of China in terms of a hazy,

self-involved reverie. This picture mirrors the treatment Barthes received in Sollers's *Femmes* (1983), which mockingly remarks that in his final years (Barthes died in 1980, a year after the death of his mother, to whom he was greatly attached) Barthes's nickname, at special parties given by his friends to give him opportunities to meet young men, was "Mammie."

CONCLUSION

1. This is not to say that contemporary China did no work for *Tel quel;* its most important legacy is the historical memory of *Tel quel*'s Maoism. Events in Communist China catalyzed the older, literary interest and gave it meaning, producing the geo-theoretical "China" that drove *Tel quel*'s Maoism and its trip. *Tel quel*'s political "dissolution" occurs in the frame of its unbecoming an audience to the Chinese "theater" of history (Macciocchi), as the move away from politics authorizes a more critical, individual, approach to the Chinese experience.

2. With this small exception: Zhaoming Qian reports that Pound, asked in a 1966 Italian documentary whether he'd like to visit China, replied, "Yes, I have always wanted to see China. It's awfully late now, but who knows?" (*Modernist*, 223).

3. For an extended critique of the sense of modernization as Westernization in treatments of China, see Paul Cohen's *Discovering History in China*. Cohen argues that the vast majority of historical discussions of China have taken modernization, Westernization, and progress all to mean the same thing, so that Chinese history from the 1800s on is judged largely through a comparison with the West. This is true, Cohen argues, in both anti-imperialist and procapitalist accounts of Chinese history.

4. For more on this poem see Tatlow, *Brechts*, 141–54.

5. Note that China's interest in the West is in most cases presumed to be natural, since it stems from a perceived *technological* lack and a desire for modernization along Western lines. For the West to be interested in China, as for Westerners interested in China, the *explanation* (why China?) is always necessary because it does not jibe with the most obvious instances of self-interest (i.e., because the West already knows what it needs to know).

6. Remember that I am translating these following Willett, and not the preferences of many other Brecht scholars.

7. One can wonder, too, about the interpretation of that "reality" and the solidity of historical "facts" in general. I see those problems as extensions of the question put forth by the *Tel quel* chapter.

8. This is not to say that without actual China these developments would not have happened. For other writers, and at other moments, other places have served similar functions; the history of European fascination with Chinese characters as against alphabetic writing, for instance, is twinned by a long-standing interest in the Egyptian hieroglyph.

9. My elaboration of the implications of the term *graphesis* owes a great deal to Lee Edelman's discussion of its possibilities in *Homographesis,* where he takes up

Logan's term in order to "name a nexus of concerns at the core of any theoretical discussion of homosexuality in relation to, and as a product of, writing or textuality" (9). The specific term *sinography,* as I am using it here, first arose as a possible description of a certain kind of work during discussions held at Stanford University in May 1999 among several scholars interested in East/West comparative literature: Christopher Bush, Timothy Billings, Steven Yao, David Porter, Haun Saussy, Robert Batchelor, Ming Xie, and Roger Hart.

10. I owe this formulation to a discussion with Haun Saussy.

11. Watson's translation follows the conventional line order of this passage. There exists an astonishing amount of debate over the interpretation of these lines. For a good summary and a soul-crushingly logical reading of the dream, see Allinson.

12. One reading is that of Jacques Lacan. Lacan argues that in the dream Zhuang Zhou "sees the butterfly in his reality as gaze." Lacan means that in the dream Zhuang Zhou experiences the "spectacle of the world," in which everything is *shown* (*donner à voir,* given to be seen) before it sees. Lacan writes: "In fact, it is when he was the butterfly that he apprehended one of the roots of his identity—that he was, and is, in his essence, that butterfly who paints himself with his own colours—and it is because of this that, in the last resort, he is Choang-tsu" (76). In other words, Zhuang Zhou, like the butterfly, is produced not by what he *sees,* but how he is given to be seen. (In *Ethics after Idealism* Rey Chow discusses the Zhuang Zhou story in the context of Lacan's reading and the David Henry Hwang play and film *M. Butterfly* [see 93–97]. I owe this connection to her.) For Lacan, this distinction is part of an attack on traditional Cartesian subjectivity, whose *cogito ergo sum* posits a subject fully at the center of his own knowledge, interpreting the world through rational observation. Lacan argues that in the "waking" world, we live with the illusion that we see things (and are therefore subjects who gaze), when in fact seeing is only a side effect, or a symptom, of a more general *gaze,* or being-looked-at, that shapes our reality. We are first shown, and being-shown, and then we build the illusion of seeing. So Zhuang Zhou (as Lacan reads him) asks the Lacanian question: What if I am simply a "dreamed" butterfly? What if, in dreaming that I have become a butterfly (one that exists within the universal gaze of being-shown), I am not simply revealing that I am a butterfly's dream (and like it, subject to being-shown in the matrix of human cognition)?

This description of Lacan's reading of Zhuang Zhou, and my reading of it, originally formed the conclusion to the book. My sense that something about the reading did not quite fit with the spirit of the rest of the text prompted me to move it to a footnote. Lacan, who just missed going to China with *Tel quel,* thus also misses out on *Chinese Dreams.*

References

Allinson, Robert E. *Chuang-Tzu for Spiritual Transformation*. Albany: State University of New York Press, 1989.

"A propos de 'La Chine sans utopie,'" *Tel quel* 59 (fall 1974): 5–9.

Baker, Edward H. "Historical Mediation in Two Translations of Ezra Pound." *Paideuma* 17 (1988): 69–86.

Barthes, Roland. *Alors, la Chine?* Paris: Christian Bourgeois, 1975.

———. *The Empire of Signs*. Trans. Richard Howard. New York: Hill and Wang, 1982. Originally published as *L'Empire des signes* (Geneva: Albert Skira, 1970).

———. *The Rustle of Language*. Trans. Richard Howard. New York: Hill and Wang, 1986.

———. "Well, and China?" *Discourse* 8 (86–87): 116–23. Translation by Lee Hildreth of *Alors, la Chine?*

Bassnett, Susan. *Translation Studies*. London: Routledge, 1991.

Baudrillard, Jean. *Simulacres et simulations*. Paris: Galilée, 1981.

Benjamin, Walter. "The Work of Art in the Age of Mechanical Reproduction." In *Illuminations*, ed. Hannah Arendt, trans. Harry Zohn, 217–52. New York: Schocken, 1985.

Berg-Pan, Renata. *Bertolt Brecht and China*. Bonn: Bouvier Verlag Herbert Grundmann, 1979.

Bock, D. Stephan. *Coining Poetry: Brechts 'Guter Mensch von Sezuan' Zur dramatischen Dichtung eines neuen Jahrhunderts*. Frankfurt am Main: Suhrkamp, 1998.

Borges, Jorge Luis. *Collected Fictions*. Trans. Andrew Hurley. New York: Penguin, 1998.

Brecht, Bertolt. *Brecht on Theatre: The Development of an Aesthetic*. Trans. John Willett. New York: Hill and Wang, 1964.

———. *The Caucasian Chalk Circle*. Trans. Eric Bentley. New York: Grove, 1966.

———. *Collected Plays*. 8 vols. Ed. and trans. John Willett and Ralph Manheim. London: Methuen, 1979.

———. *Gesammelte Werke*. 20 vols. Frankfurt am Main: Suhrkamp, 1967.

———. *The Good Woman of Setzuan*. Trans. Eric Bentley. New York: Grove, 1966.

———. *Me-Ti: Buch der Wendugen*. In *Prosa*. Frankfurt am Main: Suhrkamp, 1965.

———. *Poems*. Ed. and trans. John Willett and Ralph Manheim. London: Methuen, 1976.

References

————. *Über Lyrik*. With Elisabeth Hauptmann and Rosemarie Hill. Frankfurt am Main: Suhrkamp, 1964.

Brecht Yearbook. Annual periodical of the International Brecht Society. Madison: University of Wisconsin Press.

Bridgewater, Patrick. "Arthur Waley and Brecht." *German Life and Letters*, n.s. 18 (1964): 216–32.

Brooker, Peter. "Key Words in Brecht's Theory and Practice of Theater." In *The Cambridge Companion to Brecht*, ed. Peter Thomson and Glendyr Sacks, 185–200. Cambridge: Cambridge University Press, 1994.

————. *A Student's Guide to the Selected Poems of Ezra Pound*. London: Faber, 1979.

Bush, Christopher. Personal communication. March 24, 2001.

Bush, Ronald. "Pound and Li Po." *Ezra Pound among the Poets*. Ed. George Bornstein. Chicago: University of Chicago Press, 1985.

Calvino, Italo. *Invisible Cities*. Trans. William Weaver. New York: Harcourt Brace Jovanovich, 1974.

Carpenter, Humphrey. *A Serious Character: The Life of Ezra Pound*. New York: Delta, 1988.

Chapple, Anne. "Ezra Pound's *Cathay:* Compilation from the Fenollosa Notebooks." *Paideuma* 17 (1988): 9–46.

Cheadle, Mary Paterson. *Ezra Pound's Confucian Translations*. Ann Arbor: University of Michigan Press, 1997.

Chen, Xiaomei. *Occidentalism*. Oxford: Oxford University Press, 1995.

————. "Rediscovering Ezra Pound: A Postcolonial 'Misreading' of a Western Legacy." *Paideuma* 22 (1994): 81–105.

Chow, Rey. *Ethics after Idealism: Theory-Culture-Ethnicity-Reading*. Bloomington: Indiana University Press, 1998.

————. "On Chineseness as a Theoretical Problem." *boundary 2* 25, no. 3 (1998): 1–24.

————. *The Protestant Ethnic and the Spirit of Capitalism*. New York: Columbia University Press, 2002.

————. *Woman and Chinese Modernity*. Minneapolis: University of Minnesota Press, 1991.

————. *Writing Diaspora: Tactics of Intervention in Contemporary Cultural Studies*. Bloomington: Indiana University Press, 1993.

"Chronologie." *Tel quel* 47 (fall 1971): 142–43.

Chuang Tzu. *The Complete Works of Chuang Tzu*. Trans. Burton Watson. New York: Columbia University Press, 1968.

Cohen, Paul A. *Discovering History in China: American Historical Writing on the Recent Chinese Past*. New York: Columbia University Press, 1984.

Cookson, William. *A Guide to the Cantos of Ezra Pound*. London: Croom Helm, 1985.

Dasenbrock, Reed Way. *The Literary Vorticism of Ezra Pound and Wyndham Lewis*. Baltimore: Johns Hopkins University Press, 1985.

Davie, Donald. *Ezra Pound: Poet as Sculptor*. Oxford: Oxford University Press, 1964.

de Beauvoir, Simone. *Les mandarins*. 2 vols. Paris: Gallimard, 1954.

Debord, Guy. *The Society of the Spectacle*. New York: Zone Books, 1995. Originally published as *La société du spectacle* (Paris: Buchet/Chastel, 1967).

"Déclaration." *Tel quel* 47 (fall 1971): 133–35.

Dembo, L. S. *The Confucian Odes of Ezra Pound: A Critical Appraisal*. Berkeley and Los Angeles: University of California Press, 1963.

Derrida, Jacques. *Dissemination*. Trans. Barbara Johnson. Chicago: University of Chicago Press, 1981.

———. *Of Grammatology*. Trans. Gayatri Chakravorty Spivak. Baltimore: Johns Hopkins University Press, 1976.

Eakin, Emily. "Writing as a Block for Asians." *The New York Times*, May 3, 2003. <http://www.nytimes.com/2003/05/03/arts/03ASIA.html?ex=1052972495&ei=1&en=df4e7d18c16bd3ee>

Eddershaw, Margaret. *Performing Brecht: Forty Years of British Performances*. London: Routledge, 1996.

Edelman, Lee. *Homographesis: Essays in Gay Literary and Cultural Theory*, New York and London: Routledge, 1994.

Eliot, T. S. Introduction to *Ezra Pound: Selected Poems*. London: Faber and Faber, 1928.

Eoyang, Eugene. "The Solitary Boat: Images of the Self in Chinese Nature Poetry." *Journal of Asian Studies* 32, no. 4 (1973): 593–621.

Etiemble, René. *Quarante ans de mon maoisme: 1934–1974*. Paris: Gallimard, 1976.

Ezra Pound. Video. New York Center for Visual History. Annenberg/CPB Project, Intellimatic, 1988.

Fang, Achilles. "Fenollosa and Pound." *Harvard Journal of Asiatic Studies* 20 (1957): 213–38.

Fang, Weigui. *Brecht und Lu Xun: eine Studie zum Verfremdungseffekt*. Pfaffenweiler: Centaurus, 1991.

Fenollosa, Ernest. *The Chinese Written Character as a Medium for Poetry*. New York: Kasper and Horton, 1935.

Ffrench, Patrick. *The Time of Theory*. Oxford: Oxford University Press, 1995.

Forest, Philippe. *Histoire de "Tel quel" 1960–1982*. Paris: Seuil, 1995.

Foucault, Michel. *The Order of Things: An Archaeology of the Human Sciences*. New York: Vintage, 1970. Originally published as *Les mots et les choses: Une archéologie des sciences humaines* (Paris: Gallimard, 1966).

Fuegi, John. *Brecht and Company: Sex, Politics, and the Making of the Modern Drama*. New York: Grove Press, 1994.

———. "The Caucasian Chalk Circle in Performance." In *Brecht Heute/Brecht Today*, 137–49. Frankfurt am Main: Athenäum, 1971.

———. "The Zelda Syndrome." In *The Cambridge Companion to Brecht*, ed. Peter Thomson and Glendyr Sacks, 104–16. Cambridge: Cambridge University Press, 1994.

References

Gallop, Jane. "The Translation of Deconstruction." *Qui parle* 8, no. 1 (1994): 45–62.

Gallup, Donald. *Ezra Pound: A Bibliography*. Charlottesville: University Press of Virginia, 1983.

Giles, Herbert. *Chinese Poetry in English Verse*. London: B. Quaritch, 1898.

Granet, Marcel. *Chinese Civilization*. Trans. Kathleen E. Innes and Mabel R. Brailsford. New York: Knopf, 1930.

———. *La pensée chinoise*. 1934; New York: Arno Press, 1975.

Grimm, Reinhold. "Bertolt Brecht's Chicago—a German Myth?" In *Critical Essays on Bertolt Brecht*, ed. Sigfried Mews, 223–35. Boston: G. K. Hall, 1989.

———. *Brecht und die Weltliteratur*. Nuremberg: Verlag Hans Carl, 1961.

Ha, Marie-Paule. *Figuring the East: Segalen, Malraux, Duras, and Barthes*. Albany: State University of New York Press, 2000.

Hanssen, Paula. *Elisabeth Hauptmann: Brecht's Silent Collaborator*. Bern: Peter Lang, 1995.

Hokenson, Jan. "The Mimesis Oasis: Postmodernism's Deconstruction of 'The West' without an East." Paper presented to a meeting of the American Comparative Literature Association, Montreal, April 1999.

Huang, Yunte. *Transpacific Displacement: Intertextual Travel in Twentieth-Century American Literature*. Berkeley: University of California Press, 2002.

L'Infini. Quarterly periodical. Paris: Denoël, then Gallimard, 1983–99.

Jameson, Fredric. *Brecht and Method*. New York: Verso, 1998.

Jang, Gyung-Ryul. "*Cathay* Reconsidered: Pound as Inventor of Chinese Poetry." *Paideuma* 14 (1985): 351–62.

Jennings, Lane. "Chinese Literature and Thought in the Poetry and Prose of Bertolt Brecht." Ph.D. diss., Harvard University, 1970.

Jin, Songping. "Fenollosa and 'Hsiao Hsüeh' Tradition." *Paideuma* 22 (1993): 1–2, 71–97.

Kao, Shuxi. "Brecht et L'Autre chinois: Questions préliminaires." In *Brecht Yearbook 15*, 85–97. Madison: University of Wisconsin Press, 1990.

Karatani, Kojin. "Uses of Aesthetics: After Orientalism." *boundary 2* 25, no. 2 (1998): 145–60.

Kauppi, Niilo. *The Making of an Avant-Garde: "Tel quel."* Trans. Anne R. Epstein. Berlin and New York: Mouton de Gruyter, 1994.

Kennedy, George A. *Selected Works*. Ed. Tien-yi Li. New Haven: Yale University Press, 1964.

Kenner, Hugh. *The Poetry of Ezra Pound*. Norfolk, Conn.: New Directions, 1951.

———. *The Pound Era*. Berkeley and Los Angeles: University of California Press, 1971.

Kern, Robert. *Orientalism, Modernism, and the American Poem*. Cambridge: Cambridge University Press, 1996.

Kloepfer, Albrecht. *Poetik der Distanz: Ostasien und ostasiatischer Gestus im lyrischen Werk Bertolt Brechts*. München: Iudicium, 1997.

Knopf, Jan, ed. *Brechts Guter Mensch von Sezuan.* Frankfurt am Main: Suhrkamp, 1982.

Kodama, Sanehide. "The Eight Scenes of Sho-Sho." *Paideuma* 6 (1977): 131–45.

Kristeva, Julia. *About Chinese Women.* Trans. Anita Barrows. New York: Marion Boyars, 1977. Originally published as *Des Chinoises* (Paris: Éditions des femmes, 1974).

———. *The Kristeva Reader,* ed. Toril Moi. New York: Columbia University Press, 1986.

———. "My Memory's Hyperbole." In *The Female Autograph,* ed. Domna C. Stanton, 261–76. New York: New York Literary Forum, 1984.

———. *Revolution in Poetic Language.* Trans. Margaret Waller. New York: Columbia University Press, 1984.

———. *Les Samouraïs.* Paris: Gallimard, 1990.

———. *Séméiotiké: Recherches pour une sémanalyse.* Paris: Seuil, 1969.

———. *Strangers to Ourselves.* Trans. Leon S. Roudiez. New York: Columbia University Press, 1991.

Lacan, Jacques. "The Split between the Eye and the Gaze." In *The Four Fundamental Concepts of Psycho-Analysis,* trans. Alan Sheridan, 67–78. New York: Norton, 1977. Originally published as "La Schize de l'oeil et du regard," in *Les quatre concepts fondamentaux de la psychanalyse* (Paris: Seuil, 1973).

Leys, Simon. *Les Habits neufs du président Mao.* Paris: Editions Champ Libre, 1971.

———. *Ombres chinoises.* Trans. as *Chinese Shadows.* New York: Viking Press, 1977.

Liu, Weijian. *Die daoistische Philosophie im Werk von Hesse, Döblin und Brecht.* Bochum: Brockmeyer, 1991.

Logan, Marie-Rose. "Graphesis . . ." In *Graphesis: Perspectives in Literature and Philosophy,* special issue of *Yale French Studies* 52 (1975): 4–15.

Lombard, Denys, Catherine Champion, and Henri Chambert-Loir, eds. *Rêver l'Asie: Exotisme et literature coloniale aux Indes, en Indochine et en Insulinde.* Paris: Éditions de l'École des hautes etudes en sciences sociales, 1993.

Lowe, Lisa. *Critical Terrains: French and British Orientalisms.* Ithaca, N.Y.: Cornell University Press, 1991.

Lu Xun. *Old Tales Retold,* 2d ed. Peking: Foreign Languages Press, 1972.

Macciocchi, Maria-Antoinetta. *De la chine.* Paris: Seuil, 1971.

MacKerras, Colin. *Western Images of China.* Oxford: Oxford University Press, 1989.

———, ed. *Chinese Theater from Its Origins to the Present Day.* Honolulu: University of Hawaii Press, 1983.

Mao Zedong. *On Contradiction.* In *Four Essays in Philosophy.* Beijing: Foreign Language Press, 1968.

Marx-Scouras, Danielle. *The Cultural Politics of "Tel quel": Literature and the Left in the Wake of Engagement.* University Park: Pennsylvania State University Press, 1996.

Moyriac de Mailla, Joseph-Anne-Marie de. *Histoire générale de la Chine, ou Annales de cet empire.* 13 vols. Paris: P. D. Pierres, 1777–85.

References

Nadel, Ira. "Visualizing History: Pound and the Chinese Cantos." *A Poem Containing History: Textual Studies in "The Cantos."* Ed. Lawrence S. Rainey. Ann Arbor: University of Michigan Press, 1997.

Nolde, John. *Blossoms of the East: The Chinese Cantos of Ezra Pound.* Orono, Maine: National Poetry Foundation, 1983.

Perloff, Marjorie. "Pound/Stevens: Whose Era?" *New Literary History* 13, no. 3 (1982): 485–510.

Picon, Gaetan. "Literature Twenty Years Later." Trans. Arthur Goldhammer. In *Literary Debate: Texts and Contexts,* ed. Dennis Hollier and Jeffrey Mehlman, 373–78. New York: New Press, 1999.

Pleynet, Marcelin. "Du discours sur la Chine." *Tel quel* 60 (winter 1974): 12–20.

———. "Pourquoi la Chine populaire." *Tel quel* 59 (fall 1974): 30–39.

———. *Le Voyage en Chine: Chroniques du journal ordinaire, 11 avril–3 mai 1974: Extraits.* Paris: Hachette, 1980.

"Poems from Cathay." *Times Literary Supplement,* April 29, 1915, 144.

"The Poems of Mr. Ezra Pound." *Times Literary Supplement,* November 16, 1916, 545.

Porter, David. *Ideographia: The Chinese Cipher in Early Modern Europe.* Stanford: Stanford University Press, 2002.

"Positions du mouvement de Juin 71." *Tel quel* 47 (fall 1971): 135–41.

Pound, Ezra. *The Cantos of Ezra Pound.* New York: New Directions, 1975.

———. *Cathay.* London: Elkin Mathews, 1915.

———. *Confucius: The Unwobbling Pivot and the Great Digest.* Washington, D.C.: Square Dollar, 1951.

———. "A Few Don'ts by an Imagist." *Poetry,* 1, no. 6 (March 1913).

———. *Guide to Kulchur.* Norfolk, Conn.: New Directions, 1952.

———. *Make It New: Essays.* New Haven: Yale University Press, 1935.

———. *Selected Poems of Ezra Pound.* New York: New Directions, 1987.

———. *Selected Prose, 1909–1965.* Ed. William Cookson. New York: New Directions, 1974.

———. *Shih ching: The Classic Anthology Defined by Confucius.* Cambridge: Harvard University Press, 1954.

———. *Translations.* Westport, Conn.: Greenwood, 1978.

Pound, Ezra, and Dorothy Shakespear. *Ezra Pound and Dorothy Shakespear: Their Letters, 1909–1914.* Ed. Omar Pound and A. Walton Litz. New York: New Directions, 1984.

Pound, Ezra, and Marcella Spann, eds. *Confucius to Cummings: An Anthology of Poetry.* New York: New Directions, 1964.

Prats, A. J. *Invisible Natives: Myth and Identity in the American Western.* Ithaca and London: Cornell University Press, 2002.

Qian, Zhaoming. *The Modernist Response to Chinese Art: Pound, Moore, Stevens.* Charlottesville and London: University of Virginia Press, 2003.

———. *Orientalism and Modernism: The Legacy of China in Pound and Williams.* Durham, N.C.: Duke University Press, 1995.

———. "Translation or Invention? Three *Cathay* Poems Reconsidered." *Paideuma* 19 (1990): 51–75.

Roberts, J. A. G, ed. *China through Western Eyes: The Nineteenth Century.* Wolfeboro Falls, N.H.: A. Sutton, 1992.

———, ed. *China through Western Eyes: The Twentieth Century.* Wolfeboro Falls, N.H.: A. Sutton, 1992.

Said, Edward. *Orientalism.* New York: Vintage, 1979.

Saussy, Haun. "Always Multiple Translation: Or, How the Chinese Language Lost Its Grammar." Paper presented to a meeting of the American Comparative Literature Association, Austin, Texas, April 1998.

———. *Great Walls of Discourse and Other Adventures in Cultural China.* Cambridge: Harvard University Press, 2003.

———. "Outside the Parenthesis (Those People Were a Kind of Solution)." *MLN* 115 (2000): 849–91.

———. *The Problem of a Chinese Aesthetic.* Stanford: Stanford University Press, 1993.

Sollers, Philippe. "La Chine sans Confucius." *Tel quel* 59 (fall 1974): 12–14.

———. *Drame; roman.* Paris: Seuil, 1965.

———. *Femmes; roman.* Paris: Gallimard, 1983.

———. "La lutte philosophique dans la Chine révolutionnaire." *Tel quel* 48–49 (spring 1972): 133–42.

———. "Mao contre Confucius." *Tel quel* 59 (fall 1974): 15–18.

———. *Nombres.* Paris: Seuil, 1968.

———. *Paradis.* Paris: Seuil, 1981.

———. "Pourquoi j'ai été chinois." Interview by Shu-hsi Kao. *Tel quel* 88 (summer 1981): 10–30.

———. "Quelques thèses." *Tel quel* 59 (fall 1974): 10–11.

———. *Sur le materialisme: De l'atomisme à la dialectique révolutionaire.* Paris: Seuil, 1974.

Song, Yun-Yeop. *Bertolt Brecht und die chinesische Philosophie.* Bonn: Bouvier Verlag Herbert Grundmann, 1978.

Spence, Jonathan. *The Chan's Great Continent: China in Western Minds.* New York: Norton, 1998.

———. *God's Chinese Son: The Taiping Heavenly Kingdom of Hong Xiuquan.* New York: Norton, 1996.

Spivak, Gayatri Chakravorty. "French Feminism in an International Frame." In *In Other Worlds.* London: Routledge, 1988.

Steiner, George. *After Babel.* Oxford: Oxford University Press, 1975.

Tatlow, Antony. *Brechts chinesische Gedichte.* Frankfurt am Main: Suhrkamp, 1973.

———. *Brechts Ost Asien.* Berlin: Pathas, 1998.

———. *The Mask of Evil: Brecht's Response to the Poetry, Theatre, and Thought of China and Japan.* Bern: Peter Lang, 1977.

———. *Shakespeare, Brecht, and the Intercultural Sign.* Durham and London: Duke University Press, 2001.

References

Teele, Roy. *Through a Glass Darkly: A Study of English Translations of Chinese Poetry.* Ann Arbor: n.p., 1949.

Tel quel. Quarterly periodical, 1–94 (91 volumes). Paris: Seuil, 1960–83.

Thomson, Peter, and Glendyr Sacks, eds. *The Cambridge Companion to Brecht.* Cambridge: Cambridge University Press, 1994.

Wahl, François. "La Chine sans utopie." *Le Monde,* June 15, 16, 18, 19, 1974.

Waley, Arthur, trans. *A Hundred and Seventy Chinese Poems.* New York: Knopf, 1919.

———, trans. *The No Plays of Japan.* New York: Knopf, 1922.

———, trans. *The Poetry and Career of Li Po, A.D. 701–762.* New York: Macmillan, 1950.

———, trans. *Translations from the Chinese.* New York: Knopf, 1941.

Weber, Carl. "Brecht and the Berliner Ensemble." In *The Cambridge Companion to Brecht,* ed. Peter Thomson and Glendyr Sacks, 167–84. Cambridge: Cambridge University Press, 1994.

Weinberger, Eliot, and Octavio Paz. *Nineteen Ways of Looking at Wang Wei: How a Chinese Poem Is Translated.* New York: Moyer Bell, 1987.

Willett, John. *Brecht in Context: Comparative Approaches.* New York: Methuen, 1984.

Williams, Raymond. *Keywords: A Vocabulary of Culture and Society.* Oxford: Oxford University Press, 1976.

Witemeyer, Hugh. *The Poetry of Ezra Pound: Forms and Renewal, 1908–1920.* Berkeley and Los Angeles: University of California Press, 1969.

Xie, Ming. *Ezra Pound and the Appropriation of Chinese Poetry: "Cathay," Translation, and Imagism.* New York: Garland, 1999.

Yao, Steven. *Translation and the Languages of Modernism: Gender, Politics, Language.* New York: Palgrave Macmillan, 2002.

Yim, Han-Soon. *Bertolt Brecht und sein Verhältnis zur chinesischen Philosophie.* Bonn: Institut für Koreanische Kultur, 1984.

Yip, Wai-Lim. *Ezra Pound's "Cathay."* Princeton: Princeton University Press, 1969.

Zhang Longxi. *Mighty Opposites: From Dichotomies to Differences in the Comparative Study of China.* Stanford: Stanford University Press, 1999.

———. *The Tao and the Logos: Literary Hermeneutics, East and West.* Durham, N.C.: Duke University Press, 1992.

Zhang, Yingjin. "Introduction." In *China in a Polycentric World: Essays in Chinese Comparative Literature,* ed. Yingjin Zhang, 1–17. Stanford: Stanford University Press, 1998.

Index

Index